After History?

After History?

*Francis Fukuyama
and His
Critics*

Edited by
Timothy Burns

LITTLEFIELD ADAMS QUALITY PAPERBACKS

LITTLEFIELD ADAMS QUALITY PAPERBACKS

a division of Rowman & Littlefield Publishers, Inc.
4720 Boston Way, Lanham, Maryland 20706

3 Henrietta Street, London, WC2E 8LU, England

Published in the United States of America

British Cataloging in Publication Information Available

Published simultaneously in a cloth edition
by Rowman & Littlefield Publishers, Inc.
ISBN 0-8476-7926-8

**The Library of Congress has catalogued
the Rowman & Littlefield edition as follows:**

After history? : Francis Fukuyama and his critics / edited by Timothy
Burns.
p.   cm.
Includes index.
1. Fukuyama, Francis.   End of history.   2. History—Philosophy.
I. Burns, Timothy.   II. Title: Francis Fukuyama and his
critics.
D16.9.A46   1994   901—dc20   94-11722   CIP

ISBN 0-8226-3035-4 (pbk. : alk. paper)

Printed in the United States of America

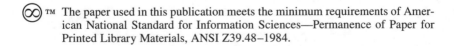

Contents

Acknowledgments

I wish to thank Joseph Knippenberg and Peter Lawler, whose advice has been most helpful in bringing this volume together. I would also like to thank the Helen Dwight Reid Educational Foundation for permission to reprint Timothy Fuller's ''The End of Socialism's Historical Theology and Its Rebirth in Fukuyama's Thesis,'' and *Interpretation, A Journal of Political Philosophy* for its kind permission to reprint Victor Gourevitch's ''The End of History?''

Introduction

In the wake of the collapse of the Soviet empire, the world's nations are moving to adopt market economies, and liberal democracy is swiftly becoming the only viable political order, the only recognized "language" of legitimate authority. But all is not well. Even the appropriately subdued celebrations of the West's victory over communism were short-lived, and not simply because of our recognition of the tasks we may face in assisting residents of the former Soviet empire, or the nagging doubts we have about the political tendencies of those residents, or our horror at the wars that quickly began raging therein. Important as these may be, the more deep-seated reason for our unease is that we do not quite know where we ourselves are now headed. We in the West inhabit nations called liberal democracies. Yet partly because its adherents have been busy conquering the globe, and partly because it was designed to keep substantive argument about the human good out of political life, liberal democracy has for some time lacked a sustained theoretical and practical defense. Now, facing no serious external enemy but experiencing an accelerating erosion of faith in its founding principles, it appears to stand in need of such a defense. With *The End of History and the Last Man*, Francis Fukuyama has attempted to provide one.

Against almost all current intellectual trends, Fukuyama has dared to argue that liberal democracy and technology, bequeathed to us by the modern world, are capable of satisfying our deepest desires—at least insofar as they can be satisfied. And with this claim, he has forced his readers to confront the question of human longing and human satisfaction, particularly the satisfaction of our sense of dignity or worth. Readers of *After History?* will find that all contributors to it have addressed the question of the satisfactory character of modernity, and hence the wisdom of the modern turn in political philosophy. That turn was made on the premise that the deepest longings of human beings can indeed be satisfied by ourselves, by means of things of this world. Each contributor raises the question of whether human longing is not, at its core, a longing for goods that we are not able to secure for ourselves, and therefore whether the modern project can ever achieve its promise of satisfying the most profound human desires. Some answer that it can and does—that there is no longing, or at least no politically relevant longing, beyond what a fully or properly articulated modernity has to offer. Others find that it cannot. They point to what has been abandoned, sacrificed, destroyed, or made obscure in the name of modernity, and view the whole modern endeavor in a critical light. Some question the sustainability of a democratic liberalism; others claim that it is already dead—the victim of an inevitable suicide.

But some readers may wonder why a debate on the satisfactory character of modernity should take the form of a debate about ''the End of History,'' or should devote much—though by no means all—of its attention to the work of G. W. F. Hegel and one of his interpreters, Alexandre Kojève. Some preliminary remarks about the Hegelian End of History may therefore prove helpful, especially to those readers unfamiliar with Hegel's, Kojève's, or Fukuyama's work.

The acceptance or rejection of modernity is the acceptance or rejection of a certain form of rationalism. ''The End of History'' is the culmination of modern, *systematic* rationalism. To see why this rationalism ends by declaring the end of history, we begin by observing that modern rationalism has from its inception stood in active opposition to biblical faith. For the Bible proclaims a radical limit to humanly achieved happiness and human knowing. It claims that our deepest longings are for something beyond us, and that the rule of the omnipotent, mysterious if just God who, according to Christianity, can transform our mortal, unsatisfactory lives is a rule that makes genuine knowledge, knowledge of permanent intelligible necessities, impossible. The characteristically modern answer to this challenge to the life of reason was a rebellion against the ''given'' or natural world, an attempt to *remake* the world (prescribe it its ''laws'') so that we can indeed know it clearly and distinctly, and can ''beneficently'' order it to our own satisfaction. This rationalism received its final, and arguably definitive, expression in the Hegelian system of science, a *humanly* created whole in which are resolved all the tensions of man's historical existence, and which thus constitutes the final realization of order within time. Hegel articulated a whole made or ordered by us, by our ideas made real, our words made flesh, and so one that required and even had at its heart what we are today in the habit of calling *technology*. As it proceeds to *remake* the world to satisfy our longings, technology gradually discloses to everyone that the world consists not of parts in a divinely ordered whole, but solely of the manipulatable, formless matter out of which we can make whatever will satisfy our longings. And as a result of its progressive transformation, the world we occupy becomes a visibly "humanized" world, a world primarily and increasingly of our making, a world that we "manage." In that world, we achieve a satisfaction unavailable in the harsh, unfriendly natural world—including the satisfaction of our desire for complete wisdom.

In the new, "developed" world, all the old tensions—between the individual and society, freedom and authority, the is and the ought—come to an end. Each *autonomous* individual comes to find satisfaction in the dutiful discharge of those public functions determined by the modern constitutional State, and in the reciprocal human recognition or esteem this brings. The society that we finally bring into being is strictly human, and its inhabitants bow to nothing and no one. It has no supernatural code of law, presumes no transcontextual knowledge, attempts no transcendence. It neither needs nor admits of the transcendent God whose existence would "delimit" our self-determining freedom, our reciprocal and full recognition of our merely autonomous selves. The new social world is, in a word, *atheistic*. Hegel's thought thus brings to completion modernity's hope for a human fulfillment (rather than a divine transformation) of our nature. It elaborates an end that brings a reconciliation, or illusionless compromise, with our mortal, temporal, re-created selves. We can know only what we make, but the world—the "historical" world—has become our product, and so our comprehension of this humanly created whole called History can provide us with the final satisfaction: full rational self-consciousness, or clear and distinct ideas of everything, or perfect wisdom.

This is the rationalism for whose fulfillment Fukuyama has expressed both his articulate hope and his deep reservations, and the rationalism that is held up to scrutiny in this book. The rejection of it as unsatisfactory leads some contributors away from reason in the name of that which modern rationalism has from its inception attempted to refute: biblical faith, and the sense of responsibility that this faith upholds and demands. It leads some contributors to a tentative articulation of something *post*modern. Other contributors argue that modern rationalism is not the only rationalism; or rather, since there could not be a host of genuine "rationalisms" contradicting one another, that modern rationalism is not rationalism at all but something—perhaps even a form of misology—posing as rationalism, and that what is needed is a serious encounter with the genuine rationalism of classical political philosophy.

Finally, apart from the assistance it has given to Fukuyama's articulation of the case for technology and liberal democracy, Kojève's thought is one of the two most important sources of what has come to call itself postmodernism. Kojève, directly and indirectly, has provided continental postmodernists with much of their vision of the modern world, of the world that they reject or from which they attempt to wrest themselves free. His playfulness and irony has also helped take the edge off their Heideggerian angst. In the middle of this century, when most Marxists were arguing that however flawed its practice, the final aims of the Soviet Union were essentially correct, Kojève declared, unsentimentally, that what the Soviets were aiming for is what we in America already had. For Kojève, as Fukuyama and other contributors to this book explain, History ended in principle with the advent of the modern, atheistic, rational self-consciousness. American postmodernists, unless they would reduce their thought to a series of attitudes in search of relief from their strict duty to be ironic, will eventually have to learn what it is that they are *after*.

The "End of History" or a Portal to the Future: Does Anything Lie Beyond Late Modernity?

Gregory Bruce Smith

Rarely does one see so many take so much trouble responding to the arrival of a new book—and what for many was a new idea—as with the release of Francis Fukuyama's *The End of History and the Last Man*, especially in light of the almost universally critical, occasionally hyperbolic, nature of the responses. This was perhaps predictable in light of the controversy generated earlier by the article that launched the book. But prediction and explanation are two different things, and an explanation is harder to come by. However, I think they clearly protest too much.

If Fukuyama's argument impacted only one side of the contemporary political spectrum to the exclusion of the other, an easy explanation might present itself. Needless to say, liberal progressives were not intrigued by having the idea of History co-opted only to be told that liberal individualism and free markets represent its terminus.[1] And conservatives were less than thrilled to be told that the victory of the liberal West in the cold war might eventuate in the moral decay and spiritual hollowness of the Nietzschean last man. Since the negative responses cut across the political spectrum, it is reasonable to suppose that there may be more here than meets the eye; Fukuyama has apparently struck a nerve. I believe that there are several explanations of this phenomenon and that they tell us something of importance about our contemporary moral, intellectual, and political environment.

I

On one level the End of History debate points to the frequent parochialism of the American academy. Similar debates, with far less fanfare, had already been conducted in France, Canada, and elsewhere. For American academics, one part of the scandal was that this debate traced its roots to a German philosopher and one of his left bank Parisian commentators.[2] The continental roots of an argument are indictment enough in some circles. But the heat generated by the present debate, even in theaters where it had already played, indicates there is far more to the matter than American parochialism. Needless to say, playing out the End of History debate at the end of the cold war was significant. The liberal West could no longer define itself simply as the demonstrably superior of two available options. The liberal West now has to look at itself in the mirror and define itself in relation to intrinsic, substantive goals and ideals—that is, articulate what we are *for* rather than take our bearings by what we are *against*. Therein lies one of the significant problems; neither the right nor the left seem well equipped at present to join that discussion.[3]

The End of History debate also came at a time of declining faith that History could be understood as linear and one-directional.[4] For a long time it has simply been assumed that the present is in principle superior to the past merely by having come later. That premise had worked its way out until it seemed like sound common sense for a series of generations.[5] But the commonsense belief in linear history is by no means obvious when one looks at the actual grist of history. Empirically, the past presents a spectacle of random occurrences. The faith that history has a meaning and direction requires a theoretical critique; it does not rest on empirical evidence. A theoretical frame must be brought to the empirical data from outside. It is precisely the status and origin of such frames—especially in the late modern world—that is at issue.

As I will argue throughout this essay, the fundamental issue with which we are confronted in the End of History debate is theoretical, not empirical. But after Hegel and Marx it has become increasingly difficult to accept the theoretical premises that underpin the notion of linear history. Nonetheless, political and moral life in the modern world has increasingly been driven by ideas. Many of those ideas lost theoretical credibility in previous generations; yet political and moral life continues to be driven by them. The premises that underlie our actions can remain suppressed for some time, but not indefinitely. When they are eventually brought to the light and seen as questionable a complicated situation arises. We live in one of those complicated times.

On the basis of a past theoretical faith in the linear, unidirectional movement of history, it was possible simply to begin from the prejudice that the past is a chronicle of ignorance and vice. To that could be added the gratifying notion that the present generation starts on a moral and political promontory simply by coming later. By extension, it was possible to adopt the conclusion that the future should in principle be superior to the present with or without reactualizing necessary antecedent virtues and circumstances that made the present what it is. If we lose our faith in linear history, our easy-going faith in all manner of commonsense opinions will be unhinged as well.[6] This is where we had arrived prior to the End of History debate, without having publicly admitted it. "We" expected further progress, perhaps indefinitely, and Fukuyama suggested that we had more or less arrived at a terminus. Without History to support our aspirations we would have to defend our idea of the good far more explicitly. But at present, no one is in a particularly strong position to do so.[7]

An adequate rejoinder to the End of History thesis would require that one furnish a substantive discussion of the good that the future *should*, rather than *inevitably will*—or at present does—offer, along with the ways in which it is plausible to believe that it can be actualized. If History does not somehow underpin the movement toward the good, substantive argument or capitulation to the status quo is all that is left. No self-respecting progressive can ever publicly accept the status quo and most are loathe to turn to nature to underpin their arguments because the left generally does not like to admit that intransigent matter, human or otherwise, might limit its utopian agendas. The left prefers instead to believe in the relative indeterminacy and malleability of human beings, as well as material reality, at the hands of clever social manipulation, education and technological mastery.

But without a fixed nature that presupposes its own end or perfection, or an inevitable history that moves only in the desired direction, one is in a very awkward position in trying to justify one's idea of the good. The left is not alone in this predicament. Most conservatives sneak in a linear conception of history along with their various "invisible hands." Invisible hands have the effect of making it equally unnecessary to discuss substantive ends and explicitly justify them. Likewise, one need not consciously foster the political prudence and moral virtue that are the only alternatives to faith in mythical inevitability.[8] Fukuyama's thesis put many in the position of the emperor with no clothes. Being forced by Fukuyama to confront their substantive nakedness was not met with gratitude by either the left or the right.

That said, it was liberal progressives who were most discomfited. Theoretically, many had backed themselves into a corner by arguing for several generations that liberalism does not rest on a substantive teaching or point to distinctive liberal virtues.[9] According to this argument, liberalism is neutral as regards ways of life and substantive ends. It is fundamentally a set of procedural norms open to a diversity of ends. This fashionable "antifoundationalism" is frequently secured by elements drawn from even more fashionable postmodern*ism* in a way that yields an entirely jury-rigged contraption.[10] However secured, this view represents the cul-de-sac that most on the present-day left have decided to colonize. Hence being forced either to accept the End of History or to be nudged into a substantive debate was particularly annoying in these circles.

Granted, arguing that history ends precisely where many neo-conservatives would wish it to end—in modern, commercial individualism—had the look of a "reactionary" maneuver. For many it was difficult to respond other than with outrage to the notion that history would not continue to progress even further in what had been assumed to be not only the desired but also the inevitable direction. The central point is this—and it is precisely the point Hegel made—one cannot know that history is linear and progressive except in light of the end toward which it moves. One cannot know of or about the end unless is has been, or soon will be, actualized. Without an End of History thesis the idea of a progressive linear history cannot stand.[11] It is impossible to conceptualize History progressing indefinitely. More to the point, if one rejects the End of History thesis, the only alternative is to show that we can somehow stand outside the flux of temporality at some fixed point. Only by standing at that atemporal point could we then presume to measure temporal movement. That atemporal standpoint is what is traditionally meant by the concept *nature*. Without being willing to openly accept the End of History, and refusing to accept nature, antifoundationalists are in a difficult position. The only consistent move they have left is to valorize "our own" as the good—and since at least Aristophanes, that has been the most traditional and conservative of maneuvers.[12]

II

While most on the left proceed from the assumption of the malleability and indeterminacy of man, Fukuyama has also been attacked by many, from both the right and the left, for not realizing that human nature does *not* change. History, they argue, cannot end because human nature will never allow itself to be satisfied by any substantive outcome, even prosperous liberal democracy. But that argument substantially begs the question. First, even such seeming absolutists on this question as Aristotle make clear that our nature requires completion by education and habit—that is, cultural variables—and those are obviously not static. It begs the question further by failing to mention that modern philosophical fellow travelers from John Locke and Jean-Jacques Rousseau to Robert Nozick and John Rawls have told us we must quit the natural condition because the good for man exists only within an artificially constructed human arena. Debate in the modern era has focused explicitly on the relation between nature and the good and by and large has concluded that the human good requires quitting the natural condition. To simply assert nature as if it operated qua efficient causality in human affairs as it does for beavers, bees, ants, and other social species does not hit the mark. The fact that there is a natural fabric to human existence does not immediately prove that it conduces to the good. The substantive question of the human good still has to be addressed even if we mechanically invoke nature.

Another variety of responses to the End of History thesis which invokes something empirically pregiven as an indication that history cannot end focuses on the renaissance of tribalism in Eastern Europe, the former Soviet Union, and elsewhere as clear evidence that secular, Western, liberal, technological commercialism has not been, and will not be, globally victorious. In a similar vein, rising Islamic fundamentalism is put forward as empirical counterevidence to the possibility of the End of History. This approach also begs the question. The modern moral, political, and technological juggernaut has confronted revealed religion before and an accommodation has been reached—and without the total secularization of religion. Someone would have to explain why Islam, which shares sacred texts and multiple principles with Judaism and Christianity, so differs that accommodation will be impossible. Is not political marginality far more accountable for the frustration that presently finds vent in Islamic fundamentalism, for example, than simple moral outrage at the Western understanding of justice and the good? If that is the primary ground of frustration, there is no reason why accommodation is not possible. Otherwise, it would be necessary to explain why, even if a radical choice for or against Islam develops, the realities of the modern world would not force a decision for modern technological civilization.

As regards the hegemony of parochialism, ethnic tribalism, and nationalism, what leads us to believe that present manifestations of tribalism will have greater staying power in their Russian, Eastern European, and Asian manifestations than they did in Western Europe? Has not the

former Soviet experience demonstrated that one cannot ultimately retain any national autonomy in the modern world without at least free
markets, and probably liberal freedoms as well? And even if we anticipate a relative withering away of the modern nation-state, and the movement toward a more homogeneous, cosmopolitan, global civilization,
there would predictably still be states competing to maintain their place
in the cosmopolitan market. Kant's vision of a cosmopolitan federation
of states is probably more plausible than any simple world state. Further, the tribal traditions to which our contemporaries turn in despera-
tion represent a response to *present* difficult circumstances and resultant
apprehensions. But such traditions emerged under entirely different
concrete circumstances than those of increasingly global, modern technological civilization. As modernity consolidates, the future world will
become increasingly foreign to the traditional world of the past. What
leads us to believe that ancient traditions have any chance of maintaining themselves in a radically transformed environment?

Any tradition is born of an attempt to explain reality and support a
shared conception of the good. It must be consistent with its concrete
present, at least to some significant degree. The real question is, is not
the modern world intrinsically at odds with the generation of stable
customs and habits and hence with living additions to traditions generated in the past? If so, old traditions will become increasingly stale and
out of touch. Why will the attempt to hold on to old traditions not
become more and more of a parody with each passing generation? The
mere fact that something is old does not make it good. It must also be
reasonable. But will reason be able to substitute something in the place
of decaying traditions? This latter question is another way of asking,
will universal Enlightenment ever be able to take the place of a shared
ethos in giving solidity to our lives?[13]

There is no doubt that we have habits in the modern, Western world.
But our habits are ones that accommodate us to constant change.[14]
There has never been a greater mechanism for constant change than
free markets, conjoined with modern technology. This is especially true
when they are likewise conjoined with an increasingly global mass
media supported by ever expanding information technologies. What
could plausibly bring this mechanism to a grinding halt? Is this not a
steamroller that will crush everything that tries to congeal in its path,
along with any remnants of past traditions? Put another way, is it possible for new traditions to form in this whirlwind?

Needless to say, near-term political and economic collapse in the former Soviet Union and elsewhere is a very real possibility, but how would it do anything but postpone the eventual march of modernity? Will Russia or its former satellites in Eastern Europe continue to turn to old traditions when they have become more successful at being modern, as seems a likely outcome sooner or later? To presume to prove empirically that History cannot end because of present manifestations of tribalism, fundamentalist religion, or any other ''facts,'' one would have to give persuasive answers to these questions and many more, not simply make empirical assertions. The real issue is, what sovereign *theoretical* understanding leads us to believe in the imperviousness of present empirical givens in the undeveloped world, in an age of cascading global technological homogenization? Have we not created a world that will inevitably destroy old traditions without providing the circumstances for the generation of new ones? Are there any rational principles that can plausibly be thought to replace the shared *ethoi* that bind classes and generations together? If there were such rational principles, has our experience in the modern world heightened or destroyed our faith in universal Enlightenment?

If we have created a world of constant, monotonous change, history could end with ongoing, monotonous agitation. We would not have proved that history was some inevitable process. But we might be forced to conclude that our unique present obliterates past possibilities and simultaneously makes unique future possibilities unlikely.[15] After a certain point humanity could very well arrive at a moment of *irreversibility*. The End of History need not require Hegelian *inevitability*. If we arrive at a moment of irreversibility, and movement forward seems implausible, we may at the very least have arrived at an extended hiatus of history. The question is, is there some nexus of variables that makes liberal, commercial, technological civilization both plausible as a global outcome and difficult, if not unlikely, to transcend—at least for a very considerable period of time? And if transcended, would our movement be in the direction of ''down'' or ''back''? That too would prove the End of History thesis; all novel possibilities have already been seen, while repetitions of past moments are still possible.[16] If one is opposed to the possibility of historical novelty—opposed to the possibility of the generation of novel ideals and ends not yet longed for—then one should accept the End of History.[17] Either there is the possibility of historical novelty or we have seen all possibilities in morality, religion, poetry, art, and politics played out at least once already.

III

It could be argued that even if human nature, understood primarily qua efficient causality, is not simply operative, human imagination and creativity are indomitable. Here we arrive at an argument that is in its own way Hegelian; it rests on the premise that genuine, concrete historical change is preceded by the generation of novel ideas. When we generate new aspirations, goals, and ideals we act differently and that eventually has concrete consequences in the world we share. But this approach also begs the question. The Hegelian point is that ideas and ideals sequence themselves in a way that leads from less comprehensive and more contradictory ideas to the most comprehensive and least contradictory ones, at which point the process of fundamental change stops because idea-novelty stops. When idea-novelty stops, and the latest ideas have been actualized in concrete institutions, history ends. Again, the only compelling empirical proof that this position is wrong would require the production of a novel ideal.[18] There simply is no evidence that has occurred since Hegel.

There have been post-Hegelian thinkers who have operated on a very high philosophical level—I have in mind especially Nietzsche and Heidegger—but they are fundamentally negative or merely hopeful. The central question is, what ideal is possible beyond a world devoted to universal equality (hence the pursuit of equal dignity and recognition), prosperity for all individuals, a secure, long, fear-free life, etc.? That ideal may not be fully manifested in present concrete reality, but what *ideal* could conceivably replace it that would win substantial acceptance? If no such ideal is imaginable, history could be at an end. If no novel ideals are possible, our only alternative—other than to continue to globally actualize the reigning ideal—is to engage in sorties through past ideas and forms in acts of remembrance. Or we could try to patch old ideals and forms together into novel pastiches (i.e., practice the ironic eclecticism of postmodern*ism*). The possibility of idea and ideal completion or exhaustion points in the direction of another fairly recent "end of" thesis—the end of political philosophy. There has surely been revived interest in the history of political philosophy in recent years, and political theory abounds—that is, working out the ramifications of already manifest ideals—but where is the evidence of a novel speculative political philosophy? Much of fashionable postmodernism seems devoted to proving both the impossibility and the undesirability of efforts to generate such political philosophies. What is at stake is the possibility of the generation of novel speculative political philosophies.

The proof that speculative political philosophy remains a possibility is an empirical one. But anyone trying to produce a truly novel speculative ideal will immediately see the difficulty. Again, precisely what is it one would wish for that we do not already have in theory? And is there an interesting, nonatavistic faction in the world that wishes something other than a long, comfortable life, self-interested and self-sufficient, devoted primarily to an industrious acquisitiveness, freedom from pain and fear of violent death, with secularized institutions, great latitude of moral belief, and so on? Where is the longing that lies beyond that modern dream? And even if there are a few who have such a longing—and they would need someone to articulate it in a theoretically serious fashion—what is the likelihood of it gaining public manifestation rather than remaining a shared private fantasy?[19] Is not the modern, bourgeois longing precisely what the majority of human beings desire everywhere and always? Other ideals are those of the few. What chance do the ideals of the few have of gaining ascendancy in an increasingly homogeneous, egalitarian age?

The two greatest philosophers of the post-Hegelian era, Nietzsche and Heidegger, give us no specific political philosophies, and Heidegger's thought, like much of contemporary philosophy, moves further and further away from concrete discussions.[20] Nietzsche, conceding Hegel's point, brings his thought to a culmination in willing the eternal recurrence of the same; in other words, Nietzsche simply wills a rerunning of history, not a novel moment. Heidegger, again conceding an Hegelian point, argues that at least an extended historical hiatus has arrived. He waits for a new god or a new dispensation of Being, neither of which, he admits, may come for a long time if at all. The record to date should not occasion great optimism about the early arrival of a genuinely *post*modern idea of justice and the good. Hence the End of History thesis is not as simple to dismiss as many on both the right and the left would lead us to believe. Simply to confront it would require that a different set of questions be addressed than those that have occupied most of Fukuyama's respondents.

It is certainly true that we have been witnessing the theoretical disintegration of faith in the principles that provide the foundation for the modern civilization that seems to be consolidating its gains globally.[21] But that fact only proves the ironic nature of our situation, not that counter-ideals exist. And when we are repeatedly told that modern liberal principles do not ground moral meaning, while allowing that meaning to intrude from a variety of traditional sources, we again see the irony of our situation. Will past traditions and norms become extinct and new ones become impossible, leaving global modern liberalism spiritually hollow—albeit materially comfortable and perhaps thereby acceptable to the majority?

Needless to say, the irony of our situation has caused more than a little shared inarticulate anxiety. The energetic responses Fukuyama has aroused are related to this pool of anxiety. But anxiety does not prove the possibility of a counter-ideal either. We should recall that the End of History thesis is just one of a series of parallel theses that we have witnessed as the twentieth century has unfolded. We could begin by pointing to the earlier twentieth-century preoccupations with the end or decline of the West, add to that the far more academic discussions of the end of ideology or the end of political philosophy and make ourselves fashionably current by pointing to the various discussions of postmod-ern*ism* that will undoubtedly preoccupy us into the twenty-first century. Add to these, terms like postindustrial society, poststructuralism, the end of man, the decline of logo-centrism, and like phrases that are all too familiar and one would have an odd mélange that seemingly shares only one idea: there is a more or less inarticulate sense that something out of the ordinary is occurring around us.

Beyond that vague sense, it remains unclear whether that which is occurring points toward a long period of stasis, a relatively quick transition to something novel, or the early stages of a novel future already deploying itself. Ambiguity always leads to uneasiness. Only a few, rare intellectuals could revel in irony and ambiguity as a way of life. Hence, anyone who revivifies an inarticulate uneasiness will run the risk of the kinds of responses Fukuyama received. But none of this proves the possibility of a novel postmodern ideal.

IV

Many of Fukuyama's critics have been generous enough to recognize that his book-length treatment adds depth and subtlety to the initial articulation of his thesis. The price one pays for subtlety is frequently the introduction of new ambiguities. In the latest account, Fukuyama offers several different engines that move the dialectic of history. There is the dialectic of modern science and technology, which overlaps with and informs a dialectic of capitalist market economies. Something similar to the Heideggerian analysis of the inevitable and unidirectional march of modern technology seems to take hegemony in this part of the account—albeit in modern fashion, technology is seen by Fukuyama as primarily emancipatory rather than alienating. There is also the spiritual or psychological dialectic of recognition, which is given two by no means identical articulations, one in *consciousness*—and here we come in contact with its modern Hegelian manifestation—and one in the *instinctive* love of honor—here we are confronted with Plato's discussion of *thymos*.[22] The spiritual dialectic leads Fukuyama to a reflection on the banality of bourgeois culture—shared substantially by authors from Tocqueville to Nietzsche, Reisman, and many others. This part of the argument is in tension with the fundamentally optimistic faith in the emancipatory goodness of technology and markets. Many of the ambiguities of Fukuyama's account come from a failure to differentiate these different engines of history, or to explain how they might converge.

Fukuyama's technological engine of history moves unavoidably in the direction of a global economy in which nation-states play a diminished role in the face of large-scale global, multinational institutions. This effect is magnified by the existence of the mass media, which increasingly give everyone access to the same culturally homogenizing influences. In this fashion Western influences consolidate their hold globally. No nation can afford not to modernize or it will lose any chance for even minimal national autonomy, whether conceived in tribal terms or in some other fashion. Despite the growing global tribalism many of his critics glory in reciting, Fukuyama concludes that the parochial—whether conceived ethnically or religiously—is on a more or less gentle and extended slippery slide toward the universal. (Fukuyama clouds the issue somewhat by observing that this outcome may be mitigated in various Asian nations by Confucian traditions. Why that would be true requires further articulation.) Brute nature itself seems to pose the only potential barrier to this outcome, since limited resources might lead to the inevitability of a zero-sum economic game. While it would be imprudent to predict with certainty the near-term outcome of the simultaneous globalization and tribalization which at present confront each other, the globalizing tendencies seem to have the upper hand.

As regards the dialectical movement of consciousness (recognition), Fukuyama openly follows Hegel—passed through the mediating lens of Alexandre Kojève.[23] The fundamentally modern turn to *consciousness* that Kojève resolutely developed,[24] shared by many of Fukuyama's critics, is that man is not primarily a fixed, determinate being but a consciousness that changes and evolves and at each stage "outers" itself, achieving thereby various concrete manifestations in different religions, art forms, cultures, constitutions, and eventually the technological transformation of the natural world. Having passed through a multitude of stages and seen the various forms of narrowness of each successive stage, humanity would return to a previous stage only on the basis of forgetfulness rather than choice.

Through an extended period of trial and error, which must be recorded in detail—and our historically conscious age is amazing in its ability to record and preserve—consciousness reaches ever more comprehensive and allegedly less contradictory states. Eventually it arrives at a point with which there is at least relatively high satisfaction on the part of the majority—taking into account the effects of the unavoidable pettiness, envy, and jealousy that would remain—having transformed the external world to correspond with its internal consciousness. In the process of its journey, consciousness not only produces ideas, but acts upon them and concretely actualizes them. In this way consciousness transforms the external world, and any adequate theory of human reality must account for our ability to do this. Eventually the world we occupy bears primarily the stamp of a human creation. Consequently, the dialectic of consciousness should ultimately dovetail with the technological dialectic. Living in a humanized world, human beings allegedly achieve a satisfaction they could not achieve in the natural world. Again, this is the modern premise par excellence, whether we take Hobbes, Locke, Rousseau, Hegel, or whomever as our favorite exemplar.

It is certainly true that Fukuyama adds a potential confusion by trying to synthesize the Hegelian discussion of recognition—a phenomenon primarily of consciousness—and Platonic *thymos*—primarily a phenomenon of fixed, instinctive being. As a result, Plato and Hegel cease to present us with fundamental alternatives. Further, Fukuyama's psychological dialectic eventually comes up against the empirical fact of significant if not universal alienation from modern, urban, global, technological civilization. That alienation can be accounted for in one of two more or less exclusive ways. Either the ideal that awaits at the end of the evolution of consciousness has not yet been perfectly manifested empirically on a sufficiently global basis, or man is not so much an evolving consciousness as a fixed being with a nature, suppression or sublimation of which within a technological civilization is necessarily alienating or dissatisfying. If the latter, nature could always rebel given the chance (barring the transformation of that nature by modern biological science). History might be irreversible, but it is never simply at an end as long as something deep in our being can repeatedly reassert itself.[25] History could be both irreversible and a terminus only if man was primarily a consciousness or if that part of his being which is fixed was irreversibly transformed.[26]

V

The central issue raised by the End of History debate has simply not been addressed by Fukuyama's critics: Is Fukuyama's point primarily theoretical or empirical? If both, how are the two related and/or which takes priority? By way of an answer, I would make the following fairly simple observation: To know on a purely theoretical level that history, or anything else, had ended would require us to know how the entirety of the human things—which is the subject matter of History—is integrated into the nonhuman. In other words, we would have to have complete knowledge of the Whole to make definitive statements about how any of the parts, particularly the human, fit into the Whole. We should admit that we will never have perfect knowledge about the Whole; hence we will never have finished knowledge about how the parts are articulated into the Whole. Likewise, we will never have final knowledge about the sense in which any of the parts could reach a terminus beyond which there is no novelty. Consequently, we cannot know with theoretical certainty whether history has or has not reached a terminus. But we can know that empirical evidence is never adequate to dispose of the issue. Where does that leave us?

This points to the fact that we should expect all articulations of the Whole to be partial. One would therefore expect a spectacle of repeated attempts to articulate the Whole, none of them perfectly adequate, with different ones publicly persuasive at different times and with the reasons that account for persuasiveness being somewhat unpredictable. If each attempt gives rise to various interpretations or "disseminations," with their own distinctive deferred ramifications and unpredictable practical consequences—as is reasonable to predict—one would expect novel ways of living to emerge. If we do not see evidence of that and see instead what looks like snowballing global homogenization, some at least temporary impasse or hiatus can legitimately be thought to have settled in and require explanation.[27] That explanation will be theoretical even though it can never be apodictic. Since it is unlikely that we will ever grasp the Whole, or if we did adequately grasp it—through some direct noetic act of apprehension—that we could articulate it comprehensively in some final form of public speech, it is unlikely we will ever arrive at the comparatively prosaic knowledge of the exact relationship between human consciousness or thought and our determinate natural being.[28] Hence perfect knowledge of precisely what we are as human is likely to remain a mystery—which is not to say that since we do not know everything, we do not know anything.

Further, as a theoretical matter it is necessary to state precisely what kind of terminus it is at which we are asserting history arrives when we say it ends. Is it the kind of end beyond which there is one or another form of nothingness or indeterminacy, or is it the kind of end that is understood as a perfection? In a significant way, Fukuyama thinks that something literally ceases in the sense that something that was part of the human scene hitherto will not be seen in the future. In another sense, Fukuyama wants to say that a form of perfection is reached, although the message is mixed, since a certain impoverishment is also possible, and the end of the possibility of novel ideas and ideals is posited as well. It would be helpful if Fukuyama could clarify the relationship between end understood teleologically and as terminus beyond which there is one kind of nothingness or another.[29] While it is plausible to project a terminus of history qua extended hiatus, it is not theoretically possible to project an end qua perfection given that we are not simply determinate beings moved only by efficient causality. If we were, there would be no History in any interesting sense.

These clarifications to the contrary notwithstanding, it should be admitted that one can "clarify" even a compelling idea out of existence and not thereby attend to what is truly compelling in it. What is it that is truly compelling in the End of History thesis? No empirical evidence exists separate from some theoretical frame, which we all use in our approaches to reality. That said, it should be recognized that it will be difficult to develop—or to mysteriously find ourselves equipped with—a post-Hegelian theoretical frame, here understood as a genuinely postmodern frame. Hence present empirical circumstances may be settling in for a long period. On this level, the End of History thesis can be *compelling* without being *conclusive*.

The End of History thesis presents a picture of an increasingly global, egalitarian, commercial, technological civilization emerging, one that at the very least may have great staying power. Yet two issues remain open: (1) Is it good? (2) If not, what is implied in the possibility of transcending it? Having arrived at those two questions, I would argue that the End of History debate would be better posed as an End of Modernity debate in which one seriously reconsiders the modern dream, the arguments in its favor and those against it. Such a reconsideration would occasion an explicit discussion of fundamental questions concerning the nature of justice and the human good. It would also require an explicit reflection on the place of the human within the larger Whole, knowing in advance that we cannot arrive at a definitive conclusion as a result of those reflections. Reflections of this kind are necessary and ones which an increasingly technological and utilitarian civilization has tried to bury in the dustbin of History—while implicitly presupposing distinct answers.

I would argue that we should engage in a fundamental questioning of modernity not with an eye to premodernity as an alternative to the possibility of a late modern hiatus of History, but with an eye to the possibility of the genuinely *post*modern.[30] As long as a fundamental, essential kind of thinking of this sort remains possible and can find some public manifestation in the concrete world—in other words, as long as thinking does not choose, nor is forced, to retreat to some epicurean garden—History cannot end in any strong sense.[31] But if such essential reflection ceases to have a public echo we would have no right to glibly dismiss the End of History thesis. The End of History thesis points toward the need for—and reflections on the possibility of—speculative political philosophy. If it remains possible, all horizons are still open.

Notes

This is a significantly enlarged and transformed version of an essay that initially appeared in *Perspectives on Political Science*, Vol. 22, Fall 1993, under the title "Endings, Transitions or Beginnings."

1. What progress means cannot be explained without some notion of History. In other words, progressives always presuppose some "metanarrative" about the course of human events, and that metanarrative rests on a theoretical picture of history as linear and one-directional.

2. The operative texts are G. W. F. Hegel, *Phenomenology of Spirit*, trans. A. V. Miller (New York: Oxford University Press, 1977), and Alexandre Kojève, *Introduction to the Reading of Hegel*, trans. James H. Nichols Jr. (New York: Basic Books, 1969).

3. The End of History debate also comes at a time when there is increasing suspicion about the meaningfulness of traditional left-right or progressive-conservative dichotomies. Progressives frequently label everything that differs from their view as "reactionary," usually on the basis of a hidden End of History premise. They know they represent the cutting edge of history, hence

only movement in the same direction they desire is legitimate. Anything that differs from the direction in which they wish to move must be a form of going back because there is nothing beyond their position that could come in the future. In this way the progressives become the defenders of the status quo. It is the conservatives who want change—either back or in some unclearly specified direction. The role reversals of progressives and conservatives may indicate the approaching end of the line for such distinctions. Terms that emerged as part of the fight for and against throne and altar, even when revamped for use in the confrontation between Marxist collectivism and liberal capitalism, will not retain their force indefinitely.

4. This can be seen clearly in the work of Nietzsche. However, history still retained a somewhat predictable circularity or repeatability for Nietzsche. It was Martin Heidegger who, in radically attacking the premises that support the Enlightenment faith in progress, opened the door to the historically random and mysterious. Heidegger presents an account of the Whole (Being) dominated by various fated historical dispensations that are altogether unpredictable. In its comings and goings, presencings and absencings, Being is simply beyond human comprehension; consequently so is history. French epigones such as Michel Foucault and Jacques Derrida build on these Heideggerian premises to the same end. Man can no longer predict and control existence as the modern thinkers had hoped. Fellow Frenchman Jean-François Lyotard codifies these efforts and announces the end of the age of ''metanarratives.'' See, especially, Jacques Derrida, *Writing and Difference* (Chicago: University of Chicago Press, 1978); Michel Foucault, *The Order of Things* (New York: Vintage Books, 1973); and Jean-François Lyotard, *The Post-Modern Condition* (Minneapolis: University of Minnesota Press, 1984).

5. What we call ''common sense'' is never something autonomous that we can use as a yardstick to measure theoretical frameworks. Today's common sense is the diluted, deferred ramification of a theory from the past.

6. Obviously, progress in limited individual areas would remain possible; together with simultaneous retrogression in others. But the larger notion of simultaneous, linear progress scientifically, morally, politically, socially, technologically, psychologically, etc., would be lost.

7. For example, if we think greater egalitarianism is necessary, then it must be defended substantively on the basis of an explicit discussion of such things as the nature of justice and the human good. In such a discussion, all manner of suppressed premises would have to be made explicit. Then we would immediately see the difficulties involved in enjoining the substantive debate.

8. One can accept the wisdom of unleashing human spontaneity from bureaucratic manipulation without falling prey to a mythic faith in an ''invisible hand''—one permutation of which is not that far from Hegel's notion of the ''cunning of reason.''

9. One exception is William Galston's *Liberal Purposes: Goods, Virtues and Diversity in the Liberal State* (New York: Cambridge University Press,

1992). Fukuyama may still be correct that the kinds of virtues Galston cata-logues are an uninspiring ensemble ill-equipped to hold the spiritual attention of the brightest and best, or even the majority.

10. Elsewhere I have differentiated what I believe could legitimately be called postmodern from postmodernism. The latter is a straightforwardly late-modern phenomenon. See my *Between Eternities: Deflections Toward a Post-modern Philosophy* (Chicago: University of Chicago Press, 1994).

11. The not so subtle irony is that many of those who attacked Fukuyama had been operating upon their own furtive, usually suppressed, End of History theses.

12. This is precisely what a self-styled "postmodern, bourgeois ironist" like Richard Rorty does. See especially *Contingency, irony, solidarity* (New York: Cambridge University Press, 1991).

13. The central issue we confront at this point is one that cannot be ade-quately dealt with at present: What is the relation between reason, habit, and tradition? The End of History thesis is the ultimate outcome of the Enlighten-ment faith that reason could replace habit and tradition completely. That was a fantastic hope from the beginning. But through acting upon that faith we have gone a long way toward destroying the habit background that is needed by any functioning society. Reason always requires law and habit as allies.

Even if reason is sufficient to grasp eternal questions and problems, that does not prove that reason can be immediately manifested in the conventional ar-rangements needed for everyday life. Indeed, reason can be adequately mani-fested in more than one set of conventional arrangements—the doctrinaire, modern, absolutist faith to the contrary notwithstanding. That is substantially what Aristotle meant when he asserted that justice is natural even though it changes.

The relation between philosophic insight and the traditions and *ethoi* that support daily existence is complicated. Unless one retains an unbounded faith in Enlightenment, shared *ethoi* are needed and must be allowed to evolve slowly over many generations. We cannot simply will traditions even if we could grasp the Whole exhaustively. We always need to find the way to articulate the truth for our time and place. How that could be accomplished in our time of unprece-dented simultaneous changeability and creeping homogeneity remains the open question.

Even if we concluded that Plato, Aristotle, Aquinas, or whomever had grasped the truth, it still has to be articulated publicly and manifested in laws, customs, and habits. And the truth must be presented in ever renewed poetic articulations. Where are the poetic articulations, habits, and traditions for our time—the time at the end of the persuasiveness and plausibility of many *mod-ern* beliefs and premises?

14. Consider in this regard, Alexis de Tocqueville, "How the Aspect of Soci-ety in the United States is at Once Agitated and Monotonous," *Democracy in America*, trans. George Lawrence (New York: Doubleday, 1969), pp. 614–16.

15. Of course, we can always believe in—or will—some version of the eternal recurrence. Even then we would be forced to explain what circumstance might return us to the beginnings. For us, the possibility of such a "return" probably would imply an apocalypse no sane person would wish for. But this would still not disprove the End of History thesis which claims only the impossibility of future novelty, not the impossibility of retrogression.

16. The collapse of Western (a.k.a. American) liberalism would in and of itself prove nothing. Likewise, natural catastrophes that reduce us to a more barbaric situation would prove nothing. The question would be, did we move to a novel set of historical possibilities, or "back" to ones that had already been lived? Having been pushed back to such a prior state, would we long for something novel in the future or would we then strive to get back to where we had already been? Everything comes back to the question, is there something novel—beyond late modernity—to long for? If not, the End of History thesis is plausible. The only point at which empirical evidence would be interesting is the empirical production of a novel ideal. We have seen none since Hegel.

17. If one accepts the argument that human nature is fixed and that there are a finite number of fundamental questions and human longings capable of playing themselves out, at some point history should have played out its finite possibilities. At that point only repetition or stagnation are possible.

18. It is no good saying that changes in material circumstances precede all changes in ideas, for one must still conceptualize, using ideas, what that change is/was. Worrying about the relation between ideas and material circumstances, one quickly gets drawn into an unsolvable chicken-egg conundrum. Rather than be drawn into this useless discussion we should bring ourselves back to more manageable observations, such as the observation that ideas have concrete consequences and no ideas are formed in a vacuum. We should add to this the understanding that truly novel ideas are rare.

19. The same response can be made to those who say that "philosophy" represents a satisfactory response to present dissatisfaction with the moral and political contours of the late modern world. "Philosophy" is hardly an alternative for any but a few—to believe otherwise is Enlightenment at its silliest. Further, if philosophy exists only in some Epicurean garden, of what public interest is it? We may grant that philosophy should not be turned into a public weapon as it has in the modern world, but as an entirely private affair of the few it would be publicly irrelevant and hence irrelevant to the present discussion. Were the privatization of philosophy to occur, we would have the Nietzschean picture of free-spirited over-men tripping quietly across the anthills that pass for civilization—what Nietzsche also termed the timeless "tombs of death." A deeper response would go to the nature of philosophy itself. Must not philosophy, in Socratic fashion, remain in the cave, and begin from speeches in the political community? If so, the Epicurean alternative is destructive for philosophy itself. Once we recognize the need to speak, we recognize simultaneously the need to be persuasive. Then we are led back to the issues we have

been discussing—what novel ideal can be persuasively argued for at present—surely not the universalization of philosophy?

20. This is not to say that in unhinging old presuppositions Heidegger's thought may not eventually have concrete, deferred ramifications. See in this regard my *Between Eternities*, especially Part 3, "Heidegger's Critique of Modernity and the Postmodern Future."

21. It is not at all easy to explain what accounts for the disintegration of faith in a moral or political dispensation—unless, of course, one turns to Hegelian premises. It is far too easy to say that it is because the old dispensation came to be seen as false. Does that mean that the reason for its initial persuasiveness was precisely its falsity? It seems to me that a dead end lurks in that direction. It is unlikely that reason is ever *fully* adequate to "prove" or "disprove" the persuasiveness of a political and moral dispensation. To claim that it is gets us in the awkward position of arguing that the "irrationalists" had, at one time, the stronger "reasons." And once again, even if we are capable of a noetic apprehension of the truth, it must still be put into speech, and unless you are Hegel, there is more than one way to do that. There is no reason to believe that what some of us might see as a compelling articulation of the truth will be publicly more persuasive than what some of us perceive to be false.

22. The idea that our fundamental humanity is to be found in our ego or consciousness rather than in our instinctive materiality is one of the central modern premises from Descartes to Hegel. It was not a premise shared by, for example, Plato. By the time this modern idea had worked its way out to Kant and Hegel, our fundamental humanity was to be found not only in consciousness, but in conscious opposition to or negation of our instinctive materiality. This consciousness/instinct dichotomy is a distinctively modern invention.

23. Many critics of the End of History thesis have dismissed Kojève as a quaint and curious volume of increasingly forgotten lore. But the customary basis for those rejections is far from weighty—usually boiling down to the observation, correct if banal, that Anglo-American academics have paid him almost no attention. But Kojève is one of those rare individuals who truly deserve to be called thinkers. He knew how to take a theoretical premise, isolate its key concepts, and follow them resolutely to wherever *they* might lead, regardless of personal rooting interests. That kind of philosophical honesty is rare. It does not prove that Kojève is correct, but it does prove he deserves respect. By the same token, that most Hegel scholars dismiss Kojève's reading of Hegel does not prove that he is wrong. It is rare to find scholars who are honest brokers. One cannot fail to see the extent to which Hegelian scholarship gives us a liberal, socialist, conservative, or simply boring Hegel.

24. This could also, to use a term coined by Rousseau, be designated our "metaphysical freedom." This is *the* premise of late modernity—shared by Rousseau, Kant, Hegel, Marx, existentialism, critical theory, etc. This is the idea upon which late modernity must make its stand. See in this regard my *Between Eternities*, Part One, "The Essence of Modernity." According to this

understanding, our metaphysical freedom is based on the fact that we are unlike all other species in that we are instinctively underdetermined. This allows us to determine ourselves, to a greater or lesser extent and more or less consciously, depending on the author. Unfortunately, the competition to determine man becomes increasingly hypothetical, abstract, and artificial, at which point one senses that this line of argument has more or less reached its terminus. For an Anglo-American example of this artificiality consider John Rawls, *A Theory of Justice* (Cambridge: Harvard University Press, 1971) and his "Original Position."

25. For reasons I will indicate shortly, I don't believe we should become overly delighted with the premise that human nature can always reassert itself. We live in a time when the mentality of limitlessness has taken hegemony. We are simultaneously equipped with techniques that allow us to assault natural limits—e.g., genetic engineering—and the desire to transcend all natural limits. Even if we could articulate what is fixed in our humanity, we are in a position to eradicate it. Hence the central question is one of ideas: should we or should we not continue further on the path to overcoming natural limits? We are then led right back into the kinds of issues we have been considering.

26. In my opinion, we are not confronted here by an either/or situation: The relationship between evolving consciousness and determinate materiality is complex. Fukuyama needs to work out more explicitly how the two are related. Perhaps he will return to this issue in the forthcoming sequel. The End of History debate confronts us with a version of the traditional nature/convention distinction. Is man primarily shaped by education, environment, culture, etc., or is he a genetically fixed and determinate being? This is in turn a version of what I would argue is an unsolvable chicken-egg problem of whether ideas cause changes in material reality or whether material changes prefigure changes in ideas. I believe it is best to conclude that the relationship is complex and that an either/or answer is not available. We have a fixed being that must be completed by habit—i.e., in a variety of different ways, albeit not an infinite variety. Our changing ideas have a significant influence on how that is accomplished.

Even here we are not confronted with a fundamentally empirical issue. Every modern "science" that presumes to speak about reality presupposes theories prior to the act of approaching empirical data; it would be naive to think that those theories were morally and politically neutral. To try to deduce anything from scientific "facts" is simply to dig up what was presupposed from the very beginning. No science is morally, politically, or metaphysically neutral. We should dismiss the contrary early modern faith as a myth. Given that modern science cannot mediate the nature/convention issue, it is probably the case that we will never get beyond the conclusion that the relationship between evolving consciousness and determinate materiality is complex. Put another way, we will never get around the need to do speculative political philosophy.

27. As mentioned above, even if we find dissatisfaction by a few—or any minority—with the present world and the prevalent articulation of the Whole,

justice and the good, it need not be interesting if global satisfaction by the majority remains. Because we live in a mass democratic age it would be unclear what ideas could come along to delegitimize the hegemony of the tastes, perceptions, and desires of the majority. Who thinks there is a plausible basis for a newly legitimate aristocracy, and from what direction might we expect its approach? Therein one may see one of the more compelling reasons why an extended hiatus of history is plausible.

28. This means we will never put to rest the fundamental nature/convention question and should be cautioned not to accept any simple invocation of either side of the equation.

29. For an important reflection on this subject see Joseph Cropsey, "The End of History in an Open-Ended Age?" in *If History Is Not Over, Then Where Is It Going? Reflections on Progress and Democracy,* eds. Arthur Melzer, Jerry Weinberger, and Richard Zinnman (Ithaca: Cornell University Press, 1994).

30. I have undertaken such a discussion in *Between Eternities.*

31. In other words, philosophy must always remain primarily dialectical political philosophy, for its own sake as well as that of the rest of the world. The retreat to some garden of shared noetic apprehension—which always raises the question of whether or not one is engaged in some subjective fantasy—points toward an ultimate alogon, "blindness." Here we should recall the Socratic metaphor of trying to grasp Being directly as an inevitably blinding staring at the sun. Religion always runs the same risk of blindness as any simply noetic philosophy. Our noetic visions, whether based on grace or otherwise, must be brought to speech. Even faith in the words of the prophets raises the question of how to tell true from false prophets. All of our endeavors require dialectical speech. There is no way to transcend the dialogue which is intrinsic to being human. As dialectical, philosophy must be of and part of its shared world, and that ultimately means it must engage in shared public speech.

2

From Fukuyama to Reality:
A Critical Essay

Theodore H. Von Laue

The assessment of Fukuyama's book here offered looks first at his formula for a "universal directional history" culminating in the worldwide adoption of liberal democracy, then analyzes its flaws. Second, it examines the commonly overlooked conditions supporting that form of government and its appeal around the world. Finally, evaluation of Fukuyama's thesis demands, at least in outline, a version of a "universal directional history" allowing a more realistic grasp of the unprecedented new age of global interdependence.

The Guiding Formula

Endowed with a bright, widely informed, well-read, spirited mind, Fukuyama has been prompted by communism's worldwide collapse to attempt a "history" of mankind. Completing his book before the dissolution of the Soviet Union and the mounting crises in Russia and the successor states, he nevertheless sensed the drift of events. The "good news has come. . . . Liberal democracy [now] remains the only coherent political aspiration that spans different regions and cultures around the globe" (xiii). Put more strongly: "As mankind approaches the end of the millennium, the twin crises of authoritarianism and socialist central planning have left only one competitor standing in the ring as an ideology of potentially universal validity: liberal democracy, the doctrine of individual freedom and popular sovereignty" (42) . . . "together with its companion, economic liberalism" (48). This optimistic exultation reverberates throughout the book. History and all the miseries so prominent in it have essentially come to an end. At this turning point in the human experience we certainly need a universal directional history rising above all traditional horizons as a compass for living at this historic moment. Fukuyama deserves credit for lifting us to a mental elevation appropriate to the end of the twentieth century, even if there are reasons to doubt that his observations realistically cover the landscape.

He bases his optimistic conclusions on two key factors. First, he considers modern natural science and technology as a "regulator or mechanism to explain the directionality and coherence of History" (xiv). It guarantees an "increasing homogenization" of all human societies regardless of their historical origins or cultural inheritances, leading to a universal consumer culture. Yet there exists an even more powerful "motor of history": the human urge for recognition, for self-esteem, persistently called in this book by the Greek term *thymos* (xviii). That urge, Fukuyama argues, promotes liberal democracy, which alone is capable of satisfying it; hence liberal democracy's universal validity. For his proof Fukuyama relies foremost on Hegel's philosophy, which traced the evolution of human self-awareness and self-esteem to the point of perfection, now achieved, according to Fukuyama, in liberal democratic society.

Fukuyama's basic perspectives are chiefly derived from the German philosophers, Hegel (as interpreted here by Alexandre Kojève, a Russian turned French philosopher in the 1930s), plus Marx and Nietzsche. All three of them have been absorbed into mainstream European thinking regardless of their German peculiarities. Yet they looked at the countries in which the foundations of liberal democracy were laid as outsiders. They were prompted by cultural values different from the insiders in France, England, or the United States. They, and Hegel most prominently, searched for philosophical frameworks capable of integrating the more practical Western with their more abstract German ways of feeling and thinking. In this manner Hegel (according to Kojève) envisaged an end of history produced by the ideals of the French revolution; Marx built that interpretation into the vision of communism as the final stage of social evolution. Fukuyama now applies it to liberal democracy, the most perfect form of human self-realization.

Fukuyama's philosophical sources give his analyses an intellectual zest. But how much did these German thinkers understand the dynamics shaping a political ideal which they knew only from afar? Fukuyama himself admits the shortcomings of his approach: "Any Universal History we can construct will inevitably give no reasonable account of many occurrences which are all too real to the people who experience them'' (130). An unsympathetic critic might even turn his rejection of pessimistic Realpolitik against him, calling his optimistic interpretations ''an impermissible reductionism concerning the motives and behavior of human societies, and failure to address the question of History'' (254). Like his guides Fukuyama looks at liberal democracy as a philosophical outsider.

His analysis is premised on the simplistic Hegelian paradigm of the slave and the master. The slave, representing all of humanity, craves recognition of his self-worth. That craving, his *thymos*, has shaped the progress of history toward ever higher levels of rationality and freedom. Emerging first, according to Hegel and Kojève, in the French Revolution, it reached its ultimate stage in the contemporary achievement of liberal democracy worldwide. ''The success of democracy in a wide variety of places and among many different peoples would suggest that the principles of liberty and equality on which they are based are not accidents or the results of ethnocentric prejudice, but are in fact discoveries about the nature of man as man, whose truth does not diminish but grows more evident as one's point of view becomes more cosmopolitan'' (51).

He finds no lack of evidence in support of his theme. Using ''a strictly formal definition of democracy,'' he argues that ''a country is democratic if it grants its people the right to choose their own government through periodic, secret-ballot, multi-party elections, on the basis of universal and equal adult suffrage'' (43). On this minimal basis Romania, Nicaragua, and Sri Lanka qualify as liberal democracies on Fukuyama's 1990 count of sixty-one liberal democracies worldwide (49–50). The impressive increase in liberal democracies (as defined by Fukuyama) prompts his triumphant conclusion: ''if we are now at a point where we cannot imagine a world substantially different from our own, in which there is no apparent or obvious way in which the future will represent a fundamental improvement over our current order, then we must also take into consideration the possibility that History itself might be at an end'' (51). We are now entering the age of post-history. Are we really?

Fukuyama himself, as he learnedly and often perceptively analyzes the many problems confronting liberal democracy, prevaricates: ''some new authoritarian alternatives perhaps never before seen in history, may assert themselves in the future'' (235). Or ''most existing liberal democracies do not yet fully measure up'' to the ideal (291). Or ''a large historical world coexists with the post-historical one'' (318). Or ''the ability of liberal democratic societies to establish and sustain them-

selves on a rational basis over the long term is open to some doubt''
(335). Fukuyama's concluding sentences lead to an even greater skepticism about the validity of his theme. Comparing mankind to "a long
wagon train strung out along a road" (338), he ends his book by saying
that "in the final analysis" we will not know whether the occupants of
these wagons, "having looked around a bit at their new surroundings
[in the post-historical era], will not find them inadequate and set their
eyes on a new and more distant journey" (339). Put more simply: the
dialectics of history are likely to go on after all ad infinitum.

Flaws

Obviously, there are many flaws in Fukuyama's argument. At one point,
for instance, he argues that "the class differences that exist in the contemporary United States . . . are due primarily to differences in education" (116). Two pages later he stresses the "profoundly cultural nature" of the differences between blacks and whites—differences that
are certainly part of the class differences. He should have done some
reading in the field of cultural anthropology. It might also have prevented his affirmation of the universality of the liberal democratic ideal
and shown him how excessively Eurocentric—or even America-cen-
tered—his thesis is. Disputing Max Weber's assertion that democracy
was the product of the specific cultural and social milieu of Western
civilization, he argues that "it was the most rational possible political
system and 'fit' a broader human personality shared across cultures"
(220–21). But he offers no evidence of indigenous non-Western liberal
democracies; in fact none exist. Liberal democracy spread as a result of
the Westernization of the world; its appeal is based on a wide range of
factors, all derived from superior power.

The most crucial flaw is Fukuyama's blindness to the centrality of
power (a common failure among Americans, who as a nation possess
the most power in the world). The "slave" does not yearn for recognition and self-respect alone. Human beings need these qualities for en-
hancing their physical and psychological security; they crave power to
dominate their natural and human environment individually and collec-
tively. In his Chapter 23, The Unreality of "Realism," Fukuyama tries
to discredit Thucydides' dictum: "Our opinion of the gods and our
knowledge of men lead us to conclude that it is a general and necessary
law of nature to rule wherever one can."[1] Liberal democracy, he pleads,
has relegated power struggles to the past: "The civil peace brought

about by liberalism should logically have its counterpart in relations between states'' (260). Well, not quite, for, following a Hegelian line of thought, he asserts that ''a liberal democracy that could fight a short and decisive war every generation or so to defend its own liberty and independence would be far healthier and more satisfied than one that experienced nothing but continuous peace'' (329).

Among human beings power, admittedly, takes many forms, ranging over a wide gamut from physical violence to saintly persuasion. The most powerful human beings, one might argue, have been prophets and founders of religious creeds, shaping the conduct of men and women over generations. Religion, the nature of which lies outside of Fukuyama's grasp, is concerned with a subtle power struggle in individual awareness between elemental human selfishness and the emotional controls necessary for peaceful human relations within a given community or even worldwide; in league with greater material comfort and civic security it has immensely civilized the perpetual Hobbesian power struggle. But as any close examination of contemporary democratic politics or at any group activities will show, the power struggle never ends; look at any church, any office, any academic department, or even at any family.

While the competition for power has become remarkably civilized in close-knit communities, it has always taken a raw form between collectives like tribes, nations, or states. When in the first and second world wars the survival of the most civilized states was threatened, what did the individual lives of their citizens count? They were sacrificed by the millions. External security was—and still is—a precondition for the continuation of civilized life at home. Lucky were those countries that had been secure from invasion by oceans, high mountains, or natural and human resources enabling them to build strong states or empires. Empires especially conveyed not only external security but also a sense of psychological assurance; they also served as models, inciting imitation among others and thereby shaping their aspirations.

As early as the eighteenth century, the framework for power politics was global. The archbishop of Goa, Ignacio de Santa Teresa, observed in 1725: ''God has deliberately chosen the Portugese out of all other nations for the rule and reform of the whole world, with command, dominion, and Empire, both pure and mixed.''[2] Other peoples, including the Spanish or French, claimed that role for themselves. At the end of the nineteenth century the British people basked in the glory of their empire, the biggest in history, sometimes (like some Americans too) carrying their pride to the extreme of racism. Whetting the political appetites of Germans, Russians, Italians, or even Japanese and Chinese—of communists and fascists—do they thereby not also share the responsibility for their enemies' actions? Let us never underestimate the power of a role model.

Americans, of course, had from the start claimed their republic to be "a city on a hill" serving as guide for all humanity. After World War II they became the universal model in the ever more subtle power politics of envious comparison. Which people did not want to live like Americans? Did Fukuyama ever consider the American ambition to extend the American way of life (including liberal democracy) around the world as a universal blessing? Such collective *megalothymia* (Fukuyama's term) is not part of his vision of liberal democracy, but is it not at work among many Americans? In any case, after the defeat of communism, the worldwide competition for wealth and power continues unabated. Relieved of nuclear-armed superpower confrontation, it is now at work in an ever more tightly interdependent world.

Basic Foundations of Liberal Democracy

At this point it seems appropriate, for the sake of commenting on Fukuyama's plea for optimism as well as contributing to an effective directional universal history, to consider for once the price paid for the exercise of power. It is an aspect commonly ignored by social scientists and historians but of crucial importance for understanding the dynamics of historical evolution and of liberal democracy.

Consider, for example, the human power over nature exercised by a simple tool, say a hammer.[3] In order to accomplish his purpose, the hammerer has to submit to the hammer, adjusting his motions in order to make his tool serve his purpose. The more complex the tool, the more extensive becomes the human submission to its peculiarities. The users of a machine must learn how to comply not only with its technical complexity but also, in a far more elaborate manner, with the extensive social organization that produces and services the machine. The machinists are part of what may be called a huge "social machine" providing the essentials that make this mechanical tool work. To mention but a few of these essentials: they include metal for the machine, the skills of engineering, the commercial organization for producing and selling it, and even more important, the social and political order that sustains all human cogs working in this "social machine." Modern technological society, dedicated to exploiting nature for human benefit, enslaves its members to a vast multitude of restraints. They gain from them and therefore, for the most part, do not even notice them.

The exercise of power over human beings entails an even more demanding submission to the necessities involved. If power is exercised by violence, the power wielders still must submit to the procurement and construction of weapons in a social support system they cannot avoid; a criminal using a shotgun is tied to some social transactions equipping him with his weapon. At the other extreme, saints exercising power through martyrdom have to submit to an internal discipline of prayer, meditation, and spiritual exercises, all suppressing their bodily promptings to a degree traditionally causing admiration and imitation among average people who are compelled, as members of a group, to practice at least some self-restraint.

Obviously, the more the vital energies of a people are tuned to the common good, the more effectively will their community enable them to manage their affairs to their socially conditioned satisfaction. Their community in turn will more effectively compete with other communities in the power struggles between them; success in this competition commonly strengthens the submission of individual citizens to the common welfare. If these community-building restraints weaken or break down, as happens in times of easy self-indulgence and excessive collective pride, people tend to revert to their raw selfishness. They are in danger of returning to the Hobbesian state of nature, which denies them any guaranty of survival in the power competition of states (unless they submit to a Leviathan).

The Commonwealth, which Hobbes considered an alternative to the Leviathan, relies on the willing submission of its members to the common good. Whether affirmed by an official church, as in much of European history, or by unofficial religious belief, or by mere conformity to established mores enforced by government, individual submission to the socializing discipline of self-restraint is the unifying cement of any community—the more of it, the better for all. In primitive communities that restraint remained limited. For modern liberal democracies with citizens counting tens or even hundreds of millions it has an all-pervasive commanding impact. Let us face reality: *the members of the most advanced industrial countries are liberal democratic organization people; they live in the most subtly regimented social order in all human experience.* Never before have so many people worked together under minimal formal compulsion in such mind-boggling complex interaction, most of them imperceptibly conditioned to submit to the disciplined cooperation that with all its imperfections creates wealth and power unmatched elsewhere in the world.

This achievement, supported by the progress of science and technology, also requires unrelenting application of human energy. The volume and intensity of work has grown with the volume and complexity of social cooperation. The burden of physical exertion may have declined, but the intellectual and cerebral effort has been impressively expanded in all aspects of life. Kojève's—and Fukuyama's—expectation of less work in the post-historical era is a gross illusion. Building the better world they envisage for the twenty-first century certainly calls for an unprecedented spurt of physical and mental energy. These facts are worth including in a universal history, as the price paid for the exercise of power.

How then does it happen that in the intense social coordination and submission the run of people feel miraculously free? In Western society the sense of freedom has grown proportionally with the intensified subjection of individuals to ''the social machine'' and to the political discipline of liberal democracy. The answer lies in the fact that for the majority of the people, including the working class that stayed away from Marxism, the submission fulfilled their chief desires. In a geographic setting uniquely favored in the world they obtained not only more material comfort but, more importantly, the psychological satisfaction of promoting progress. The key agent in this subtle psychological transformation of submission into liberating fulfillment was an optimistic pride, a collective sense of victory in the universal competition for superiority mixed with a spiritual commitment to human perfection. Despite all imperfections, hardships, and even wars, people were building a better world for all humanity. Such was the common state of mind among the insiders, foremost the people in France, England, or the United States, who from the age of Enlightenment onward exercised global leadership.

But look now at the hostile outsiders barred from these material and psychological satisfactions. Listen to Marx or Nietzsche, and to intellectuals from the border areas of the West or from the Third World (and also of some of their allies on the inside). The expansion of Western influence around the world has raised bitter outcries among its victims against the intolerable pressures of life and work in the metropolitan center. By their values there exists no freedom in capitalist liberal democracy; people without inner depth live there in an enslaving conformity; work there means exploitation; individuals can't be themselves. They preach the pessimism which Fukuyama is determined to combat.

But is he right in saying that ''the twentieth century . . . has made all of us into deep historical pessimists'' (3)? Steeped in the writings of the outsiders, he minimizes the popular optimistic belief in progress that has traditionally propelled—and still propels—Western and especially American ambition for global leadership. Admittedly, at present pessimism is spreading among American intellectuals, as the economy deteriorates and American power in the world declines. As a result, optimism has become a political issue, especially for conservatives. There are good reasons to fear that if the traditional optimism weakens, the unifying bonds of voluntary cooperation will disintegrate. As the flaws in the American system become more obvious, pessimism grows; the polity becomes more splintered and divisive; liberal democracy is endangered. For the politically correct, therefore, the times call for an intellectually refined reaffirmation of the American dream and its optimism buttressing liberal democracy—just what Fukuyama tries to provide.

Obviously, under American influence, that optimistic faith in liberal democracy still flourishes around the world. But—to take issue once more with Fukuyama's conviction that liberal democracy is a conscious aim of all humanity—that belief is merely a part of the Western model's overall attraction. What seems to count most in that model is the opportunity for liberation from the humiliations of backwardness, the escape from poverty and powerlessness, rather than the form of government. To be sure, the model also promises personal liberation from political control—to outsiders who are blind to the huge burden of obligations operating within the much admired model. As immigrants in a liberal democracy they commonly stay outside the civic process, ignorant of its demands and often disillusioned with liberal democratic society.

If they stay at home and try, as leaders of liberation movements, to introduce the economic and political benefits supposedly flowing from liberal democracy, they face immense obstacles. How can they reshape their peoples to act and work like the citizens of the model country? The crucial answer, still relevant after the collapse of communism, was supplied by Lenin in 1902. *"What is to a great extent automatic in a politically free country, must in Russia be done deliberately and systematically by our organizations."*[4] In other words, the subconscious social discipline of liberal democracy developed over many centuries in highly favored geographical and historical settings has to be quickly matched by an all-pervasive system of command. Not surprisingly, therefore, the imposition of liberal democracy upon unprepared societies after World War I led, in much of Europe, or in Russia and China, to the rise of one-party rule or dictatorship. The victims cried for liberation, even though they themselves (like the leaders of the Tiananmen demonstration in 1989) still shared the prevailing anarchic self-centeredness that made their societies, in Sun Yatsen's phrase of 1924, into an ungovernable "sheet of loose sand."[5]

Under the extreme conditions prevailing in the Russian empire at the end of World War I, when the very survival of the country was threatened, Lenin's prescription created Soviet totalitarianism (a subject poorly understood by Fukuyama). As a Russian patriot in Marxist disguise Lenin optimistically adapted the Western promise of liberation and pride of global superiority to Russian conditions; Soviet communism was to be the culmination of human perfection. At the same time he was compelled to substitute rigid political control by his Communist party for the missing spontaneity of civic cooperation. Even more aware of the country's danger than Lenin, Stalin, with harrowing brutality, subsequently imposed upon the raw peasant masses of Eurasia the disciplined solidarity needed to repel Hitler's even more brutal plans for ruling Russia. Stalin thereby raised the Soviet Union to the position of a super power.

But while granting the country an external security unknown in its history, those artificially imposed restraints by their very nature prevented the creativity-enhancing growth of voluntary cooperation. In the incessant power politics of envious comparison (to which the handicapped Russians, in contrast to the traditionally victorious Americans, are keenly sensitive)[6] the Soviet system, designed for a country in a most disadvantaged area of the globe, could not compete with the most favored Western democracies. When Gorbachev allowed unrestricted comparison with Western prosperity by opening his country to what he described as the "unprecedented richness of foreign contracts," the Soviet system collapsed—to Fukuyama's delight. The reason, however, was not the superiority of liberal democracy, as he argues, but the profound difference in the factors shaping Western and Russian culture.

Would that Fukuyama had some insight into the totality of factors shaping political systems or, more basically, universal history. Instead he, like most other Americans in their habitual cultural imperialism, imposes American perspectives grown in the American setting upon the rest of the world, with dubious results. For instance, assessing the conduct of the Russians under perestroika, he notes "an increasingly broad and vigorous civil society began to spring up spontaneously in 1990–91" (221). What wishful thinking about that brittle society composed of obstinate and self-centered people hardened by adversities beyond their control and utterly unknown in America! In the foreseeable future establishing liberal democracy in the Eurasian space is a utopian dream.

Realistic Perspectives for a Universal Directional History

What now, in the barest outline, would a universal directional history based on all factors shaping the human urge to survive by domination look like? To establish a meaningful pattern, we have to start with geography, commonly overlooked in historical analysis. The highly diverse land surface of the earth created different human responses to its challenges, all legitimate but tragically unequal when matched against each other in competitive interaction. From the start people in cool and wet climates had the advantage over those coping with heat and drought, as did people protected by oceans or mountains over those living in wide-open plains. Crucial minerals and food resources likewise were unequally distributed. Through the ages the intensity of human interaction facilitated by easy communications was a vital factor, responsible for advancing human creativity, most cruelly in war and more peacefully in trade and commerce. Both distributed to those capable of receiving them the instruments of power: weapons, goods, and knowledge in all its forms.

In the competitive interaction diverse power centers originated, the largest the Chinese empire, the smallest the city-states of ancient Greece. The latter benefited from the keen cultural exchanges in the eastern Mediterranean and from their highly charged internal politics, bequeathing their civic insights to western Europe until the very present. History records a long succession of dynasties and empires rising and falling in the vast Afro-Eurasian space, interlinked by military campaigns and trade networks that enlarged the scope of human skills, all harnessed to the desire for victory in the unceasing rivalry for domination in all its forms.

At the dawn of modern history, that competition was keenest in the area of the Mediterranean. Islamic rulers had expanded their domain into Spain, and the Islamic Turks advanced toward central Europe. Christian explorers based along the Atlantic coast searched for opportunities on the high seas, taking hold of the American continent and enlarging the sea power of their political masters into the Far East. From the Renaissance onward western Europe, aided by its geographic advantages, turned into a unique cultural hothouse, as city-states, feudal monarchies, and eventually nation-states interacted in all fields of human endeavor through peace and war. The embattled competitiveness of the peoples of western Europe and the ambitions of their rulers were constructively held in check by their common Greco-Roman roots and their Christian faith. The combination of diversity and unity produced in short order impressive advances in all fields of human achievement, including constitutional government and military power.

By the end of the nineteenth century the peoples of western Europe, led by the British and soon joined by the Americans (all summarily called "the West"), had extended their sway around the world. Western imperialism revealed the inequality of the power resources developed in different parts of the world. Everywhere people had engaged in the pursuit of power. But favored by factors essentially beyond human control the Westerners had prevailed. Under the banner of freedom they had carried the skills of power-creating human cooperation to the highest level in human experience. By victoriously penetrating all societies and all countries around the world, they set the direction in which humanity must henceforth march.

Thus began "the world revolution of westernization," the harrowing process of westernizing the non-Western peoples around the world caught in disabling disorientation between their indigenous traditions and the irresistible Western impact. Resistance, ever present, had to be undertaken on Western terms (no matter how eagerly denied).

Not surprisingly, imitation of Western achievements and power by their most envious rivals was the dominant theme of the twentieth century, leading to unprecedentedly brutal "world" wars. The first of these wars, in which the Germans tried to gain "a place in the sun" of imperial glory, set off a worldwide challenge to Western superiority. Soviet communism, appealing to the world's exploited majority, claimed to be the leader of the future. Fascist leaders like Mussolini and Hitler aspired to building worldwide empires. According to Japanese Prime Minister Tanaka, Japan was to conquer all of Asia and even Europe. World War II, raising the United States to super power status, ended the aggressive challenges of Germany and Japan. The Soviet Union, thanks to Stalin now the second super power, remained as the only challenger, until its collapse at the end of 1991.

In that year the worldwide sway of Western civilization and power was triumphally secured; all challenges had been defeated. Never before had all humanity been united under one dominant culture. It was the profoundest turning point so far in all human existence. Fukuyama is right in stressing its fundamental significance. In this utterly novel human condition we need a truly universal directional history to tell us where we are headed—complacently to the end of history, or apprehensively, even with alarm, to a perilous new beginning?

Let us face reality (here but briefly sketched). Never before have so many people—five and a half billion now, twice as many in the next century—encroached upon the limited resources of the earth. Never before, despite the immense differences in human capacities, have they existed in such irreversibly tight interdependence. Instant communications and high visibility have brought unprepared people into unprecedented intense interaction. The westernization of the world has created a global city crowded with highly assertive citizens trading in a single market of goods, money, and political influence. Humanity now lives in a cultural hothouse more competitive than its European predecessor and more divided.

In global politics the end of the super power rivalry has raised to prominence the many smaller local tensions hitherto festering on the sidelines. The American dominance has globalized the ideals of freedom and self-determination, with dangerous consequences. Now national, ethnic, or religious minorities claim political recognition or even independence, threatening the cohesion of states of which traditionally they had been part. The Soviet Union has collapsed, and Russia itself is in danger of splitting up. The splintering of Yugoslavia sets an infectious precedent in eastern Europe, the mid-East, India, Africa, and the Americas. Inclusive economic and political units are experimentally progressing in the European Community, in North America between Canada, the United States, and Mexico, and among the states of the Pacific rim. But even here separatism is rife, as among Cataláns and Basques in Spain, the Quebecois in Canada, or the people of Timor. The ideology radiating from the United States promotes a new divisiveness underneath the westernized surface at a time when global interdependence demands cooperation in larger units, if not worldwide. The new separatist movements, incidentally, are hardly run in a democratic fashion.

The American worldwide preponderance has another negative effect. It radiates American materialistic self-indulgence around the world, raising expectations for material well-being that not only cannot be met but also undermine all efforts to improve living standards. The underlying invisible social discipline still supporting the American (or Western, and certainly the Japanese) style of life is not transferable to other people. Among the latter, most of them caught in cultural disorientation, the impact of Western consumerism tends to promote corruption, just when an investment-oriented disciplined austerity is needed. It also prompts an elemental surge of migration from poor to rich countries, swamping the latter with unwanted immigrants. As a result, local violence is on the rise worldwide—as it is in the United States.

How sound is liberal democracy in the United States? Its economy is in disarray, burdened by a large national debt, continuing government deficits, and a high volume of private indebtedness. Insufficient funds are available for improving education or the infrastructure of communications. Worse, the cohesion of American society is becoming more brittle; people are more contentious, less inclined to voluntary cooperation. More alarming is the decline of public and private morality, the shrinkage of public awareness, the loss of common convictions. Open to the world as never before, Americans too are caught in cultural disorientation. In their midst different ethnic groups, reflecting the worldwide trend, aggressively affirm their cultural identity. Trying to escape the spreading cultural relativism, disturbed people turn to religious fundamentalism, which here as in other parts of the world acts as a source of disunity. Life has become too complicated; too many demands—or distractions—overload the human attention span; the global world has grown over people's heads. As a result democratic consensus has become more elusive (in matters of national security a measure of authoritarianism has been in effect since the 1950s). How under these conditions can the country retain its leadership in the global hothouse? That ambition obviously persists as a strong trend in American opinion. But how can it be realized, given the patent unwillingness among the bewildered public to change its self-centered ways and reorient its values? A conflict between global ambition and declining resources certainly looms ominously over the American horizon.

In addition that ambition is bound to run up against a much more disorderly world trapped between two contradictory tendencies. On the one hand, global interdependence is irreversible, calling for ever more active peaceful cooperation. On the other hand, the perspective-shrinking pressures of the global overload, combined with the intensified urge for collective and individual self-assertion in the name of freedom and human dignity, create a counter-global divisiveness. Both tendencies coexist in perpetual friction, creating ever new uncertainties. The North American Free Trade association, the European Community, and the Pacific Rim states, promising mutual integration, may in fact develop into economic rivals protecting their own regional turf. In addition, these centers too are bound to suffer from the worldwide malaise of cultural disorientation and from the rise of violence. And let us never forget: nuclear weapons are always available.

Everywhere the tensions between domestic priorities and the demands of foreign policy, between local self-assertion and global collaboration, are increasing. The dominant reality in the novel historical era of the global confluence is that the complexity of the world has grown beyond public comprehension. Under the overload, human perspectives are shrinking in the world just when they should expand. People tend to harden their traditional ways just when they should practice openness toward others.

In sum, difficult times lie ahead worldwide. In order to avoid the crises or catastrophes arising from ignorantly drifting into an unknown future handicapped by fancy philosophical optimism, we need a vision-enlarging pessimism in order to gain a realistic overview of the new era of global interdependence.

The times call for a new state of mind built around a heightened moral alertness that helps people to adjust their lives, their societies, and the world to peaceful cooperation in harmony with their natural environment. Human beings possess the intellectual and spiritual potential for improving their lives. But creating that new mind-set among a majority of the world's peoples will take a very long stretch of time indeed. The End of History beginning now? A Western ideology of optimistic complacency replacing the now defunct communist illusion? Let us ready our minds for a New History.

Notes

1. Thucydides. *The Peloponnesian War*, trans. Rex Warner (New York: Penguin Classics, 1954), p. 363.

2. Quoted by C. R. Boxer, *The Portuguese Seaborne Empire*, 1415–1825 (1991), p. 374.

3. See my essay elaborating this aspect: "Technology, Society, and Freedom in the Tower of Babel," *Technology in Society* (1983), vol. 5, 119–138.

4. *The Lenin Anthology*, ed. Robert E. Tucker (New York), 1975, p. 83.

5. Sun Yatsen, *The Three Principles of the People, San Min Chu I* (Taipei: 1963), p. 5.

6. Even among Americans alarm about challenges to their country's preeminence is now rising.

3

Fukuyama and the End of History

Susan Shell

What sort of thing must history be to end, where end implies neither material destruction of the earth (through its collision, say, with an errant asteroid) nor religious deliverance (by the coming, say, of the Messiah), but something like a culmination and completion inherent in the historical process itself? What, in other words, does Francis Fukuyama mean by history ending? And what "larger conceptual framework,"[1] to use his own language, enables him to distinguish the "essential" from the merely "accidental" in such a way as to conclude that history may have ended?

Fukuyama's implicit answer to these questions draws on a mixture of Kant, Hegel, and Nietzsche, a mixture that would seem idiosyncratic if Alexandre Kojève's shadow were not visible in the wings. Still, Fukuyama's brilliant and provocative essay presents itself as more or other than a footlight or footnote to Kojève. It may be useful, then, to turn briefly to the earlier sources of the idea of history on which the author at least partially relies.

I

The first celebrated proponent of the "idea of history" was Kant—the idol who has for some time been riding the crest of a resurgent wave of liberal/international optimism. It is thus chastening to recall that Kant himself was not quite an optimist, as the reference to the possibility of natural catastrophe in his essay *A Renewed Question* might well remind us.[2] A thinker who dwells on the stark possibilities that nature may have in store for us is not likely to be overly sanguine about man's ability to secure his own happiness in any final sense. What Kant meant by the "idea" of history was not a recipe for success, nor an outright prediction, but what he was inclined to call a "hope."

The idea of history is the idea of culture, understood as the process by which the human race progressively enlightens itself by freeing itself from nature's tutelage. (Such enlightenment resembles but also differs from the earlier Baconian ideal [to which Kant often alludes] of technological mastery.) The guiding idea that both legitimates and drives Kant's concept of history is that of justice or *Rechtlichkeit*—that state or condition (embodied in what Kant calls the perfect republic) in which the maximum freedom of each can coexist with the maximum freedom of all. One goal of human enlightenment is thus the universal liberal state, or to speak more precisely, a universal *federation* of liberal states (for Kant was wary of the tyrannical potential of a single homogeneous world order).[3] The proximate goal of history is a state or condition in which the fundamental human right (to maximum external freedom consistent with the rights of others) is fully guaranteed. What gives this goal its *ultimate* force for Kant is not its empirical likelihood but its moral necessity. The juridical condition is an a priori idea that we are all morally required to strive to actualize. And yet concerns about the practicality of the idea emerge, for how are we to strive to realize the idea with all our might if we harbor doubts about the possibility of success?

Kant's account (it is not quite a philosophy) of history arises as an attempt to quiet these doubts. If we can read into the seemingly meaningless treadmill of human folly and suffering a dynamic mechanism of progress—if such an interpretation is even possible—then something morally helpful will have been achieved. What is more, to the extent that human beings generally adopt this hopeful perspective, the end of justice will in fact be advanced, inasmuch as hope in progress is a spring to progressive action. In this way the idea of history can become, in Kant's words, a "self-fulfilling prophecy," unique among cosmological predictions because the objects of knowledge are themselves actual or potential *subjects* of knowledge. The *telos* or essence that is missing from our knowledge of the natural world (and which is available, according to Kant, only to God) is present in the case of history because the "purpose" is one in which all human beings (do or can) knowingly share. The story of history—and it is literally a "story" for Kant—can thus be a whole in a way that our knowledge of nature cannot. History is the human (or moral) world in a state of tentative and perpetual becoming—the only world whose end man can grasp because in this single case the goal or inner essence of the subject and that of the object are or can be one.

To be sure, justice alone cannot secure this end, which requires not merely reciprocity of right, but a genuine harmony of inner purposes, an ethical commonwealth in which men are united not only by their outward use of means but also by their inner ends. Outer freedom or justice is at best only a way station on the endless trajectory of the human race toward virtue or inner self-perfection. Few have been as emphatic as Kant about the spiritual limits of liberalism narrowly and selfishly conceived—a liberalism that amounts to little more than the ''glittering misery'' of self-regulating devils—unless and until it is accompanied by a genuine moral transformation of the inner man.

Kant's account of history (in which the Baconian ideal of mastering nature is somehow conflated with the ethical ideal of mastering oneself) can thus be understood both as a moral tool, and (more ambiguously) as a substitute for the shattered dreams of metaphysical dogmatism, a compensation for man's inability to fully know the natural whole. This double function (which emerges with particular clarity in Kant's *Critique of Judgment* —Hegel's favorite Kantian work) furnishes a clue to Hegel's own fully realized philosophy of history. Hegel's basic argument with Kant stems from what he perceives as Kantian otherworldliness. Theoretically, Kant assumes a noumenal world accessible to God alone and in relation to which human reason is found wanting. Practically, Kant projects the noumenal world as a moral ideal, approachable by man but unattainable—in this life at any rate. Kant's error on both scores lies in what Hegel calls his ''bad infinity,'' his obstinate blindness to the identity that unites the infinite and the finite. Kant's belief that human reason sets itself a task that it cannot complete rests on a mistaken understanding of the nature of that task. The comprehensive unity that theoretical reason seeks is not an achievement reserved to an otherworldly God but already accomplished in and through history. And the moral perfection that practical reason demands is not a state reserved to the hereafter, but a condition already accomplished in and by the actual political communities with which history culminates. Genuine freedom is not something purely inward and noumenal as Kant insists, something radically separate from the outer phenomenal nature that is addressed by politics; rather, freedom is the goal of history, which finds its fulfillment in the modern rational state and the universal mutual recognition and substantial satisfaction it secures to every citizen. Thus—and this is crucial—Hegel's History stands together with his Logic. Hegel can do away with practical otherworldliness (for this is what the Kantian idea-as-object-of-perpetual-approximation amounts to) only by doing away with theoretical otherworldliness, by showing (by way of the *Logic*) that the human mind can do and know what Kant reserved to a transcendent and creative God. Hegel's *Philosophy of Right* begins with an allusion to his *Logic*, without which, he insists, the concept of freedom—the very kernel of the idea—cannot be comprehended.[4] Until this kernel is understood, it could be argued, all bets are off as to whether history in the Hegelian sense has or hasn't ended.

But the history that Fukuyama has in mind is also Kojève's, and thus as much Marxian and Nietzschean as Hegelian. Again, the question: on what basis can one claim that history has ended? And by what right can anyone claim that the liberal idea has ended it? For Kojève, the course of history is epitomized in the struggle for recognition between master and slave—between one who for the sake of recognition risks his life, and one who, succumbing to the fear of death, becomes a slave who transforms nature through his own labor. History essentially ends, for Kojève, with the principles of the French Revolution as embodied and enacted by Napoleon: for it is here that the slave is fully transformed into the worker-citizen, willing to engage in the struggle to the death for recognition, and at the same time genuinely at home in a world made human by his labor.

Kojève's tour de force, which points to the "Universal and Homogeneous State" as the essential truth about the modern world, reads out of Hegel much that Hegel insisted upon—the continuing importance of a plurality of nation-states, for example, or the moral necessity of war, or the continued need for a constitutional monarch and a hereditary nobility to offset the homogenizing effects of market society. Indeed Kojèvean reason sometimes seems to owe less to Hegel than to Kant, albeit a Kant stripped of the last vestiges of moral and spiritual otherworldliness. What Kojève appeals to, and what makes his thought finally so compelling, is, I think, less its selective Hegelian scaffolding than a singular perceptiveness (almost Nietzschean in its pessimism) about basic features of the modern world. Thirty years ago Kojève's claim that there was no essential difference between the Soviet Union and the United States seemed ludicrous if not downright criminal. Today, the fall of the Berlin Wall and the constitutional equivocations of the former Soviet Union (not to speak of the international postmodern aesthetic Kojève helped to inspire) make his claims for convergence seem almost eerily prescient. In keeping with this Nietzschean mood, the end of history for Kojève is less a triumphant culmination—less the rational made real—than an exhaustion of possibilities and unbending of the bow, a final playing out of the negativity whose dialectical energy and *frisson* made history possible. The realization of freedom is thus for Kojève the abolition of freedom. The end of history is the end of man. Faced with such a dénouement, those who insist on clinging to the idea of history may wish to return (with relief) to the hopefulness of Kant, whose prediction that the spiraling cost of arms would finally put an end to war (a prediction that only a few years ago seemed laughably naive) no longer seems laughable. Better peace and prosperity (plus inner spiritual transformation) than peace, prosperity, and the end of man.

The trouble is, of course, that Kant's predictions were only hopes, grounded in moral convictions and speculative longings we may not fully share. The idea of history, however, has a peculiarly seductive power of its own, a power that may beguile us into reading a necessity into events that is absent from the events themselves. The precipitous collapse of communism as a worldview capable of claiming widespread allegiance and the simultaneous spread of an international consumer culture may lead us to imagine that we are at some sort of ''end,'' be it dispiriting or inspiring. Many of the world events that are currently unfolding are themselves the effect and afterglow of the idea of history in its various permutations. One should therefore be wary of reading in them independent evidence of the necessity of the doctrines that inspired them. Kant insisted that the predictive value of philosophic history is only as great as its capacity to make self-fulfilling prophecies. To forget the limits of such prophecy is to breach the distinction, on which Kant's measured optimism rests, between permissible hope and wishful delusion.

Current developments in Europe put one in mind of another, at least equally portentous prophecy.

> Owing to the pathological estrangement which the insanity of nationality has induced, and still induces, among the peoples of Europe, owing also to the shortsighted and quick-handed politicians who are at the top today with the help of this insanity, without any inkling that their separatist policies can of necessity only be entr'acte policies, owing to all this and to much else that simply cannot be said, the most unequivocal portents are now being overlooked, or arbitrarily and mendaciously reinterpreted—that Europe wants to become one.[5]

These words, uttered one hundred years ago by Nietzsche, whose own youthful health was shattered by the Franco-Prussian War, seem to anticipate not only the political catastrophes of this century but also the hopeful prospect of what Nietzsche elsewhere called (as Thomas Pangle has recently reminded us[6]) the ''good European.'' What counters that hope is the consideration that it is the *fact*, not necessarily the *meaning*, of Europe's yearning that Nietzsche calls "unequivocal." Given this fact, definitive pronouncement of the end of history and the victory of the liberal (that is to say, American) idea may be especially premature.

II

Fukuyama, however, is not (if I read him correctly) making any such pronouncement. In his pursuit of the reasons for liberal democracy's ascendancy, he is ultimately guided, not by Hegel or Nietzsche, but by Plato, that is, by a thinker lacking in (or superior to) what has been called the historical sense. Fukuyama discovers in Plato's typology of the human soul a template or model for understanding the politics of our time, and it is this model—not Kojève's dialectical logic—that gives Fukuyama's timely observations their untimely philosophic mooring. (His references to the "rationality" of the modern state must thus be taken as in some sense ironic.) The modern regime succeeds above all because it meets the demands of desire, spirit, and reason—the three parts of the soul enumerated by Plato—in a manner peculiarly suited to the requirements of a universal political order. The end of history rests, in Fukuyama's account, upon the dual supports of a progressive science that yields ever increasing material benefits, and a prevailing principle of justice or "recognition" that both presupposes and secures the equal dignity of all human beings. The modern liberal/technological state both liberates and harnesses desire; it also gives moderate scope to the spirited aspiration to excel while checking the latter's destabilizing pretensions. At the same time alternative ways of life find themselves doubly assaulted: first, military considerations, if nothing else, require adoption of the fruits of science, and with them—disregarding exceptional cases—such science's supporting habits, including (but not limited to) participation in a universal and culturally homogenizing world economy. Second, alternative standards of legitimacy find it ever harder to compete with a principle of justice deemed rational, not least because peculiarly suited to the twin demands of science and commerce.

Fukuyama concludes, however, by wondering whether the claims of human spiritedness can be answered so reasonably; he thus calls implicitly into question the rationality of the principle by which the contemporary world is guided, and with it the degree to which thoughtful people should, as Hegel claimed and urged, be satisfied. The harmonics of the soul defy techniques of mass production. The end of history is in fact an uneasy compromise, whose relative stability may mask future prospects not yet imagined.

If the modern rational state does not satisfy human beings (as Kojève came in a certain sense to admit),[7] it also lacks the character of dialectical necessity (on which Kojève continued, albeit ambiguously, to insist). Fukuyama's forceful demonstration of this double failure, combined with his extraordinary openness to the facts as they present themselves, make his work invaluable as a guide to the directions in which our politics may be taking us.[8]

Two questions, however, occur to me. I wonder, first, whether piety in a traditional sense figures in as relatively minor a way in the contemporary world as Fukuyama suggests. And I wonder, second, if the liberal principle of equal rights and freedoms does not owe more to such piety, however secularized, than to the dialectical logic of Hegelian recognition that Fukuyama implicitly discounts. That, in any case, is one way to understand the Lincolnian register in which America's liberal principles arguably find their deepest and most spiritual resonance. If either of these questions has merit, then the alternatives with which the author leaves us in this most pessimistic of optimistic books—Nietzschean love of fate or classical resignation to the intractability of politics—may not in fact exhaust the possibilities.

Notes

1. See Fukuyama, "The End of History," *The National Interest* (Summer 1989), 3.

2. See Immanuel Kant, *Political Writings*, ed. Hans Reiss (Cambridge: Cambridge University Press, 1991), p. 185.

3. Kant, *Political Writings*, p. 113.

4. G. W. F. Hegel, *Elements of the Philosophy of Right*, ed. Allen W. Wood (Cambridge: Cambridge University Press, 1991), p. 10.

5. Friedrich Nietzsche, *Beyond Good and Evil*, paragraph 256.

6. Thomas L. Pangle, *The Ennobling of Democracy: The Challenge of the Postmodern Era* (Baltimore: Johns Hopkins University Press, 1992), p. 81.

7. In becoming satisfied, human beings, according to Kojève, cease to be genuinely human. In the second edition of his *Introduction à la lecture de Hegel* (Paris: Gallimard, 1968), he corrects an earlier statement to the effect that people living post-historically are "happy," and instead claims that they enjoy only an animal contentment. The "snobbism" of Japan, where everyone is capable of committing "gratuitous" or contentless suicide, is the one human

possibility remaining (pp. 434n–37n). See also Fukuyama, *The End of History and the Last Man*, pp. 319–20.

8. The celebrity of Fukuyama's own work would thus seem to bear out (at least in this one instance) the Kojèvean claim that at the end of history recognition and desert converge.

4

Kant, *Thymos*, and the End of History

Joseph M. Knippenberg

There is much to admire in Fukuyama's ambitious effort to explain our situation after the demise of communism. Synthesizing social scientific development theory, political history, and political philosophy, he has offered us an account of "universal history" that purports to show its comprehensive meaning. There are, he says, two mechanisms that give history its direction and force. One is the combination of desire and reason that offers a competitive advantage to market mechanisms that promote and implement technological innovation. The other is the thymotic demand for recognition that can apparently best be satisfied in the universal respect for human dignity enforced by liberal democracy. Given the reductionism of much of contemporary social science, the former mechanism is hardly novel and reasonably well understood. Fukuyama's genuine contribution to the debates about the new world order is his demand that we take human *thymos* or spiritedness seriously.

Thymos and Politics

Following the tripartite division of the human soul first articulated in Plato's *Republic*, Fukuyama argues that it is spiritedness that is uniquely constitutive of the political realm. While desire and reason have satisfactions that are essentially private and only incidentally involve others,[1] spiritedness absolutely requires relations of respect and acknowledgment among human beings. Indeed, it is the various manifestations of spiritedness that pose the problems with which political thinkers have grappled through the ages. To take only the simplest examples, both Hobbes and Rousseau identify vainglory and vanity as forces that must in some way be overcome or managed in order to establish a healthy civil society. But rather than suppress or submerge *thymos*—the route by and large taken by the Anglo-American liberals who have followed Hobbes—Fukuyama takes his cue from a continental tradition that suggests that it is possible to transform and work with this passion.

To this end, he proposes a distinction between two varieties of *thymos*: *megalothymia* and *isothymia*. Megalothymia is the spiritedness characteristic of ambitious lovers of honor, who seek to extract from others, forcibly if necessary, acknowledgment of the high regard in which they hold themselves. This passion is characteristically satisfied by a fundamentally inegalitarian political order in which the few demand obeisance and respect from the many. On the other hand, isothymia signifies the longing to be treated, not as a superior, but as an equal. The isothymotic person wishes to be regarded as just as good as the next guy. He or she would be impatient with an inegalitarian order that makes it impossible to claim this regard, but could be satisfied with one that either gives everyone equal respect or affords everyone the opportunity to earn it. In short, while a megalothymotic individual can be satisfied only at the expense of others, an isothymotic person's satisfaction is in principle consistent with that of others. It is possible to imagine a political order constituted by the mutual respect of citizens for one another. Indeed, there is no need to imagine such an order, for liberal democracies that profess to respect human dignity embody such an understanding, at least in aspiration.[2] We can thus reconceive the political challenge posed by spiritedness in the following terms: how can we make certain that isothymia prevails over or supplants megalothymia?

Borrowing from a number of sources, Fukuyama offers a richly detailed account of how this development might occur. First, liberal institutions, such as those designed by the American founders, provide "a benign way to indulge man's natural pride and inclination toward thymotic self-assertion . . ." (187).[3] Second, the arena of activity made possible by a vital and growing capitalist economy offers an outlet for a kind of heroic approach to commerce: the pursuit of wealth is an economized, privatized, and largely constructive version of the struggle for unequal recognition that has such destabilizing effects in politics (cf. 315–16).[4] In the third place, there are also ambiguous human phenomena—like religion and nationalism—that derive much of their force from *thymos*. However much these have, at earlier stages in our history, served as sources and instigators of conflict, they can quite literally be domesticated, that is, relegated to the private or cultural, subpolitical sphere. Whatever the mechanism of this transformation—whether it be the conscious efforts at pacification on the part of those who have experienced the horrors of religious or national conflict or simply the gradual diminution of an initial "unnatural" fervor—the fact is that "mature" religions and nationalisms seem to be largely consistent with a liberal order of mutual respect.[5] Indeed, it can be argued that Christianity lays the groundwork for universal and mutual respect by teaching that "all men are equally endowed with one specific faculty, the faculty for moral choice" (196). Fourth, it should be possible to enlist *thymos* in defense of the principles of liberal democracy by cultivating in citizens "a certain irrational thymotic pride in their political system and way of life" (215). In sum, since the objects on behalf of which thymotic self-assertion is enlisted are in large measure fungible, megalothymia can be either sublimated, channeled into productive endeavors, privatized, or collectivized.

These transformative processes are not only possible but indeed choiceworthy because "*rational recognition,* that is, recognition on a universal basis in which the dignity of each person as a free and autonomous human being is recognized by all" is, at least in the view of Alexandre Kojève, "*completely satisfying* to man . . ." (200, 206; emphasis supplied). Fukuyama recognizes this contention as the linchpin of his entire argument and devotes a good deal of effort to examining it: "The question of the end of history . . . amounts to a question of the future of *thymos*: whether liberal democracy adequately satisfies the desire for recognition or whether it will remain radically unfulfilled and therefore capable of manifesting itself in an entirely different form" (289).

Fukuyama's answer to this question is a tentative and qualified "yes." Liberal democracy continues to face challenges from both the left and the right. The former, partisans of isothymia, insist on the incompleteness or indeed falsity of the equal recognition offered in a liberal democratic order and seek to spread equality still further, obliterating in the process all distinctions of rank. Those on the right who object do so on behalf of those very differences in rank. In Hegelian-Nietzschean terms, the promise of equality does not elevate the slave, but merely diminishes the master and therewith the human prospect altogether. What makes freedom attractive and ultimately dignifies humanity is creative self-assertion, not simple respiration or even the self-conscious capacity for choice. It is Fukuyama's "intuition" (314) that the latter challenge is more serious than the former. Natural differences in rank cannot be abolished by legislative fiat and consequently must eventually be recognized and accommodated. But the accommodations he identifies are by and large repetitions of devices he has discussed earlier: entrepreneurship, democratic politics (especially the conduct of foreign policy and war so long as there remain countries opposed to liberal democratic principles), and "purely formal activities like sports, mountain climbing, auto racing, and the like" (318). As a result, he must acknowledge that this "horizon of human possibilities" may not "be ultimately satisfying for the most thymotic natures," so that mega-lothymia may return in an extreme and pathological form" (328). In the end, "[n]o regime . . . is able to satisfy all men in all places" (334).

In short, if the sorts of recognition available in a liberal democratic society cannot plausibly be said to be completely satisfying, we must seek other grounds for preferring it to the alternatives, for promoting and implementing the devices that channel and sublimate *thymos*, if only imperfectly. While a commonsensical appreciation of the superiority of liberal democracy to its current alternatives and a natural "loyalty to our inherited values and traditions" (287) are readily available grounds for this preference, Fukuyama—unlike, say, Richard Rorty—does not insist that they are sufficient. They will persuade neither the megalothymotic few nor those who do not happen to share democratic traditions. As a result, "those who remain dissatisfied will always have the potential to restart history" (334). Furthermore, these grounds may not be adequate banners behind which to rally either a populace or an intellectual elite on behalf of a liberal democratic order.

Kant and the Moral Interest in History

To the extent that this *aporia* is to be taken seriously, Fukuyama might be well advised to examine further the continental tradition that makes so much of *thymos*. While he refers constantly to Hegel, Tocqueville, and Nietzsche, he is less dependent on Kant, from whose thought can be constructed a detailed account of the connection between *thymos* and the morality of mutual and reciprocal respect.

From a Kantian point of view, what is missing from Fukuyama's book is a discussion of how education and enlightenment can serve to transform the objects of *thymos*. The institutional solutions he proffers may not be sufficient, for, as Rousseau puts it, "the same vices that make social institutions necessary, make their abuse inevitable."[6] Furthermore, it is in considering how pride can be cultivated and edified as part of a moral education that we learn a great deal about the inner workings of this passion.[7] Appealing to the love of honor is, for Kant, an integral part of moral education, for that passion can be "the constant companion of virtue." While it is of course possible to desire honor in a manner conducive to conflict and vice—that is, megalothymotically— it is also possible to love it in a different way. According to Kant, those educated as "noble" lovers of honor seek mainly to avoid dishonor, for they compare themselves to an absolute and innate standard—the moral law—not to the status of others. From their subjection to this standard, they gain a sense of their dignity as human beings and a sense of humil- ity in seeing how far short of moral perfection they fall.

This sense of worth is the psychological sine qua non of the cultiva- tion and practice of moral virtue. Only when people feel that they owe it to themselves to live up to their potential, only when they take pride in it, will they try to control their desires, not to increase their pleasure, but to assert their inner dignity. While this self-control may not produce "objectively" praiseworthy acts, it can help avoid those that incur blame. A moral person's aversion to falling short of his moral potential, thereby dishonoring himself, is reinforced by his sense of the great dis- tance between his present condition and the moral perfection of which he is capable. Knowing the sublime heights to which he ought to as- cend, he cannot be satisfied with anything less. The humility intimately connected with this conception of human dignity can be an effective antidote to the arrogant pride that might otherwise follow from the love of honor.

Elicited by an education that "emphasize[s] above all . . . the *shame- fulness* of vice," the moral love of honor can replace its divisive coun- terparts. Because it depends on an absolute standard, it does not foster competition: one person's success does not require another's failure. It thus resembles Fukuyama's isothymia, but with a crucial difference: while the bare consciousness of the capacity for choice might lend itself to a kind of egalitarian assertiveness and arrogance, Kant's proper pride necessarily comes with an admixture of humility. The source of human dignity is not a formal capacity, whose content may well be arbitrary and hence susceptible to self-serving and self-flattering interpretation, but rather one whose exercise is intimately connected with the con- sciousness of a high vocation.

Stated in another way, we are much more certain of our subjugation to the moral law and of our capacity for living up to it than we are of *actually* living up to it. We may wish to hold others to high standards, but cannot confidently claim that we already live up to them ourselves.

Indeed, under the circumstances, we can only legitimately complain about others to the extent that we are willing to "complain" about ourselves. The assertive or agonic aspect of *thymos* can just as well be enlisted in the conquest of oneself as in the conquest of others.[8]

This sort of thymotic self-conquest cannot be prompted simply by the kinds of institutional devices that Fukuyama favors. While they may channel competition into peaceful, productive, or innocuous arenas, they do not turn *thymos* in on itself. What is necessary, from the Kantian point of view, is a serious religious and moral education that stresses both sinfulness and perfectibility, associating two elements that are typically separated.[9]

Another way in which Kant attempts to balance pride and humility is his treatment of the highest good, the systematic connection of virtue and happiness, for which he says human beings inevitably hope. We wish that our happiness be deserved, that is, that it be meaningfully apportioned, not simply the arbitrary product of chance. At the same time, we recognize that the world as we experience it does not correspond to our morally inspired hopes. While we might respond either with despair or anger, Kant attempts to offer grounds for hopeful and productive effort. His treatment of the highest good in this world and the next—in history and religion—aims to inspire our confidence without turning it into arrogance. We are indeterminately and illimitably potent in our capacity to transform nature (including human nature), to make it bend to our wishes, yet at the same time we are not masters of the universe. That is, we do not stand outside the world as its comprehensive cause. The completion of our efforts seems to require a divine supplement, a just God who ultimately makes certain that we get what we deserve. Still, Kant does not specify the limits of the human and divine contributions; as the former grows, the latter shrinks. He intends thereby to counteract despair by fostering pride and then to qualify or limit pride with a reminder of human finitude. Proper pride in our capacity to promote the attainment of our highest hopes is the product of this delicate balancing act.[10]

Now it is possible to take these contentions on two levels. On the one hand, we might ask whether Kant has gotten his moral philosophy and theology right. To the extent that an adequate defense of liberal democracy depends on eminently contestable claims about human acknowledgment of the moral law and about the primacy of morality to theology, we cannot flinch from this inquiry. Nonetheless, while such an inquiry may lead to conclusions no more assuring to liberal democrats than Fukuyama's own, I do not propose to undertake it here.

On the other hand, Kant's arguments may be taken simply as reflections of his insight into human moral psychology. We may then, in the spirit of Fukuyama's eclecticism, borrow from them in order to accomplish more or less practical goals.

In this latter vein, let me briefly summarize the "Kantian" contribution to Fukuyama's project. First, the proper balance between encouraging and discouraging human pride requires that human beings be brought to understand their dignity in moral terms. They have to be made to hold themselves to a standard whose very existence will humble them. Liberal institutions may more or less adequately channel *thymos* without ultimately containing it; liberal moral education is necessary if we are actually to transform it. Second, history has to be understood, as well, in moral terms. Its "end" cannot merely be a political state, but must be a moral one as well. We are, after all, much more likely to be humbled by a consciousness of our moral shortcomings than by one of our political or technological shortcomings. The last frontier, the moral conquest of human nature, would stand as a challenge to both resignation and arrogance.

In short, while Fukuyama admirably attends to the psychological, as opposed to the merely material, engines of history, he ultimately does not have enough to say about the human soul. Remaining wedded to an—albeit deeper and more comprehensive—Anglo-American institutionalism, he does not adequately explore the prospects held out by a politics that makes education more central to its mission.

Notes

1. Consider the city of sows and the Isles of the Blessed in the *Republic.*
2. Fukuyama observes that while much of the original language of the American founding is Hobbesian-Lockean, its self-understanding is better expressed in the Hegelian language of dignity and respect. Cf. Fukuyama, *The End of History and the Last Man* , p. 203.
3. All citations in the body of the text of this essay are to Fukuyama.
4. Cf. Alexis de Tocqueville, *Democracy in America,* trans. George Lawrence, ed. J. P. Mayer (New York: Harper and Row, 1969), vol. II, part III, ch. 18 (pp. 621–23).
5. For analyses of nationalism that agree with Fukuyama's conclusion, cf. Ernest Gellner, *Nations and Nationalism* (Oxford: Blackwell, 1983), and E. J. Hobsbawm, *Nations and Nationalism Since 1780,* 2nd ed. (Cambridge: Cambridge University Press, 1992). Both regard nationalism as a response to a specific set of historical conditions associated with modernization.

6. Jean-Jacques Rousseau, *Discourse on the Origin and Foundations of Inequality Among Men*, in *The First and Second Discourses Together with the Replies to Critics and Essay on the Origin of Languages,* ed. and trans. Victor Gourevitch (New York: Harper and Row, 1986), p. 193.

7. The argument of the next three paragraphs is drawn from my "Moving Beyond Fear: Rousseau and Kant on Cosmopolitan Education," *Journal of Politics* LI (November 1989), 809–27. The quotations are taken from Kant, *The Doctrine of Virtue*, trans. Mary J. Gregor (Philadelphia: University of Pennsylvania Press, 1964); *Anthropology from a Pragmatic Point of View*, trans. Mary J. Gregor (The Hague: Martinus Nijhoff, 1974); and *Lectures on Ethics* trans. Louis Infield (Indianapolis: Hackett, 1979). Full citations may be found in my article.

8. The best treatment of this is Susan Shell, *The Rights of Reason* (Toronto: University of Toronto Press, 1980).

9. For other suggestions about democratic education, cf. Thomas L. Pangle, *The Ennobling of Democracy* (Baltimore: Johns Hopkins University Press, 1992).

10. For an extended treatment of this subject, see my "The Political Significance of Kant's Treatment of Religion" (unpublished manuscript). I develop some of the arguments in "From Marx to Kant: The Perils of Liberal Idealism," *Political Science Reviewer* XX (1991), 101–43.

5

The End of Socialism's Historical Theology and Its Rebirth in Fukuyama's Thesis

Timothy Fuller

Fukuyama's assertion of the "end of history," the debate it incited, and his restatement and qualification of his thesis in *The End of History and the Last Man* converge to pose a proposition to American society that, although consistent with America's historic millennialism, we have yet to address in so many words: American foreign policy should be completed by articulating a specific ethico-theological standpoint and America's role in the world must have world-historical significance. We cannot grasp fully and explicitly the issue posed by Fukuyama's thesis unless we see it as a philosophy of history that attempts to be a civil theology for informing our political deliberations. America's role in the world is to be defined by a speculative philosophical thesis about the meaning of history that cannot be derived from the events of history alone, but which must be shown plausibly to fit the events of history as we know them.

The attempted union of the philosophical and the historical has been a matter of fundamental controversy since Hegel insisted that the philosopher's task was to contemplate the past and to theorize history in order to restore the sense of history's providential character, which traditional Christian doctrine could no longer provide in an intellectually commanding way. In the contemporary American context, we might say, the corresponding task would be to show how the sense of America's providential role in world history can be reformulated against the skeptical, demythologizing tendencies of the modern professional historians and the pressures of a multicultural worldview.

Analysts frequently insist that there are fundamental disagreements among Americans; that diversity is becoming an end in itself; and that relativism stalks the land, celebrated in the media and lent scholarly verisimilitude in the universities. Traditionalists argue that American culture is devoted to a perilous experiment of discovering if its social fabric can be beat to airy thinness without disintegrating altogether. They fear that we will only find out after we have gone beyond manageable limits into irreparable social chaos.

It should not be surprising, then, if many may, secretly or openly, wish for an anchor to establish a vantage point of evaluation and commitment in the midst of flux and blur. Equally, it is not surprising that many look with suspicion upon and resist this quest for anchorage—or feel guilty in seeking it—as a temptation to abandon what they consider the genius of the modern liberal tradition for a new, but possibly illiberal, orthodoxy. We are caught between aspirations to perfection and the uncomfortable awareness of the fickleness and the insubstantiality of what is thought and said in each generation. The perennial question of what to keep and what to change does not—I would say cannot—disappear from political life. One person's liberation is to another an iron cage.

Fukuyama's thesis caters to both aspects of our divided mind. Viewed in one way, the thesis celebrates the triumph of the West's existing liberal democratic regimes, contradicting the many predictions of the West's decline that have been grounded on the radical critiques of that very liberal democratic character. Viewed in another way, the thesis laments the passing of the age of the universalizing but dismal sciences of economics and management, leaving implicit the hint that we might want to resist the fulfillment that our age holds out to us.

As such, Fukuyama's prophecy actually does not surpass, but merely manifests, the kind of ethico-theological imagination that dominates our time. It also reveals how watery and cramped that imagination is, leaving little impetus to see beyond the immanent situation. For all of the elaborations of his argument in *The End of History and the Last Man*, Fukuyama takes the view that what is not historical is not real.

In Fukuyama's scheme, which recounts the inevitable triumph of the modern over the ancient, the passing of the primacy of politics has been under way for a long time. The triumph of liberalism is the triumph of the private over the high art of politics, and of the managerial over the heroic. The destruction of communism is unquestionably justified because it is a perversion of the human spirit. Liberalism is much more attuned to the human spirit, although liberalism seems to truncate the human spirit and is thus an incomplete and drab achievement. Liberalism is not perhaps exactly what we were hoping for when we set out on the modern path. Or perhaps, if it was what we thought we wanted, we did not understand fully what it would be like to have it. The globalization of Western liberalism does not preclude the possibility that liberalism will universalize its own internal tendency to decompose certainties and to disappoint us in assisting the direction of our lives. If liberalism is an incomplete or disappointing end, it is difficult to see how (even leaving aside commonsense observations about the unknowability of the future, which remain the simplest and most obvious objections to any speculation of Fukuyama's sort) it can be the vehicle to bring history either materially or imaginatively to an end.

The liberal tradition encourages individuals to have purposes and ideas of "good" while accepting simultaneously an inevitable plurality of purposes and of ideas of good. What validates plans, purposes, or projects is that these are *chosen* by particular individuals. This fits with the commitment to pluralism. On the one hand, all acts of self-expression are morally arbitrary because they can make no special claims. On the other hand, self-expression is intrinsically good. Thus, freedom and equality are strongly reinforced in our attitudes toward our typical associations, and agency—though taken to be intrinsically valuable—cannot set apart or designate particular acts or accomplishments of agents as intrinsically valuable. In the post-Hegelian tradition that informs Fukuyama's thought, a universal form is assumed: the liberal democratic, but it must realize itself in the individual rather than in the general. Individual realizations are espoused and applauded but not validated beyond themselves. The form of the age is not to be crystallized in a substantive achievement.

Recall the critique of liberalism delivered to us by Alexander Solzhenitsyn in his Harvard Commencement Address of June 1978. We live, he said, in a historic moment of transformation equal in its sweep to the transition from the Middle Ages to the Renaissance. The latter change was dominated by the rise of the liberal tradition whose custodianship of civilization—as he saw it in 1978—was under severe attack. For all its scientific and rationalist advances, the liberal tradition is imperiled by challenges that, if successful, would destroy the human spirit. Solzhenitsyn identified two weaknesses in liberalism requiring correction. First, liberalism needs a less self-deceiving diagnosis of what challenges it; second, liberalism must renovate its understanding of the human condition in light of the diagnosis and in light of certain ancient verities that are fast being forgotten. The great achievements of the Western legal systems have been, he insisted, vitiated by "legalism" that teaches not that the law is the practical actualization of a "higher law" of human fulfillment or flourishing; rather, legalism teaches that the law is the imposition of procedural control, for the sake of self-preservation, on the unruly but ethically neutral surges of human passion. Solzhenitsyn connected this to a foolish belief in the nonexistence of any necessary evil and a superficial optimism that we can take our destiny into our own hands.

Against self-congratulatory claims of enlightenment and progress, Solzhenitsyn identified a decline of thought into shallow hopes for the continuation of a comfortable life. His prescription was to revitalize the life of the spirit, to throw off "rationalistic humanism," and to recover the courage to reject the so-called emancipation from the moral heritage of the Christian centuries.

As powerful as Solzhenitsyn's critique of Western liberal democracy may have been, it was largely rejected as both a misunderstanding of the West's creation of a symbiosis between freedom and security, and an underestimation of the West's staying power. The collapse of the Soviet empire lends plausibility to this reaction to Solzhenitsyn. Yet obviously, the power of Solzhenitsyn's critique and the sharpness of the rebuke it elicited derived from his evocation of a traditional ethico-theological outlook that certifies what is real not solely in the events of history but instead in an experience of a permanent and transcendent wisdom.

Fukuyama's thesis, in proclaiming the triumph of the West, but also the decline of humankind, concedes much to the critique of liberalism that came to us prophetically from the East. However, it was inadequately and perversely incarnated by the regimes of the East and revealed the existence of residual elements within the liberal tradition that result from the old theological ways. The critique could come to us either from the East or from the residual internal critics because it is based in a theological framework different from the modern, progressivist, and historicistic one. It could come from anywhere that the ancient philosophical and theological reflections have previously held sway and are still remembered.

The Fukuyama thesis reveals both the reasons for the strong appeal of the Hegelian foundation (from which it springs) and the intellectual weakness of that foundation. According to Hegel's philosophy of history, ideas are powerful because they grip the imagination, energizing and channeling our passions into projects, which when fulfilled, will become evident in the materialization of ideas into the world. This will be their true realization: in political, moral, legal, ecclesiastical, economic, artistic, educational, and other institutions.

The power of the human spirit is found in its ability to achieve what it sets out to achieve. Of course, many projected achievements go unrealized; these are the "irrational" ideas because they cannot be put into practice successfully. Thus, there remains a mystery about why some projects succeed and others fail. In considerable degree, therefore, Hegelian prophecies gain plausibility by fitting in with some state of affairs in the world that is regarded at the time as successful. Nothing precludes a need to alter speculations on the shape of history while new events occur that alter the observable picture. Within the lifetime of people alive since, say, 1940, both the decline of the West and its triumph have been proclaimed plausibly—provided that those involved remained willing to accept terms like *decline* and *triumph* as theoretically adequate for understanding the human condition. But it should also be noted that speculative formulations of this kind seldom fail from their own point of view. Thus, even those who shift from foretelling decline to celebrating triumph are still thinking in the same terms of discovering immanent meaning and necessary conclusions in the procession of historical events.

History, in such worldviews, is constituted in the human spirit's continuous mediating power to reconcile the imagined and projected but not yet realized cultural environment with the initially resistant materials of the natural world. We do this through our shaping of the matter by imposing imagined form. We humans, as the intersection of idea and matter, thus constantly create culture in which ideas become real or are "realized" through our capacity to mediate ideas and nature. A powerful idea—one that excites the human imagination—will never remain merely an idea, but will become something real in the world; having been imagined, it must actually come to be seen.

This is an incarnational theology in a special sense. Unlike the Christian idea of incarnation, originally developed in orthodox Christian theology, this version assumes that human beings can define the good and then find ways to bring it to be without deterioration of the idea in the process. The power of "divine" creation is here reassigned to the realm of human spirit. It is also the inversion of the Platonic insight that the best in speech loses something in its materialization. It is the divine (the idea of possibility) made "flesh" (instituted as it should have been without loss). Through Hegel, this theological idea is developed into a doctrine of the irresistible power of the human spirit, which realizes itself through its historically relevant, and therefore destined, earthly agents. This understanding of realization contradicts the sense of the transcendent as that present to us but also beyond us, which was evoked by Solzhenitsyn in his critique of the progressive West. Fukuyama's thesis promises the capacity not merely to live in faith for the things unseen, but also to enjoy the security of the unseen's revelation in the fully visible.

Certainly, many find a sense of reassurance in the belief that what we now see, or soon will see, is all there is to be seen; that the sense of mystery is abated nearly to the vanishing point; and that there is nothing we need to know that we cannot know or perhaps that we do not already know. But, as Fukuyama himself has admitted, the perfectly visible may also be boring. Implicit in this observation is the acknowledgment that the mystery, which is not mysterious, does not entirely abate the mystery that is genuinely mysterious but that, by definition, is excluded. What is boring is the self-limitation of the creative imagination in denying its own capacity to look beyond itself.

Hegel said that what is real is exactly what can be incarnated by human imagination and will. The validity of human institutions or culture is certified by their appearance and persistence in history. Thus, the collapse of the Soviet empire means its existence was irrational (not "real") because it could not sustain itself. By contrast, the West's reality persists; thus, it is more real than its vanquished foe.

In a sophisticated sense, this offers little consolation. There is no logical reason why what presently persists as opposed to what presently fails to persist must continue to persist in the future. Yet, it is not uncommon to feel safe when the crisis that we feared is not the crisis that we actually undergo. But should we be confident that the crisis averted or avoided is the one we ought to fear? Nothing guarantees permanent sustainability for any humanly made institutions simply because some alternatives come and go in the meantime. History is hardly reassuring on this point. Is not history an apparently interminable succession of endings and beginnings? These occur at different levels and on different time spans, from the individual to the societal. Each moment of historical change may and will necessitate a revision of our view of what the past and we are about.

The end of an era is not identical to the end of history. Nor is it a foregone conclusion that the end of an era is the end of meaning, even if it often imposes upon us the experience of meaninglessness, therefore necessitating the reformulation of what we think the meaning of life is. Do we not need to make a much more serious effort to assess the intellectual character of a century in which both the decline and the triumph of the West have been affirmed? Does this not include reexamining the use of the expressions of decline and triumph, assessing their theoretical adequacy and grasping the character of historical existence?

On the other hand, in a superficial sense that disregards detailed examination of or reflection on history, there is a temporary plausibility to the triumph of the West—so long as there is no obvious external threat and so long as the West does not confront its own brand of internal disintegration that may look quite different from the disintegration that led to the exhaustion of the Soviet empire.

Yet, even at the unsophisticated level, a sense of uncertainty and fear lurks for the sustainability of our ways. There is a residual doubt about whether something we have made can be perpetuated indefinitely into the future. In our having made it is its sign of contingency. It is precisely the implicit claim to perpetuation that marks off the modernizing, millennialist theology of the Fukuyama thesis from the Augustinian theology of Solzhenitsyn. For these reasons, it seems to me, we need to speak of the great theological debate of our age.

Perhaps we are in a good position, if we are capable of recognizing it, to theologize creatively once again (I do not mean this to imply a specific theological position or dogma). What seems to me to underlie all the debates about history today is a reawakened sense of the fundamental temporality of human existence. The sheer experience of temporality or "changingness" in human existence is more basic than any speculative interpretation of its significance and cannot be fully captured in any theory about it. The search for meaning in history is itself an effort to theorize the radical changingness of our experience. In fact, the effort to explain ourselves to ourselves in historical terms is itself a doctrine about how we are to think about our temporality. Not every age that is aware of its temporality is historically minded in our post-Hegelian sense. Indeed, one could argue that the historically minded approach is a peculiarly pronounced feature of modern life, and is no less subject to the potential for change. In short, theorization of change is prone to exempting itself from that feature of experience that it has set about to understand. In the tension between the experience and its theorization, we must find our bearings. But to do so is to abandon speculative historical hypotheses of the sort Fukuyama has presented, and this is something we are not altogether inclined to do since, in the short run, it will seem to be a deepening of the loss of purpose and direction from which the speculative hypotheses were designed to rescue us.

The true demise of socialism requires a more radical rejection of speculative historical hypotheses. The death of socialism in some regimes is not the end of the story. The Fukuyama thesis about the triumph of the liberal democratic West is the inversion of the socialist politico-theological hypothesis about history and can only be hostage to further historical developments that inspire other, contradictory speculations. These will, no doubt, temporarily capture the imagination of the intelligentia, without assuaging their longings.

Acknowledgment

This essay originally appeared in *Perspectives on Political Science* 21, No. 4 (Fall 1992), pp.189–92. Published by Heldref Publications, 1319 Eighteenth St. N.W., Washington, D.C. 20036-1802. Copyright © 1992. It is reprinted here with permission of the Helen Dwight Reid Educational Foundation.

6

Fukuyama versus the End of History

Peter Augustine Lawler

The revolution of 1989, which brought down most existing socialist regimes and discredited the idea of socialism, was arguably the last of the modern revolutions. It is open to at least two extreme or radical interpretations.

The first is radically modern. Socialism failed because it contained reactionary "idealism," which opposed the free development of modern liberty and prosperity. Its failure shows that human beings were already definitively satisfied with the "classless society" of the United States, imitated by the other "advanced" nations of the world. Socialism and the revolution against it were the last manifestations of human spiritedness, what produces human action or history, in the world. History or human liberty has now come to an end. Human beings will now come to live everywhere as docile members of a "welfare state," gradually surrendering the details of the humanity or human liberty they have already surrendered in principle. Eventually even the state itself will wither away. This end of history, with its eradication of the disorder of human liberty, is the culmination of modern or systematic rationalism. This view, we shall see, is found in the thought of Alexandre Kojève, although it was anticipated by the musings of Tocqueville about "soft despotism."

A second view of the revolution of 1989, in its way almost as radical, is that the end of the modern world may mean the inauguration of a postmodern world. This world will be a new birth of human liberty or plurality, one free from the pretentious and misanthropic illusions of modern rationalism. The postmodern view is found in many places today. Most strikingly, it was the interpretation given to the revolution by the dissident opponents to socialism or communism in Central and Eastern Europe.

Fukuyama's book attempts to find a middle way between Kojève's misanthropic view of modern rationalism and the postmodern rejection of that rationalism on behalf of human liberty or dignity. He wishes to combine that rationalism with the concern for the perception or even revitalization of the conditions for human liberty. He searches for an account of the end of history that is full of human or free and dignified beings. He fails, although perhaps nobly. The position he wishes to defend is indefensible.

Fukuyama argues that the worldwide triumph of liberal democracy is the end of history. His book's main deficiency is that it does not really make clear what the end of history must necessarily be. Fukuyama shares this deficiency with Marx, who also said, quite incoherently, that at the end of history man will remain a social and so human being. Incoherence is not necessarily a criticism of a book about human beings. But Fukuyama almost claims that he is a wise man because he views history, and so human existence, as a coherent whole.

The most misleading incoherence of Fukuyama's book is his combination of a seemingly moderate defense of human dignity and liberal democracy with comprehensive atheism. He seems to hold that human liberty can be perpetuated in the absence of the distinction between man and God. With this suggestion, he departs from the rigor of the comprehensive atheism of his mentor, Kojève, as well as from that of Nietzsche, whom he regards as Kojève's most thoughtful antagonist. Kojève and Nietzsche agree that the death of God, or, as Fukuyama puts it, the banishing of religion from the West by liberalism (271), signals the end of human liberty or distinctiveness.[1]

One sign of Fukuyama's incoherence is that he interprets the revolution of 1989 in a way that is both radically modern and a celebration of human dignity. He says, in effect, that that revolution can be viewed as the completion of the atheistic project of the modern philosophers to transform the world in the service of their thought. Man now has no need for God, because the Kingdom of God has come to earth, and there man rules.

The dominant view, of course, is that the revolution of 1989 was not the final stage in the revelation of the truth of this theology of liberation. It discredited that theology, and reinvigorated other forms that retained the distinction between man and God. For the most eloquent and profound of the dissidents, Alexander Solzhenitsyn and Václav Havel, the collapse of socialist totalitarianism was part of the modern world revealing itself to itself as an error.[2] The error is that there could be a systematic or merely historical or social solution to the disorder or liberty that characterizes human existence. For the dissidents, human liberty is, in part, freedom from such determination.

Any solution to the human problem, for Solzhenitsyn and Havel, must be individual and spiritual. That thought is the foundation for the reconstitution of a world that supports the individual's free spiritual development. This world depends on the recovery of the key human distinctions between good and evil and man and God, as well as the human person's openness to eternity. These distinctions are the foundation of human responsibility, which can still be exercised in our time. From this dissident perspective, Fukuyama's book seems misanthropic and reactionary.

Kojève never hid the misanthropy of his description of the end of history as the here and now. He sought to show that human liberty or distinctiveness no longer exists, and he affirmed their disappearance as according to reason and according to nature. For him, human liberty is an error that manifested itself in and was finally corrected by history. According to Kojève, there is no difference worth considering between today's Western liberal democracies and the socialist societies that used to make up the Soviet bloc. Both are forms of the universal and homogeneous state, or the end of history. They recognize, in principle, the dignity or liberty of all human beings as citizens equally well, and they both, in principle, reduce all human beings to "automatons."[3] It would seem that the recognition of dignity is a momentary prelude to the end of human liberty and self-consciousness.

But Fukuyama distinguishes clearly between the freedom and dignity of liberal democracy and the systematic efforts to destroy it under socialist or communist totalitarianism. He quite strikingly voices his agreement with Havel's account of human dignity and communism's futile attempt to negate it. He disguises his disagreement with Havel by not showing that, for Havel, dignity is "living in the truth," which is, in part, living with one's awareness that one is not most fundamentally a historical being. In Fukuyama's hands, Havel's account of dignity becomes merely an assertion of one's freedom from fear, although he also says that this assertion characteristically mocks the truth about itself to itself.[4]

Havel draws a quite different lesson for the West from the human victory in his nation. His people's successful resistance against efforts at systemization ought to inspire the Western nations to resist the systematic tendencies that animate their own societies. Human beings act humanly, or in accord with their dignity and openness to the truth, precisely when they resist all efforts to bring history to an end.

For Havel and Solzhenitsyn, liberal democracy remains superior to socialism only because it is not simply animated by the modern pretensions that fill the thought that history has or can end. But for Fukuyama, liberal democracy is superior to socialism because it is history's true end. He aims to improve upon Kojève and satisfy Havel by purging the argument for the end of history of its misanthropy. He even suggests, quite incoherently, that the end of history cannot be simply systematic, because to perpetuate itself over time it must make room for human irrationality or disorder. History can come to an end only if it does not come to an end.

Such subtle thinking, of course, is really equivocation. Fukuyama also attempts to do justice to the strongest argument, in his view, against history's end. It comes from Nietzsche, on behalf of human dignity. But Nietzsche's view, finally, is much closer to Kojève's than Havel's. Kojève and Nietzsche both agree with the radically modern perception that God is dead. He had been killed by the development of human self-consciousness over time or history. God disappears either because men have become gods or because they have become unhistorical and so unfree and contented animals. Kojève says, in fact, they have become both. For Nietzsche, the alternatives, in the absence of God, are the "last man," who, if not simply an animal, is without dignity or spirit, and the "overman," who surpasses mere humanity in his radical or self-consciously divine creativity. Fukuyama's book describes a world without God yet full of free and dignified men.

But Fukuyama's description of a godless world of unprecedented freedom and dignity sometimes seems not to be his last word. He tacks on accounts of Nietzsche's view of the "last man" and Kojève's description of the return of man to simple animality. But these radical views, in Fukuyama's hands, are defanged and hence are remarkably uncompelling. He never even presents Kojève's simple argument for the conclusion that man must disappear at the end of history. If man is a historical being and nothing more, which he must be if he is to recognize his perfection in history's end, then his recognition of that end is also a recognition of his own disappearance.

What I miss most in Fukuyama's book is a clear, consistent articulation of the view that man is a historical being. He does not show how that view of man can claim to be the only empirical verifiable atheism, or the only atheism properly so-called. So he makes it far too easy for us to believe something Kojève and Nietzsche (and Havel and Solzhenitsyn) do not, that human beings can live well in freedom and dignity without God.

The extent to which Fukuyama misuses Kojève in this way is sometimes astounding. He says, again most incoherently, that Kojève is wrong not to employ a teleological view of human nature to support his view that history has definitively satisfied human desire (138–39). He makes it seem possible to use Socrates's tripartite account of human nature or the soul to judge the results of history (162–65, 139). At the end of history, the rational, spirited, and desiring parts of the soul are all satisfied. Science has conquered nature, producing the material plenty required to satisfy bodily desire. The spirited part of the soul is realistically or historically redefined as the desire for recognition, which is satisfied by the universal and homogeneous recognition of citizen by citizen in a world of liberal democracies. The rational part of the soul is satisfied by the fact that history has an order or system, and it is readily comprehensible as history's end. At the end of history, philosophy is replaced by wisdom, or complete knowledge or self-consciousness. What the wise man (Fukuyama) possesses, in Fukuyama's eyes, is a complete account of the perfection of human nature. With this seemingly natural yet historically won wisdom, Fukuyama can affirm history's success.

Fukuyama confuses us quite deliberately by presenting this teleological view in the text while leaving Kojève's empirical objection to it for the notes (364n7). Human nature, in Kojève's eyes, is an oxymoron. The evidence is that what distinguishes man is his historical being, not his nature. His nature really is the same as that of other bodies in motion, obeying the same predictable, even mechanical, laws. Nature, so understood, has no *telos*, or at least no human end. If human beings have a purpose, it must be historical. It can only be known at the end of history, when their historical or distinctively human desire can be known to have received historical satisfaction.

Fukuyama's correction of Kojève about nature merely produces confusion. He relies on the authority of a letter of Leo Strauss to Kojève to support this correction.[5] The letter's point, as a whole, is that only a teleological conception of nature can keep man's existence or distinctiveness from seeming radically contingent. This observation is true. But it is hard to see how it is a criticism. The radical contingency of human existence is a necessary consequence of the radical distinction between nature and history. That distinction is required if one is to speak of the end of history.

The relationship between history and nature is contingent or accidental. Why man emerges in opposition to nature man cannot know. That history is inexplicable according to nature is a necessary premise of human freedom historically understood. That freedom must be complete freedom from all that is given by nature.

Strauss does say that without a teleological conception of nature Kojève cannot know whether the historical process he describes is unique. It may repeat itself here on earth or somewhere else. But Kojève cannot and does not deny that history might occur again. There is no reason why or why not. The accident might happen again. That fact has nothing to do with the rationality or circularity of Kojève's description of human freedom, and so of his satisfaction at history's end. Although history emerges accidentally against nature, it can still be shown to be an ordered or rational and human whole.

A human being is given a nature, as is every other animal, but he makes himself human. Human motion is actually a mixture of natural givenness and historical acquisition. But only the latter motion is distinctively human, or free from nature. With the disappearance of historical motion or action at the end of history, man once again becomes wholly determined, like every other animal, by nature.

Fukuyama reveals in a note that the identification of human with historical existence was first made not by Kojève or Hegel, but by Rousseau. He does not assess the significance of this fact or show the relationship between Rousseau's thought and Hegel's. In Rousseau's view, man, at the beginning or in the state of nature, was simply an animal.[6] Rousseau also anticipates that the end of history will be a return to man's beginning, to his wholly natural, asocial, and brutish existence.[7] The great merit of Kojève's wonderfully consistent Hegelianism is that he sees the necessity of this return clearly and without equivocation.

According to Rousseau, human beings begin as brutes, but with an inexplicable or accidental capacity for perfectibility or undetermined development away from nature. They make themselves more free in their attempts to satisfy their desires. But in the process they also create new desires which are more difficult to satisfy. History is, in part, human desires expanding more rapidly than the capacities to satisfy them.

As human beings become more free from nature, they become more self-conscious, or more aware of what they have made. Almost the first moment in the development of this self-consciousness is the awareness of one's mortality and so consciousness of time. Human beings become progressively more conscious of time, or self-conscious, over time. Human beings are historical and so temporal beings, the beings with time in them.

Historical development is in response to human discontent. Natural man is almost content; animals are content. Over time, man makes himself progressively more discontent in response to his discontent. He becomes more conscious of time, the consciousness which is the source of all distinctively human misery. That misery, in turn, is the source of all human disorder, including poverty, disease, inequality, hatred, vanity, and so forth. History, for Rousseau, is the record of human misery and disorder.

Human beings cannot be understood to have aimed to make themselves progressively more discontent. From the perspective of individual human beings, historical development must be understood as accidental. They move away from the health and contentment they were given by nature. From the perspective of nature, history is a misery-producing accident and nothing more.

So the lesson of history, according to nature, is that history is an error. Human beings ought to live according to nature, which means they ought to surrender what is distinctively human about their existence. Perfectly self-conscious mortals reject that consciousness. They may, at first, prefer their humanity or history in their pride. But they cannot help but see that all pride is vanity, because everything human is accidental. To be human, as we seem to see so clearly today, is to be a victim of one's place in history, to be deserving of compassion, not pride.

Hegelians such as Kojève agree with almost all of Rousseau's account of the relation between nature and history. Where they seem to differ from Rousseau is that they deny that human pride is vanity. The total independence of historical motion or action from the givenness of nature is proof of the existence of human freedom. At the end of history, human beings are perfectly conscious of their freedom. One knows that what one perceives about one's own freedom is true, because it is recognized by other free beings. Human self-consciousness is necessarily social or reciprocal. So, paradoxically, the self-sufficiency of each particular human being can be recognized only in the social or political setting of the universal and homogeneous state, the end of all historical action. There, free citizens recognize one another's freedom, their dignity in being undetermined by nature.

But Kojève makes it clear that this reciprocal recognition of human freedom occurs only for a moment. Unlike Fukuyama, he does not worry about the conditions for its perpetuation, because he knows it is impossible. Human freedom is historical, or action in response to human desire. For Kojève, the only human or historical desire is for prideful consciousness of one's freedom from nature, or the desire for recognition. If that desire is satisfied, as it is in the universal and homogeneous state, then human beings will no longer act. They will no longer manifest or give evidence of their freedom in history. They will be satisfied, but it is not human to be satisfied. The end of history must be the end of humanity.

Despite differences on details, Kojève shows that the Rousseauean and Hegelian conclusions are virtually indistinguishable. Man is an historical being. History is time. Man is the being with time in him. If he is historical, his existence is temporary. He comes into being and passes away in a cosmos indifferent to his existence. His disappearance, in retrospect, was inevitable and, as Kojève laconically says, no cosmic catastrophe. The species *Homo sapiens* lives on in harmony with nature. What disappears is only the historical being, man properly so-called. The end of history is, if anything, good for nature. The disorder of historical or human existence, as the ecologists say, mixes with, corrupts, and so threatens almost all natural order.[8]

Man disappears when he recognizes his total independence or freedom from nature. He realizes his self-consciousness is "nothing," or merely negation, and so he negates it. He disappears, as the Hegelians say, as a consequence of his wisdom. He sees history as a whole, and so sees himself as a misery-producing error. His pride as a citizen or his human satisfaction is certainly not an adequate compensation for his misery. Finally, the wise man does not, most fundamentally, affirm history's rationality, but the fact that a rational or well-ordered world is one without human self-consciousness or history. Only a world without history is one without contradiction, a system.

How could a self-conscious mortal, the being with time in him and nothing more, really be satisfied by political recognition? Fukuyama's attempt to defend this possibility against obvious criticisms is half-hearted and unconvincing, even to himself. The remaining contradictions are too clear, perhaps more clear than ever before. For the coming of the universal and homogeneous state, the state with no credible opposition, makes more clear than ever before that there is no political or social solution to the problem of human individuality or self-consciousness.

So Kojève is right to say that the end of history would have to include man's rational self-destruction. He follows Rousseau in showing that man returns to a simple, natural existence, his beginning. He agrees with Tocqueville that the universal and homogeneous state aims not to preserve the freedom and dignity of active citizens.[9] It means to replace politics by the automatic rule of automatons, or docile animals.[10] Human action is to be replaced by behavior as predictable and regular as that of any other animal.

The dissidents have shown us to our satisfaction that this reduction of human action and thought to systematic behavior was the aim of totalitarianism. They showed us what we already half-knew from writers such as George Orwell. But Kojève adds that this "classless society" is the American as well as the Soviet aim. Solzhenitsyn and Havel at least almost agree, seeing it as the aim of modern rationalism as such. The spirit of resistance which they affirm comes not from any rational or historical understanding of dignity, but from premodern sources, such as Christianity, that cause human beings to view themselves as immortal or eternal in some way.

Fukuyama, again, distinguishes himself by considering the end of history as a conceivably sustainable state full of human beings. He claims not to know why Kojève disagrees with Hegel by saying there will be no war or other form of human struggle at the end of history. War is caused by human desire, which will have disappeared. The "need for struggle" is what animated history. Absent the need, there will be no struggle (389n1). Kojève's correction to Hegel here is on an Hegelian basis, and Fukuyama's inability to see why it was made shows that he has little idea of what the end of history *must* be like.

So Fukuyama is no wise man, and Kojève may be. Kojève affirms the end of history as a partisan of reason. He prefers a rational existence to the illusions or incomplete self-consciousness that supported various conceptions of human nature or human dignity. Fukuyama, in his eyes, would be like the dissidents or Tocqueville in preferring the illusions. Kojève never expressed any interest in or sympathy for Nietzsche's or Strauss's moralistic opposition to the "last man."[11] For him, it is or must be enough that the real is the rational, even if his moment of self-conscious wisdom is necessarily replaced by the simply unconscious or impersonal rule of reason. Strauss opposed the end of history because its coming would mean that philosophy would disappear from the world. For Kojève, Strauss forgets that the aim or *telos* of philosophy is to disappear, or to be replaced by wisdom.

According to Kojève, the wisdom available at the end of history is the only definitive or empirically verifiable atheism. Without that wisdom, philosophy itself is only a faith or prejudice. Those who speak of human nature cannot really be atheists. They lack the necessary evidence, and they cannot help but distinguish between man and God. Kojève knew as well as anyone that Strauss was not a believer in any conventional sense. But he still called him a theologian.[12]

Contrary to Fukuyama's equivocation, the fundamental alternative for Kojève is between those who speak of human nature and those who know that man is an essentially historical being. The former do not believe that history can come to an end, because they do not believe that human satisfaction could be simply historical. They do not believe that human beings can become wise, and they understand the distinction between man and God to be permanent.

Those who distinguish radically between nature and history hold open the possibility that man might transform or has transformed himself into a god. By so doing, he can prove to himself that there is no god but himself, and so also prove the truth of atheism. Kojève actually said that Kojève was a god, and that man at the end of history is somehow both divine and brutish. But such audacious and paradoxical statements do not find their way into Fukuyama's book.

Kojève also says that the wise man at the end of history is both divine and mortal. He is a particular individual in possession of divine or complete, universal science.[13] He must be divine, because he is no longer a man or the historical being who acts to transform his existence. He cannot be, at first glance, a brute, because he possesses the complete self-consciousness characteristic of God. But, from another perspective, he must be a brute, because he is mortal and unhistorical. What has happened is that human beings have lost their specifically human or historical attributes or acquisitions while retaining the physical or biological characteristics of their species. They live according to their nature, and so not according to their human or spiritual freedom from material determination.

It is still far from clear how man can be simultaneously divine and brutish, or how all I have just described can be simultaneously true. But we have already seen why we do well to search for a beginning of an explanation in Rousseau. He reported that his most choiceworthy condition, and his experience which was closest to man's uncorrupted or unhistorical nature, was a radical forgetfulness of his historical condition in an atemporal reverie. Such reveries contained no awareness of time, mortality, or one's sociality. They are without, or almost without, what the human being acquired historically or over time. They include, in fact, "[n]othing external" to oneself. One's existence is radically solitary, but it includes all that exists. All there is is "[t]he sentiment of existence, stripped of every other emotion." "As long as this state lasts," Rousseau remembered, "we are sufficient unto ourselves, like God."[14]

The asocial individual who lives wholly in the present is not human or historical. He seems to be the brute of Rousseau's state of nature. But he is also divine in his self-sufficiency, including his genuine independence from other human beings. For him, it seems, everything is simultaneously divine and brutish. He experiences nothing external to himself. With the disappearance of history or human distinctiveness, all other distinctions disappear. What remains, as Tocqueville explained, is nothing but the experience of the truth of pantheism. Pantheism, Tocqueville understood, is the most seductive philosophy in modern or very self-conscious times. It is the complete negation of the misery of self-consciousness or individuality. Far more than any State or form of political organization, it is perfect in its universality and homogeneity.[15]

From the perspective of Kojève's wisdom, Rousseau's reveries at first seem very far from the end of history. Unlike Jean-Paul Sartre, whom he classed among the "tasteless" existentialists,[16] Kojève held that affirmation of history is not a reverie or diversion from the truth or self-consciousness. Kojève emphatically opposed the self-forgetfulness that can animate historical idealism, the attempt to lose oneself in the historical process. An account of history is simply an account of the truth, and so the human beings who live at the end of history can be perfectly self-conscious. The wise man lives wholly in the light of the truth, sees reveries for what they are, and has no interest in them.

Rousseau calls his reverie a "pleasurable fiction," a conscious negation of the truth about Rousseau in view of its misery. But to negate the truth one must know it. Rousseau's affirmation of the reverie is based on his theoretical conclusion that the wholly human or historical or social being is a miserable accident and nothing more. So his "fiction" is a response to a wisdom that anticipates the end of history.

Rousseau's fiction, with its approximation of man's ahistorical beginning, is an approximation of man's genuine existence at the end of history. The end of history might almost be described as the universalization of Rousseau's extraordinarily asocial experience. In Kojève's time, the wise are wise because they see the whole of history as an error from the perspective of nature. In their divinity they affirm the universality of the experience of the brute's wholly natural existence. That experience—far more than the recognition all citizens receive in the universal and homogeneous state—is the self-sufficiency that man has always longed for and expressed in his conception of divinity. Both God and animal (or at least the self-sufficient, asocial being Rousseau describes in the state of nature) have no experience of time, and so at least very minimal social needs or dependence.

From this perspective, it is unsurprising that the wisdom of Rousseau would become especially clear at the time of the collapse of socialist idealism. The error of socialism was always that there could be a social solution to the problem of human disorder or dissatisfaction. The social- ists, beginning with Marx, have always said that human beings will remain social and so human at the end of history. They have always viewed the end of history, like Fukuyama, as full of human beings. But if human beings remain human, they remain conscious of time, and so humanly miserable and dissatisfied. Contrary to Marx (and Fukuyama), the fundamental human scarcity is scarcity of time, and no amount of material prosperity can eradicate that scarcity. Human misery and, if Marx is right about its cause,[17] religion, will remain as long as human beings remain self-conscious mortals.

Generally speaking, Fukuyama's book is unconvincing because he knows too well the problems with the premise that human satisfaction could be both social and self-sufficient. As Rousseau shows, a social being simply is not a self-sufficient one. We have just suggested that material scarcity will not disappear as long as material desire is bloated by self-consciousness, as long as it is, in part, the feverish desire for luxury. Material scarcity will disappear, as Rousseau explained, only if material desire is reduced to its simply natural dimension, and so is satisfied quite easily or with hardly any work.

The desire for recognition, as the Christians see, seems really to be the desire for full and complete recognition, for a being who sees you as you really are. Social recognition, obviously, will always be partial. Human beings experience themselves as more than citizens, and their spirited desire to be recognized in their uniqueness will never be satis- fied completely through social or political reform. Fukuyama says, quite rightly, that some will remain dissatisfied with merely receiving the recognition received equally by all. I would add that no human being would be fully satisfied, if only because the awareness that one's free- dom depends on intersubjective recognition is as much a recognition of dependence as of independence.

As Marx first noted in opposition to Hegel, the recognition of citizen by citizen seems particularly abstract in the modern world, the world of secularized Christianity. And as post-Hegelian or postmodern critics of many sorts observe, the modern state has not obliterated alienation, loneliness, restlessness anxiety, and so forth. Today's critics, from Solz- henitsyn to Jean-François Lyotard, observe[18] that religious longings re- main. They echo Tocqueville's account of American restlessness in the midst of prosperity and even the Marx of "On the Jewish Question."

Fukuyama knows, of course, that human beings are spirited or angry because they want to be free from their bodily limitations. But they want more than to win their freedom from fear in a life-risking struggle for pure prestige, the struggle that culminates in the universal freedom of citizens. They want actually to be immortal or eternal, or genuinely self-sufficient. The end of history freed from contingency and dependence reveals that there is no *human* satisfaction for the longing for immortality which, as Tocqueville says, equally torments every human heart.

Probably the obliteration of immortality or eternity as a *human possibility*, the end of all illusion, is what causes man's self-destruction at the end of history. That this possibility is not raised by Fukuyama suggests that he really believes that history has eradicated ''religious'' longing or successfully focused it wholly on this world. But the destruction of socialism should have shown him that any theology of the historical liberation of human beings is untrue. Human beings will have religious longings as long as they remain human or social. Religion will not wither away unless man withers away.

Finally, the social basis of Fukuyama's view of the end of history seems to undermine the possibility of genuine wisdom. At the end of history, man is wise because he knows that history is all there is, and he comprehends history as an intelligible whole. But, in truth, he knows that history is not all there is. It is just all that he can comprehend, given the premise that man can only know what he can make, which is the historical or social world. But, in truth, it is not all he can comprehend. He also is aware of the contradiction between the historical and natural worlds, one which remains present in Kojève's thought that one can be both divine and mortal. As long as that contradiction remains inexplicable, man is not wise.

So the completion of human wisdom must be the thought that human distinctiveness must be negated. Kojève, the wise man, claims to know that man no longer exists. If Fukuyama is a wise man, or comprehends what it means for history to end, he must unequivocally reach the same conclusion. Fukuyama, from Kojève's perspective, is much less wise than reactionary, finally joining Nietzsche, Tocqueville, Havel, and so forth in preferring human liberty to the end of history. Fukuyama actually seems to regard the end of history as Kojève describes it as a future possibility to be resisted.

But if I have correctly described Fukuyama's lack of wisdom, then he compromises his partisanship fatally by calling liberal democracy the end of history. He does not clearly see liberal democracy as *limited* government. He sometimes knows that the principles of the universal and homogeneous state must inform all of human or social life for history to be over. He means to do justice to the Marxian criticism of a merely political and so merely abstract conclusion to history. Liberty in the sense of disorder or plurality must completely disappear. There is necessarily something totalitarian about this historical definition of liberty, something opposed to any idea of privacy or the transpolitical openness the American founders left for conscience, or our duties to the Creator.

But Fukuyama, to repeat, also sometimes says that some room for irrationality and even religion must remain for the end of history to work. This incoherence comes as the result of his refinement of the Marxian thought that the end of history will be full of human beings with social desires. The end of history, unlike human liberty, cannot really be a struggle to perpetuate itself over time.

Kojève restored the wisdom of Rousseau against the Marxists by being perfectly aware of the incoherence of socialism, which is the same incoherence found in Fukuyama's description of liberal democracy as the end of history. He said that human beings cannot remain human, or conscious of time, at the end of history.[19] Today perhaps this wisdom is in the process of becoming universalized. It is easy to see in the various forms of "postmaterialism," especially the ecological or New Age injunctions to live in harmony with nature. This pantheistic idealism, which is the view that history, in both its capitalist and socialist manifestations, is a nature-threatening disorder that must be extinguished in the name of health and security, is obviously more consistently post-historical than its socialist predecessors. Postmaterialism really opposes the disorder that results from the mixing of material desire with self-consciousness. So it is actually *the* consistent materialism. It sees, as Rousseau did, that material scarcity will always be a human perception, no matter how much human beings produce, until human self-consciousness withers away.

Fukuyama is well aware of this growth in post-historical wisdom, although he mistakenly presents it as evidence for the possibility that history has not come to an end after all. He notes, following Tocqueville (who, on this, followed Rousseau), that compassion, or secularized Christianity, grows in strength in the world. What really intensifies is the awareness that human beings, as such, are deserving of compassion and nothing more, because they are miserable accidents and nothing more.

This awareness, Fukuyama says, can be explained as a result of the working out over time of the consequences of modern science, which cannot distinguish qualitatively between human and nonhuman being. Hence it denies the genuine existence of human liberty or "moral choice." More precisely, from Fukuyama's perspective, modern science denies the existence of history, or the realm of human existence free from material determination.

But if history has ended, modern science would now be completely true, even if it had not always been completely true. There can be no more human choices or action. What distinguishes human existence no longer exists. The contemporary inability to give an account of human dignity, or to find evidence of its genuine existence, might be the dawning of post-historical awareness.

If there is no longer "any basis for saying that man has a superior dignity," then there is no longer any basis for man's conquest of or opposition to nature. This desire for consistency is what Fukuyama, following Tocqueville, calls "[t]he egalitarian passion that denies the existence of significant differences between human beings." He says it "can be extended to a denial of significant difference between man and the higher animals" (297–98). At the end of history, human distinctiveness is negated, and the laughably incoherent "animal rights" movement exists a moment before the nonexistence of rights.

This egalitarian line of thought, Fukuyama rightly says, opposes the idea that liberal democracy, animated by a "liberal concept of equal and universal humanity with a specifically human dignity," is the end of history. But it does not oppose the idea that history has ended. It aims at the consistent articulation of the end of history.

If liberal democracy is defensible, it is because history has not come to an end. It is because human beings remain human, between beast and God. It is because human beings are not essentially historical beings. They have longings which elude historical satisfaction. They point to some other foundation of moral choice or responsibility, one that opens human existence to eternity. The choice, it seems to me, is between the sober forms of this postmodern thought found, for example, in the thought of the dissidents, and the audacious vigor of Kojève's consistent articulation of the end of history, which expresses the culmination of the deepest modern aspirations. Fukuyama confuses us by not making this choice. He at least obscures both the brilliant plausibility of Kojève's analysis and the genuine greatness of both human liberty and liberal democracy.

Let me conclude by returning to the observation that Fukuyama assumes without proof that Kojève's atheism is true. He also assumes, without proof, that man can live well without God. He cannot think clearly about these assumptions because he does not really know whether man is a historical being, or a being with a nature, or a created being. His lack of wisdom about the human condition ought to make him a very modest or pluralistic liberal, one devoted to a regime full of unwise and dissatisfied and so human beings. The dignity of man, he might have concluded, depends on his elusiveness, and so on his insurmountable resistance to systematic or scientific determination.

Notes

1. My essay is a criticism of one aspect of *The End of History and the Last Man*. Let me add here that there is much to admire in it, and that I am not doing justice here to what I learned from Fukuyama about contemporary affairs.

2. For an introduction to Solzhenitsyn's postmodernism, see his 1978 Harvard Commencement Address, "A World Split Apart," especially its conclusion, with his *Rebuilding Russia*, trans. A. Klimoff (New York: Farrar, Straus & Giroux, 1991). On Havel, see his Address to the U.S. Congress (February 21, 1990) with his "Politics and Conscience," *Open Letters: Selected Writing 1965–90*, trans. P. Wilson (New York: Knopf, 1990) and *Summer Meditations*, trans. P. Wilson (New York: Knopf, 1992).

3. See Alexandre Kojève, *Introduction to the Reading of Hegel*, ed. A. Bloom, trans. J. Nichols Jr. (Ithaca: Cornell University Press, 1968), pp. 158–62, note 6 with Kojève, Letter to Leo Strauss (September 19, 1950) in Leo Strauss, *On Tyranny: Revised and Expanded Edition*, eds. V. Gourevitch and M. Roth (New York: Free Press, 1991), pp. 255–56.

My understanding of Kojève's thought is greatly indebted to two intelligent and penetrating books: Michael S. Roth, *Knowing and History: Appropriations of Hegel in Twentieth-Century France* (Ithaca: Cornell University Press, 1988), and especially Barry Cooper, *The End of History: An Essay on Modern Hegelianism* (Toronto: University of Toronto Press, 1984).

The importance of the Strauss-Kojève correspondence for Fukuyama's book is obvious even in its title. Kojève argues for the end of history. Strauss is not convinced, calling attention, "for the sake of simplicity," to "Nietzsche's 'last men'" (Letter to Kojève, August 22, 1948, *On Tyranny*, p. 239).

4. Compare Fukuyama's account of a portion of Havel's "The Power of the Powerless" (pp. 166–69) with Havel's essay, found in *Open Letters*, as a whole. Consider, in particular, Fukuyama's sidestepping of what Havel means by the ideological denial of reality, an extreme manifestation of "living within the lie." This self-denial, for Havel, is a perennial human temptation. Resisting this temptation is the foundation of what Fukuyama calls "moral choice" for Havel.

5. Fukuyama, p. 364n8, where Strauss's letter of August 22, 1948 is quoted. Fukuyama's use of this letter is confusing, because he does not actually quote or mention Strauss's key criticism.

6. See Rousseau, *Discourse on the Origin and Foundation of Inequality*

Among Men. All my accounts of Rousseau's view of the relation between history and nature are based on this, his most theoretical, work.

7. Near the end of the *Discourse on Inequality*, Rousseau describes "the extreme point which closes the circle and touches the point from which we started. . . . Here all individuals become equals again because they are nothing." His conclusion is not quite expressed in Hegel's or Kojève's terms, but we can say that he anticipates what Marx and, more consistently, Kojève describe as the end of history. Perhaps we can say that Rousseau should have said that if the end is a return to the beginning, then it is a return to the state of nature or the end of humanity. See Kojève, Letter to Strauss (October 29, 1953), *On Tyranny*, p. 262.

8. See Rousseau, *Discourse on Inequality*, Note i, in light of Kojève, *Introduction*, Chapter 6. Almost all of the presentation of Kojève's view of the end of history as the end of human distinctiveness is based on this chapter. According to Kojève, "when specifically human error is finally transformed into the truth of absolute Science, Man ceases to exist as Man and History comes to an end. The overcoming of Man (that is, of Time, that is, of Action) in favor of static Being (that is, Space, that is, Nature), therefore, is the overcoming of Error in favor of Truth" (p. 156).

9. Alexis de Tocqueville, *Democracy in America*, vol. 2, part 3, ch. 6, in the context of vol. 2 as a whole.

10. Kojève, Letter to Strauss (September 19, 1950), p. 255.

11. Note the absence of this interest or sympathy in his letters to Strauss.

12. Roth, p. 134n22: "In Kojève's copy of the typescript of Strauss's lecture 'What is Political Philosophy,' Kojève wrote 'Strauss = Theology,' alongside Strauss's discussion of political theology."

13. See Cooper, p. 274.

14. Rousseau, *Reveries of a Solitary Walker*, Walk 5.

15. Tocqueville, *Democracy*, vol. 2, part 1, ch. 7.

16. Kojève, Letter to Strauss (October 29, 1953), p. 262.

17. See Marx, "Critique of Hegel's *Philosophy of Right*" with his "On the Jewish Question." The latter shows that the Americans living in the universal and homogeneous state remain religious because they experience their true or human existence as miserably whimsical.

18. On Lyotard's defense of religious longing against Kojève's systematic rationalism, see Thomas L. Pangle, *The Ennobling of Democracy: The Challenge of the Postmodern Age* (Baltimore: Johns Hopkins University Press, 1992), pp. 20–33, 48–56.

19. See Kojève, *Introduction*, pp. 154–66, especially note 6.

7

A Clarity Interfered With

G. M. Tamás

> One sleeps among the omens and among one's opinions of
> things named as objective and shown as objects and as
> dramas, each an example of clarity of vision convincingly;
> and this goes on for a while if no one interrupts your sleep
> and wakes you. A clarity interfered with.
>
> Harold Brodkey, *The Runaway Soul*[1]

Francis Fukuyama's famous book[2] settles a few scores and, what is
most important, expresses forcefully the feeling we all share: something
momentous has come to an end. We are stepping over a mysterious
threshold into a twilight zone where all the combats we fought seem all
of a sudden bewilderingly irrelevant. Keepers and poachers, princes and
rebels, believers and doubters are staring at each other incredulously: a
both decadent and barbarous chaos appears to engulf everything. Some
call it the triumph of liberal democracy. Some think it is the end of
socialism, nay, of all totalitarian Grand Vision. As Mr. Fukuyama puts
it,

> [T]he fact that there will be setbacks and disappointments in the process
> of democratization, or that not every market economy will prosper, should
> not distract us from the larger pattern that is emerging in world history.
> The apparent number of choices that countries face in determining how
> they will organize themselves politically and economically has been *di-
> minishing* over time. Of the different types of regimes that have emerged
> in the course of human history, from monarchies and aristocracies, to reli-
> gious theocracies, to the fascist and communist dictatorships of this cen-
> tury, the only form of government that has survived intact to the end of
> the twentieth century has been liberal democracy.

What is emerging victorious, in other words, is not so much liberal practice, as the liberal *idea*. That is to say, for a very large part of the world, there is now no ideology with pretensions to universality that is in a position to challenge liberal democracy, and no universal principle other than the sovereignty of the people. (45)

In his recent book, *Spectres de Marx*,[3] a critic no less famous than the author, Jacques Derrida, alleges that Mr. Fukuyama's thesis is of a deeply Christian nature, since it announces a millenarian "good news," thus misreading Kojève, avowedly Mr. Fukuyama's main inspiration (apart, of course, from Hegel and Leo Strauss). M. Derrida emphasizes the heathen ambiguity of Kojève, according to whom the end of history is no good news at all; in fact, it is no *news*. Indeed, if we are trying to be faithful to Hegel, we must realize that the end of history means the end of an age characterized by history and the beginning of one characterized by something else. The Hegelian idea is rooted in the Kantian notion of the "end of all things," which is not an event in time, but the eschatological aspect of all things human that are subject to redemption because they are finite.

Unlike Mr. Fukuyama, I think that the "end of history" is part of the liberal utopia, and it is both the liberal and the socialist utopias that have been defeated. I believe that it is precisely the idea of the "end of history" that has come to an end, a concept common to liberals and socialists alike. But I guess M. Derrida is only partly right. The Christian expectation of the Last Judgment followed by eternal heavenly peace is, after all, different from the main idea of modernity, which might be described as a hope for an end to history. Heaven is not solely a metaphor for bliss. Resurrection and redemption are supposed to change our nature—the "end of history" is not. On the contrary, it is deemed to fulfill it. Announcing, as Mr. Fukuyama does, that our nature will now be reconciled with the rules of societal being is not tantamount to announcing, as Christians do, that all reconciliation is canceled due to the end of any need for it. A state of affairs true to our nature ("the end of history") is rather dissimilar to a state of affairs where our (sinful) nature is simply obliterated. Good news, perhaps, but definitely not an evangel or a gospel. An evangel (literally, "good news") trumpets abroad a spiritual revolution, actually, the most radical one: an evangel will say that human nature is all wrong and we should not be afraid of disregarding it altogether. An evangel would spurn procreation, work, and obedience to the law, the mainstays of all well-ordered human civilization. An apologia for the "end of history," on the other hand, will have a placatory tone; it will plead for what Hegel called *Versöhnung*, reconciliation, an illusionless compromise with what we are: mortal souls with mortal bodies.

Strangely enough, this inviting reconciliation with our nature, with man accepted together with his desires and ambitions, is the result of another revolution of reason: utopia. Evangel and utopia are opposites.

I do believe that Mr. Fukuyama is justified in thinking that socialist utopia is finished. But I also think that the liberal and the socialist utopia are closely related. I shall argue therefore that *both* have been defeated, that the collapse of communism is heralding the end of what Alasdair MacIntyre has called the "Enlightenment project,"[4] and that the fruitful Hegel/Kojève approach—which it is Mr. Fukuyama's merit to have once again excavated—can be used in a different manner to illuminate the terminal crisis of the Enlightenment. I shall not depart very far from Mr. Fukuyama's sources—that would be ungentlemanlike. They are in any case instruments good enough for my purpose, which is to show the hitherto neglected parallels of liberal and socialist utopias, and of their fall.

A Society without the State

A philosophy that does not want to call itself evangel nor utopia is usually held to be moral philosophy.

While political philosophy is as old as Plato's Socrates, moral philosophy is something more recent. Moral philosophy emerges, as a rule, when reason and nature are divorced for some lofty purpose or are regarded as irreconcilable. Be the motive cheerful or gloomy, the question of harmony between the two arises, either in the form of a more or less open admonition to better our nature, or in the shape of sensible despair. Sensible despair, sometimes sporting the sobriquet of "science," will endeavor to enroll reason to observe and describe nature presumed to be the Other, thus making reason appear passive, even dispassionate, and so forcing us to turn elsewhere when trying to account for our motives. Sensible despair will not allow us to interpret our motives as straightforward reasons for action. That "elsewhere" lies necessarily somewhere outside reason, perhaps in the area of that Wholly Other which reason is supposed to watch. Motives embedded in observed nature are passions, maybe instinctive or subconscious, the very opposite of "free" regarded as the outcome of rational choice.

To the extent that our motives are purely passional, they are part and parcel of nature. Reason can criticize or adapt. It is an age-old debate whether we should follow our nature or break it like a bridling mare. If reason is what moral philosophy says it is, it can indeed either like it or lump it. Of course we can say with a characteristically modern twist that reason too is nature of a kind, therefore harmony is pre-ordained or pre-established, by evolution or whatever. Nature watching nature will dispose of the problem of freedom; furthermore we can merrily abandon striving for any understanding that is not subservient to passion—and even boast about our "weak thinking."

Utopia offers a way out from these unsavory *dilemmata* by claiming that we can will a reconciliation; that the harmony of reason and nature might be pre-ordained in the sense of its being planned; but this plan has to be brought to fruition by human action. Utopian action need not change human nature; it has only to fulfill the hidden program encoded by an imagined narrative comprising that portion of history that lies before, not behind us.

Charles Taylor reminds us of the Enlightenment origins of the reason/nature dichotomy and of the essential part it has played in all thought since Kant.

> Kant wants to recover the integrity of the moral, which he sees in an entirely different quality of motivation. To be moved by this is freedom, but it also entails a radical break with nature, a disengagement in a sense more radical than the naturalistic Enlightenment had envisaged. The understanding of nature as source takes a different path. It is also meant to rescue the moral dimension, but this is now to be discovered in the élan of nature itself, from which we have cut ourselves off. [. . .] The Kantian view finds its second dimension in the notion of a radical autonomy of rational agents. The life of mere desire-fulfillment is not only flat but also heteronomous. This critique has been the point of origin of a family of theories which have defined human dignity in terms of freedom. The fully significant life is the one which is self-chosen.[5]

This is a very good description of the modern liberal—and as we shall see, also of the socialist—utopia. "Disengagement" and "autonomy" are the key words here. The classical view stipulated that freedom was freedom *from* the servitude of passions, *from* the bondage of sensual desire. Clearly the classical view was evangelic rather than utopian (if you accept my typology) since its summons was that of a change of our nature. Not a "break with nature," mind you, but its conscious transformation by the meditative-contemplative way sometimes called philosophy. The ancients did not seek an autonomous region for rational moral agents where they could take refuge from nature, theirs and others', but sought to make reason our new nature. In other words, freedom meant rationality. Fighting nature is not a denial of nature. Liberation from under the dominion of passions is not a canting or prudish clothing of instinct with the outer garment of spiritual respectability. The dominion of reason is no less harsh a rule than that of the passions. Philosophic or eremitic *ascesis* ("training," "drill") is war: war on the senses, on desires, on immediacy.

The moderns, on the contrary, are trying to pacify nature through separation. The dominant moral psychology of the age is conjuring up the image of a pluralistic nature: we are determined by our passions, but these passions are variegated and further diversified by changing cultural horizons. We perceive our motivations as a rush of contingencies, a tempest of stochastic flukes. Freedom appears to consist in our ability to draw a map, to choose between routes conducive to goals pre-determined by our character, by our individual emotional make-up (called once by Heraclitus our *daemon*). Freedom for the moderns is not a state wherein reason reigns supreme, but a potentiality of choosing, of what Hegel would call a *reflection* on our subjectivity, what Professor Taylor calls our "self-choice." And all this depends on whether nature is really pluralistic. This is why we need history so. History will show wildly divergent patterns of behavior, the study of civilizations will offer a potentially infinite variety of modes of reflections on subjectivity—that is, of interpretations of available choices. Nature does not give itself to us as a sheer generality, but as a plurality of motivations, desires, passions pluralized by class, gender, beliefs, customs, competing discourses, and the like. Being able to map them, to find advantageous routes to our aims, understanding this storm of determinations we are swaying under (determinations that would be only limitations if they were static) will redefine both freedom and reason. Freedom as a choice between aspects of the given, reason as a state "above" nature merely in the sense of a consciousness of natural plurality, puts an end to the nature/reason conflict.

A helpful picture of the freedom of the moderns can be found in that extraordinary chapter of Hegel's first ethics (1802), "The Negative, or: Freedom, or: Crime."[6] This abstruse text, difficult even by the young Hegel's standards, contains the first intimation of what is demonic in modern morality, long before Nietzsche and Dostoevsky. It can be summarized perhaps by translating it into his later idiom.[7]

In a curious simile, Hegel says that murder and morality do the same thing to a person: they both annihilate his particularity. Morality will annihilate his subjectivity (it will reduce a person to what is general) and murder will obliterate his objectivity (his being a part of nature) by reducing him to his objective aspect (being an inert body). Freedom, more precisely, pure freedom, is negative because (rather like murder) it ignores what is objective about someone, since it defines him as a subject who chooses. A person reduced to choice is not really someone; he has no substance proper, but is just a sum of decisions that can go any way. Being conceived thus, a person is pure negativity (circumscribed only by his decisions and actions, not his substance or "being") and, says Hegel, if something or someone is defined by negativity, its or his essence is nothing else but indifference. Theft is property subsumed or subordinated to desire, the negation of the indifference (the person as negative generality). At the same time, theft ceases to be theft, or appropriation of what belongs to another. For if a person is reduced to his choices, decisions, desires, then his relation to the object that is his is *violence* (his relationship to his property is volitional, willed, subjective); therefore the counter-violence that robs him of his property is not different in kind from his; it is only stronger. Theft merely shows the greater strength of the thief compared to that of the owner.

Later, at Jena (1805) Hegel writes that in a contract a person's being is not separated from its pure will.[8] Here the will is reality. In the contract the other recognizes my absent, represented *will*; it is the will that is valid; the contract is indifferent to being and time. The contract is coercion against my will, and it has nothing to do with my individual morality, with my way of thinking. The contract holds each individual will as a generality. In the contractual position, i.e., *not* in a state of nature, I am opposed not to a conscious activity but to another will. The idea of contract paves the way for a notion of evil that Hegel defines juridically as *culpa* or *dolus*. For in a contractual relationship intentions are made obvious, freeing one from the exculpatory plea of ignorance.

According to the young Hegel, then, (modern) freedom is dependent on what we consider to be a person. The limits to this freedom are the limits of force or strength, since *what* is free is one's choice, decision, action, desire. These can be stopped in their tracks only by some equivalent force. Freedom, to recapitulate, is not a state, let alone a superior state of a human being (as it was for the ancients). It is merely a configuration of clashing desires of unequal strength. Recognition is due to one in accordance with the strength of his desire (characterized by Mr. Fukuyama through the revived Hellenic concept of *megalothymia*, the generous strength of one's personality[9]), not according to one's quality or intrinsic worth. The ability to secure recognition, that is, to have one's own way in a public manner, is the measure of one's freedom. As a consequence, freedom becomes an attribute that can be strengthened or weakened. Freedom increased would mean an imposition of one's desire on the plurality of wills deemed to be "nature" (Hegel's "spiritual fauna"); freedom lost would appear to be an acquiescence in someone else's desire, a submission to someone else's intention or choice.

The question is, if freedom is an event rather than a state, how is freedom for everyone to be achieved? If "self-choice," as Professor Taylor puts it, is the only version of a "fully significant life" one can have, how are we to proceed in order to bar injustice resulting from the differing levels of strength people appear to exhibit when making decisions and trying to impose them on a contingent, chaotic, unpredictable reality?

The answer is supplied by the liberal/socialist utopia.

One can prevent injustice (different degrees of realized freedom) from solidifying into a permanent state where suprapersonal coercion might prevent even strong individuals from achieving a freedom commensurate with their *thymos* (striving soul), and where sheer bad luck and misadventure can conspire to thwart desires worthy of fulfillment, only by inventing an antidote to institutional coercion. Institutional coercion will cut down on the free play of desires, intentions, decisions; it will unavoidably prefer some types suitable to one given institutional order (chivalry will be richly recompensed in a feudal dukedom, celibacy in theocracy, conformism and hard work in a democracy, and so on), thus rewarding people for what they are rather than for what they do. If so, the demonic negativity of modern freedom, discovered by Hegel, will become unthinkable, will and action will become irrelevant, comparisons will be made between groups of people adhering to different creeds and behavior patterns rather than comparisons between the terms of choices. Such comparisons between groups of people and their ways of life (the bread and butter of ancient moral psychology) are odious to the modern sensibility, which does not wish to recognize that, say, monks are superior to tarts, or vice versa.

Freedom must consist (according to the moderns) in would-be monks being able to become monks and would-be tarts becoming tarts if they so wish. Freedom cannot be *one state*, determined by rational moral criteria to which anyone can aspire, and beneath which one is less free than those who have ascended to that (supposedly) perfect realm impervious to external compulsion. For us moderns, compulsion or coercion is not bad in itself if it is merely the mute resistance of speechless nature expressed by chance or accident. If there is no permanent rule prohibiting us from acting as we wish, we can put up with being unable to do as we wish: in principle there can always be a future moment when we can, provided we desire strongly enough and are sure of our purpose. *Amor fati*, love for our destiny, acceptance of the intricacy of the great web, is possible if fate is no more that just that, a combination of inner force and statistics.

But where there is an obstacle in the nature of a human will that is not solely a chance impediment (i.e., that is not merely some blind intention emanating from a member of the "spiritual fauna"), fatality ceases to be significant for us. The liberal and socialist utopia rooted in this quintessentially modern view of freedom, while glorifying will and therefore promoting individual victory, cannot accept defeat for anybody. Choices will have to be made in an unencumbered fashion from a virtually infinite menu of potentialities. But we do, also, realize that the menu is by no means infinite, that the moral and physical world available to humans is rather limited, and that therefore some will get what they want and some probably will not. This is a raw deal for the defeated, to be sure. It appears to the moderns that encountering necessity embodied by the will of others is particularly intolerable. The liberal and socialist utopia will—Nietzsche saw it well—attempt to tame the will of the strong.

The race to win the rewards, limited in number, of our moral and physical world should not have winners and losers, say the moderns; there should be compensations for the whole field. But lacking prizes for victory, what would induce people to participate in the race at all?

One solution (a version vaguely advocated by the new evangel of radical feminism) could perhaps be to change human nature, eradicate the competitive elements therefrom, and institute harmony within people's souls *before* trying to establish it between people. This is a quasi-religious idea; some socialists had been attracted to it or, at least, had hoped to see such a transformation of human nature brought about by communism as the final stage of history. They had hoped that the limitedness of resources would be overcome when the promised redemption changed Nature as such.

But the more common, or characteristically modern—that is, liberal and socialist—solution was instead *to glorify consent.*

What does this mean? It does not mean achieving compromises. People can indeed compromise over some of the different rewards offered, since not everybody will want the same rewards. But competition is meaningless if we cannot hope for satisfactions that would fulfill our personal desires. A gentleman fighting to win the heart of a lady will not be made happy with a sum of money. A desire to rule will not be satisfied by amorous conquest. A thirst for truth cannot be quenched by a life of pleasure. How, then, are we to manufacture consent? First, we shall have to recognize the variety of desires. Second, we shall have to remove all barriers that might bar people from participating in the great contest; all such barriers appear to the moderns as artificial or alienating.

Marx thought that the dynamic element in human nature—the needs which transcend the present state of the world—would make us, under favorable circumstances, well-rounded and universal beings (*Gattung-swesen,* "species-beings") for whom contest and consent would be one and the same. But he believed also that science and technology would redeem the limitedness of resources. If so, of course, every wish could be gratified. In Marx's paradise, unlike in any other, we are not supposed to lose our desires and thus to be pacified for ever and ever, but to have them with a great intensity, and there we shall each be able to be happy and active without hurting anybody, as life's horizon becomes an ever-receding frontier.

Socialists, then, agree with liberals on the meaning of freedom. Both will deem a society free (1) when the expression of the full variety of desires is not thwarted by a moral ban on any of them and (2) if there is no aristocratic principle excluding disadvantaged human groups from the game—which means, naturally, the end of religion and hierarchy.

In spite of half-hearted protestations to the contrary, law and the state are not able to fulfill these two conditions. Try as we might today to "free" law from moral constraints and from imposing a definite morality, and to make the state "ideologically" neutral, self-evidently and necessarily law will profit some types of people (in tune with the morality propounded by that very law and custom) and the state will always differentiate between superiors and underlings. Institutions designed to uphold a certain kind of human life can hardly do otherwise. There might be an element of equality in democratic conformism—banality is a majority thing—but if it is dominant, rebels and heroes will have a difficult time, unlike under the robber kingdoms of old.

If we think as the moderns do that no moral act is valid when induced by ethical principles established outside one's individual will, i.e., under the compulsion of someone else's superior will, and if we think likewise that "autonomy" is a necessary condition for morality—that is, the law we obey is, in a manner of speaking, *our law,* a law both general and in accordance with our own personal idea of what is good—then it eventually becomes clear that living under the dominion of a state is morally unacceptable. If freedom is choice or the ability to choose, being prevented by a pre-designed institution from deciding for ourselves will mean servitude, something undignified and revolting. If there is nothing "objective"—no recognized law that is exterior or external to our own volitional and emotive selves—then only those rules will apply to which we have voluntarily acquiesced.

"The withering away of the state" is the heart of the historical construct I call the liberal/socialist utopia. The aim is to keep us free from institutional interference while we are making our choices and securing a smooth path for the satisfaction of our desires. What is human becomes *par excellence* non-institutional. Institutions are seen as bad on two counts: first, because they are trying to impose a rigid, conceptual, thus "artificial" order on autonomous persons who are embodying nature by virtue of the spontaneity and dynamism of their desires and, second, because institutions are making their own servants into mere expressions of another set of conceptual, abstract, "artificial" roles by compelling them to behave in a uniform, synchronized, predictable, patterned fashion, "according to the book." Since institutions are prescribing roles (spheres of authority) within themselves, and establishing a hierarchy between them, they are held to make any person subordinated to institutional authority, either within or outside institutions, non-free. After all, institutions prescribe actions and are therefore inimical to the "significant life" grounded in "self-choice."

From the vantage point of the liberal/socialist utopia, society is nothing else but the political community without the state. Society (or "civil society") is presumed to be anti-authoritarian and non-hierarchical. For both authority and hierarchy reside in the institutional order whose paradigm is the state, invested with the privilege of issuing obligatory rules outside of a contractual relationship, i.e., "absolutely." Unlike the state, society (or "civil society") is presumed to be informal (not rule-abiding) and non-oppressive, and is characterized by an extreme nominalism that does not even try to go beyond the personal, the transient, the local, the contingent. People with desires might disregard other people's desires, and selfishness might threaten the paradisiac freedom from institutions, but this peril can be alleviated by voluntary associations and contracts. There is nothing detrimental to individual liberty in imposing self-restraint if this is our conscious choice, nor is liberty damaged by making and keeping contractual promises—so long as there is no general rule compelling us to do so. The point is, in a stateless society perhaps more rather than fewer decisions are made, but all these decisions must have our consent.

Romanticism and the Modern Utopia

Replacing coercion with consent is the regulative idea of freedom in the liberal/socialist utopia. But what makes a binding contract superior to a binding statute? What is the psychological difference between a statute and a contract, provided that both are equally compulsory? We might suffer punishment if we fail to perform our contractual obligations, but these obligations are self-imposed. The imposition of someone else's superior *will*, on the other hand (as opposed to merely facing disagreeable consequences of whatever nature), rankles. If that superior will is impersonal—for example, institutional—then we will have left the realm in which we oppose only "spiritual fauna": we cannot confront, plead with, suck up to, impress, cheat on, seduce, sadden, or amuse an agent that is an abstract Behemoth. With the modern emphasis on the transient, the local, the emotional, and the corporeal, law and the state are seen as "abstractions" and must appear as the enemy. It would hurt moral equality (always according to the modern sensibility) if we had to assert our liberty against something radically different from us, against something that is not personal. And of course there is always the suspicion that impersonal institutions serve powerful people or groups of people whose discernibly "human" interests are merely veiled by the institutional scum nicknamed "law and the state." Modernity's instinctive nominalism and anti-Platonism has not only a liberal but also a romantic aspect.

It was the romantics who, besides convincing us that only "the moment" expressed our essence, that caprice and adventure were more telling than rules and design, paved the way for the liberal/socialist utopia which they achieved through their criticism of the Enlightenment. The romantics had a powerful hankering after the hierarchical communities of the Middle Ages, but—as good moderns—they changed the authoritarian argument forever. They worshipped tradition not because it appeared *good* or *true* to them (establishing what is good and true by unassisted reason seemed godless and irreverent) but simply because it was theirs.

The end of questioning (be it Socratic or Voltairian) meant that faith should be *blindly* attached to custom and tradition, the tradition of the place we happen to live in, in the shape that happens to be respected at the moment. The romantics did not want to believe in religion because it was true (what if it was not?) but solely because they were religious. A very irreligious attitude, of course. The romantics did not bow to authority because they thought it was good or fair or just, but merely because it happened to have been imposed. A very anti-authoritarian attitude, of course. The romantics did not obey the law of the land because that law satisfied the loftiest, nay divine ideas of justice, but— like Rousseau's Hottentot—only because it was the law *of the land* that happened to be *their country*. Surely this does not betray a very profound respect for legality. Thus the old quarrel of the ancients and moderns was changed forever. The Party of the Ancients, now led by the romantics, advocated policies that were abhorrent to liberals and progressives, but did so *for the same reason* that the latter preferred equality, democracy, liberty, toleration, and the like: it was the belief of *both* camps from then on that the only comprehensible foundation for politics is personhood. And personhood among them meant the free reign of the transient, the local, the emotive, and the corporeal. Whatever curtailed the room for maneuver of persons so conceived (circumscribed by this foursome of adjectives) had henceforward to be fought mercilessly. Philosophy, with its inherent universalism, was seen by romantics like Herder (before the multiculturalists, Foucault and Virilio) as the imposition of an alien cultural discourse; philosophy was not parochial, so it had to go.

All of a sudden, liberals were confronted not by believers in the goodness of the moral and legal Behemoth, but by people who spoke like masochistic perverts who prefer to kneel and to kowtow when others would rather stand up or lounge comfortably away from authority. But if humility and love of the lord is nothing else than an emotion, then a submissive subculture can employ at will its master or dominatrix, ''if it makes them feel good.'' And of course Joseph de Maistre is the twin brother of the Marquis de Sade.

The Human Cosmos of the Modern Utopia

The nominalism, emotivism, and voluntarism of modern moral psychology is the background of the liberal/socialist utopia wherein the best that can be said of institutional coercion is that it might be a necessary evil in a period of transition to complete liberty. The state can be accepted provisionally as a self-destroying device that (by blowing itself up, as it were) will be replaced by a new order that is voluntary, consensual, and contractual.

All polities, be they real or imaginary, have their own ideas of excellence. The polity of the liberal/socialist utopia is no exception; it is constrained by the moral psychology on which it is based to propound social ideals that are in keeping with its (non-coercive) nature. Although this utopia has never been realized, its ethical program has proved to be quite successful. The perfect Free Man who can be praised and popularized by liberals and socialists does not pretend to be good and just: he wishes to appear "authentic," that is, to have a public persona that is intensely, even passionately identical with his private one. He does not presume to be thought perfect; on the contrary, he will show his blemishes, anxieties, worries, and whims as witnesses to his life being true to the transient and local character of modern moral perceptions. The Free Man will be susceptible to change, a change dictated by his inner needs. His assertions will be credited not by proofs supplied by anything external—such as logic or reality—but by their being deeply adhered to or "felt"; sincerity, not truth, is the aim. Even if Free Man is a leader or a public figure, he is expected to be suspicious of anything "public": he can be a leader by being more strongly private, personal, subjective, even more biased than others in order to gain a following. For an adherence to allegedly objective standards appears to be hypocrisy to the dominant liberal moral psychology. You will recognize in this description many a political and artistic success story where intensity won over wisdom, capriciousness over knowledge—over knowledge that is never wholly personal.

This emotivist view of man, coupled with democratic conformism caused by the dominance of egalitarian public opinion, gives us the identikit portrait of the Man of the Age: he is both intensely, uniquely, unmistakably his private self and at the same time earnestly banal.[10]

What is the order of a free society as proposed by modern socialists and liberals? How can law be preserved and observed in a society without the state? The answer had been furnished by Hegel a long time ago, but it took a twentieth-century Hegelian—the greatest apart from Kojève—Michael Oakeshott, to explain it clearly to those who lived under the aegis of the liberal/socialist utopia, although of course Oakeshott, a conservative, never subscribed to it:

> *Das Recht* here [. . .] is a system of known, positive, self-authenticating, non-instrumental rules of law (*Gesetze*) enacted by human beings according to a procedure authorized in a system of law; capable of being considered in terms of their desirability and deliberately altered; related to the contingent conduct of persons within their jurisdiction in a judicial procedure which is further empowered to penalize inadequate subscription to the conditions they prescribe. . . . To be associated in terms of *das Gesetz* is to be related in terms of conditions which can be observed only in being understood, which can be subscribed to only in self-chosen actions and

cannot themselves prescribe substantive conduct; which not only allow "free" agency but postulate "free" agents as their Subjects. Acknowledgment of their authority does not entail approval of what they prescribe; they can demand nothing which might compromise the authenticity of the conduct they govern; they neither enjoin nor forbid any other mode of association.[11]

This is the classical image of a well-ordered society without the state, where there is no human action that is as limited as the law itself is. The law must give way to subjectivity as far as a "reflection" on it—that is, our understanding of it—is concerned: I shall observe or obey the law if it coincides with the law of my autonomy. The law, having thus been transformed into subjectivity, has no intrinsic authority; actions in accordance with or in contravention to it are not intrinsically good or bad. The only *general* function of the law is to assert the subject's freedom; and the freedom of the subject is of course not subsumed under any substantive general rule, since the subject as subject ("personhood") consists in its own immediacy, in what is local and transient. The obstacle to an individual desire is, even if not strictly personal, subjective or at least it partakes of a titular subjectivity inasmuch as it appears as a psychological (subjective) *force* opposed to the peculiar force of my desire and will.

The Hegelian version of a "play of forces" within a political community or a polity is described by Hans-Georg Gadamer in the following fashion:

> . . . The assertion that there "exists" a force by itself apart from its expression and isolated from the context of all forces is also a false abstraction. What exists are forces and their interplay. [. . .] [T]he appearance [as such] is not just an expression of force which, when the force weakens, nullifies itself and its effect. Rather, it is the whole of reality. It not only has its ground; it is as the essence showing itself. As opposed to shallow talk of a thing "having" properties, indeed even as opposed to the insight that penetrated behind that force which either expresses itself or remains potential, there opens up now a view into the inner essence of things as the "absolute reciprocity" of the play of forces.[12]

This is the human cosmos of modern utopia. There is nothing solid, nothing fixed; there are only "subjectivities" set against one another; there is no substance "behind"; appearance (*Schein*) is all there is: an animated cosmos of desires.

The Dialectic of Desire

The moment Mr. Fukuyama calls "the end of history" is the defeat of socialism by liberal capitalism, a defeat which has put an end to the dream of a non-institutional, stateless civil society. Yet phenomena in Eastern Europe, the Caucasus, and Central Asia show that we have chaotic uprisings aiming at nothing other than the stateless civil society.[13] What we might have on our hands, then, is an unsuspected victory of socialism. The collapse of communism has been a revolt against hierarchy and coercion, thus it was both a liberal and a socialist revolution. The unprecedented decay of state authority shows not the weakness of socialism (or liberalism), but the strength of the liberal/socialist utopia.

With a difference.

The revolutions at "the end of history" are not proclaiming the liberal/socialist utopia, but are taking it for granted. These revolutions have no "regulative idea" or utopia at all; they are revolutions in the original sense of the word (reversal, restitution, rolling back) since they want to restore the original position contained in the modern idea, a society that is "purely human," i.e., a society without a supernatural code, without a presumption of transcontextual knowledge, *without attempts at transcending the corporeal and the temporal.* If socialism has come to an end, so has liberalism. The rebellions against Soviet-style regimes were directed—like all revolutions—against what was perceived as unjust privilege or the iron rule of an immovable hierarchy. In the wake of this revolution, freedom is accepted as the reduction of the polity to non-servile, that is, personal, "subjective" relationships; "civil society" is opposed to politics, the common good is ineffable, the public interest meaningless. The only true justification of political power, unselfish service to a higher good that might or might not coincide with the sum of individual desires (*la volonté de tous* as opposed to *la volonté générale*) is unthinkable with the conceptual instruments we possess at the moment. It is in fact believed to be a sheer impossibility, a whimsical fancy of ill-informed, conservative doctrinaires.

The liberal/socialist utopia wins hands down against what had been achieved against its grain during its nominal reign. Inequality in liberal societies, brutal coercion in socialist societies is attacked successfully by an unthinking return to the original idea. This is what Alexandre Kojève calls "cyclical" in his magnificent (and slightly mad) introduction to his *Essai d'une histoire raisonnée de la philosophie païenne,*[14] where he also says that the history that comes to an end is a history which speaks.[15] For a history defined by what is local and transient can no longer be addressed by philosophy—it cannot speak; it becomes mute. Liberal and socialist societies are defeated by liberal and socialist resistance (modernity is challenged and defeated by itself)—which only shows the extent to which modernity is unresolved, the extent to which it has not fulfilled itself. To assert the liberal/socialist utopia *positively* would be totally ineffective, but its *de facto* triumph shuts up the history that speaks: it is indeed the end of history as we know it. Why? Because it is impossible to enunciate its principle. What is happening today is identical to what happened yesterday, with the difference that nobody believes in our ability to speak today with the utopian ideas of yesterday. The defeat touches speech, not the deed.

This is a, not *the*, barbarous state of affairs. Non-utopian liberalism or socialism appears barbaric because it stays unhistorically the same, without an "externalized consciousness,"[16] *Bildung, paideia.* And without *Bildung*, history and culture become separated. And in my opinion this is the essence of this counter-historical moment: inarticulateness, speechlessness, the availability of testimony (the remains of a high culture hitherto in existence), and the concomitant inability to philosophize.

It is always hard to tell barbarism from decadence. "The end of history" is as good a metaphor as fall, decay, decadence, obsolescence could possibly be, but if we specify that it is conscious, "speaking" history that has come to an end, then these terms are virtually synonymous or coterminous. The collapse of communism made us understand that its adversary, Western liberalism, has collapsed as well. The lease of life neoconservatism had offered it, a welcome and useful leg-up, has also expired. A modest tinkering or *bricolage* is advocated today by "the best element," accompanied by a profound cultural dissatisfaction temporarily remedied by feeble-minded fads and *cris de coeur,* by knowing glances shot at poor Matisse, or by embarrassing quotes from Matthew Arnold.

In his intelligent reconstruction of Kojève, Mr. Fukuyama[17] tries to characterize the present moment through a dialectic of recognition and desire. I shall attempt myself an interpretation of what I believe Kojève thinks through a reading of his magisterial *Esquisse d'une phénoménologie du droit.*[18]

According to Kojève, man is constituted by what he calls *le désir anthropogène*,[19] which in fact gives birth to man. An animal satisfies its desire by assimilating natural reality. Its being is its action. But by realizing (satisfying) its desire, it annihilates this desire as desire: it fills its void, replaces absence by presence. The animal is natural reality; therefore its desire, which is the absence of this reality, annihilates itself in order to become the presence of this same reality.

Human desire is the desire of a desire that can be satisfied only by itself, by an absence that annihilates (*néantit*). But man, this being of desire, is the negation or absence of the real being—man is an ideal or unreal being since it exists in its annihilation of its real being while desiring it. This self-negation is the specifically human existence. Desiring a desire, that is, desiring to be desired by someone else, means wanting to assimilate someone else's desire, to make it one's own, to obliterate it as something external. In other words, says Kojève, one wants to become oneself the object of the desired desire. I am going to be completely satisfied when that being whom I desire to desire me will have *no other desire* but his or her desire of me. That desire will then have become a part of me; it will not be external to me, since it is a desire of me; it will be part and parcel of my own self while being all this time someone else's desire. The other being, wanting what I want through wanting me, identifies with me, becomes *me,* while remaining his or her own self. Is this the same thing as wanting to be loved? Kojève professes to speak of something more general. Desiring someone else's desire is to desire to play for that other the role of an absolute value. The desire of desire, *le désir anthropogène,* is a desire for recognition (*Anerkennen*).

Man as desire can annul himself as an animal (since man is part of animal nature too); his "anthropogenous" desire could obliterate his natural instinct of self-preservation. In fact, for someone to realize himself as a human being it is *necessary* to be capable of risking his life for recognition. This risk is the veritable birth of man, when the risking of one's life occurs solely in order to secure recognition.

The essential difference between humans, according to Kojève, is created by this willingness to die for recognition. Those who prefer mere life or self-preservation will have to submit to the superior will of the man seeking recognition. The winner becomes the Master, the loser becomes the Servant (the usual translation of the *Knecht* in the *Phänomenologie* is "slave," but I find it too narrow and exaggerated); while the defeated one is not recognized by the victor, the victor is recognized by the defeated. But the "actuality," the true existence of the Master, says Kojève, is pure illusion. For since the Master does not want to become a Servant, the desire cannot be mutual, and the "anthropogenous" desire becomes impossible. There is no pleasure in being recognized by a Servant because this is tantamount to being recognized by someone whom one does not recognize oneself. Being what he is, the Master cannot stop being Master, nor can his desire for recognition be assuaged. The Master is unfulfilled as a human being. One can only *die* as a Master, one cannot *live* as one. The Master appears in history only to disappear; he is present only in order that the Servant be. The Servant wants to change, since he is aware of the fact that he is human only to the extent to which he recognizes the reality, dignity, and valor of the Master—that he is human only to the extent that he has got the idea of humanity in himself. He is not wholly human, as he knows, because he is not recognized. And even if he, the Servant, has got a stomach for fighting, he cannot become a Master because the Master does not recognize him. Hence, the Master does not recognize the one who recognizes the Master, and the Servant would recognize only him who would compel recognition. The Servant, then, could never become a Master, but he will become a *Citizen*. It is only the Citizen who will be satisfied, only he who will be recognized in turn by the one whom he recognizes. The Citizen is both Servant and Master: a Servant, because he recognizes others, and a Master because he is recognized by others. The only "real" man is the Citizen: Master and Servant are merely "logical principles."

This is the *hégélisant* version of the modern (the liberal/socialist) utopia which, unlike other versions, gives a frank, albeit somewhat convoluted, account of suffering and humiliation. As I have argued elsewhere,[20] the main task of political philosophy is social theodicy: the justification of suffering and humiliation. We are under an obligation to obey whomever, or whatever, only if it can be shown that the servitude, inherent in all obedience, is good.

The suffering in a state of nature of a Hobbesian kind, in the absence of authority and law, is in no need of justification, since we are constrained to bow to sheer personal and physical force rather than to authority. In a Hobbesian state of nature suffering is inflicted without justification. While the State is supposed to alleviate sufferings of precisely that kind, the suffering of those upon whom an impersonal authority seeks to impose rules not of their doing—rules indifferent to their personal inclinations—is humiliation or servitude. You can be free from unauthorized coercion if you accept that you will have to obey state authority. But authority, unlike the imposition of sheer force, is in need of moral justification; people do not obey the state because they are subjected to a relentless physical harassment or violence by the agents of state authority; they obey because they have come to believe that the kind of authority they think fit to obey is good. This does not mean that obedience to authority is a question of voluntary choice. People have to make up their minds as to whether authority is good while already obeying it, therefore finally they will have to judge for themselves whether the fact of their obedience is good or not. A voluntary submission to authority (because this is what we undertake when we reckon that resisting authority would be too cumbersome) will be a terrible thing and a source of bitter humiliation if it turns out to have been sinful to start with.[21] This is why the claims of authority made by state agencies will always be examined by their subjects who do not wish to suffer the humiliation inherent in obedience (however useful it should be in practical terms) without good reason.

The task of offering a *social theodicy* is not easily performed by Western political philosophy because our main cultural tradition, Christianity, refuses pointedly to admit of such. Christianity is utterly anarchistic in this respect (and in others as well, of course) since it makes clear that all the wrongs of social life, including obedience to legitimate authority, will be redeemed only in the nether world. The indifference of Christianity to the question of authority (however this indifference was modified by later Hellenization in church history) made it necessary for modern political philosophy to recognize itself—first in Hegel, then in Kojève—as *pagan* philosophy, so much so that Kojève thought himself able to summarize the essence of Hegel's "System of Knowledge" through a "reasoned history of *pagan* philosophy," i.e., of Greek philosophy. Christian theodicy justifies suffering with predestination, grace, and redemption, but this justification contains "the social" as a subordinate element in the overall scheme of things, thus tacitly assuming that it belongs—quite independent of the kind of political order in which the man in need of justification finds himself—to a sphere of injustice.

Modern (liberal/socialist) utopia is in part an answer to the question of how to work out a social theodicy (a justification of the suffering of obedience) by removing the basis for the question rather than answering it directly. I think that Kojève's Hegelian theory of desire and servitude is just another variant of this utopia, although a rather critical and ambivalent one. This ambivalence is inherited by Mr. Fukuyama, who compounds his apparently unconditional endorsement of liberal democracy with a quite gloomy Nietzschean critique of the same.

Since seemingly there is no acceptable answer to the question of how to find a non-utilitarian theory of reasons for obedience, liberal utopia will put forward a picture of a social cosmos where there is no authority to obey (thus secularizing the anarchistic skepticism of Christianity).

Far from being the "pagan" philosophy it purports to be, it continues to mirror the profound ambiguity of all Peoples of the Book towards secular authority. Even while the Good Book is not any longer seriously believed in (and with this faith go all dreams of a divine regiment on earth, be it theocracy or a philosophic *politeia* or whatever—let us not forget that Christianity is Platonism for the masses), the distaste of Western civilization for power remains unambiguous. Enlightenment and Marxism, the two greatest attempts to eradicate religion, failed to uproot the modern distaste for authority, and paid the price by setting themselves up as this-worldly "religions." The recourse one could always have—through the agency of natural law—to Higher Authorities, whereby one could ask in principle always for reasons for obedience, ask for guidance to the common good, had to be upheld. But it was not upheld by a theory of just government; it was upheld by a promise to end all government. The historicist and positivist critique of natural right practiced by liberals and socialists was so thorough that no alternative remained other than a blind acquiescence in authority on prudential or mystical grounds (Joseph de Maistre or Simone Weil are not all that different from Machiavelli and Hobbes), or anarchism.

Anarchism won.

The fact that there is "only" a fundamental identity between anarchism and the liberal/socialist utopia (all political consequences drawn are strikingly different) cannot hide the fact that the quintessentially modern answer to the question of authority, i.e., to the question of politics, stems from the anarchist notion that very few had the guts to enunciate clearly, and the boldest political writing we have is still La Boétie's *Servitude volontaire*, written by a boy,[22] and most certainly not written for immediate publication. (It is hardly surprising, by the way, that such radicalism has since been displayed only by two other boys, Arthur Rimbaud and Raymond Radiguet.) But this is neither here nor there. Whether or not anarchism is the secret doctrine of modernity, it is still "the truth," as Hegelians would say, of the liberal/socialist utopia. Autonomy or self-rule is the polite name for anarchy, non-rule. Either someone else is prescribing rules to me, or I am prescribing rules to myself; I can get others to make a deal with me about mutual arrangements on a voluntary basis, and these arrangements will be called valid if all concerned agree (this is what people call "democracy" today in Eastern Europe). But be our provisional mutual arrangements what they will, the point is that someone else—the Other—is not allowed to establish binding rules for me, much less to force me to follow.

The Other for the moderns is everything that is beyond what is transient, local, emotive, and corporeal. For the moderns believe that everything social can in the last instance be reduced to the personal. Marx's poetic analysis of commodity fetishism, whereby he reduces the great holistic concepts of political economy to what is subjective in work, is a characteristic example of what we could call "personal reductionism," a view backed not only by Marx but especially by late modern literature with the exception of some solitaries like Franz Kafka. The state is a metaphor, institutions are merely human groups.[23] The state is a metaphor for regulated domination by strong groups of Masters (including *maîtres-penseurs*), institutions are gangs with charters. A notion like "capital" is too remote from what is corporeal or emotional in man; and the moderns feel they have to find the "revolutionary" component within the universal, the one which will blow it up conceptually, will dismember it and show that there are no self-sustaining ideas that cannot be analyzed asunder into atoms of personal-human activity. Latter-day liberals hope that individual rights (chunks of unfettered personal activity) will gradually fritter away the state, making the state a mere idea subordinated to persons, something that vouches for privacy being kept untouched, and thus something that "belongs" to the citizens in the sense that the state is increasingly prohibited from representing anything impersonal, such as authority itself.

Anyway, the faith in supra-personal entities seems to be culturally and psychologically dependent on theistic metaphysics. And of course, as one of the greatest Marxist thinkers noted, there is atheism in Christianity, since the reduction of divinity to its appearance in the flesh, which is central to the Christian faith, closely parallels the revolutionary feeling of early Christians which moved them to debunk the haughty claims of secular authority, an authority which being Gentile and unjust was doubly alien to them.[24] Theistic metaphysics is difficult not only today; it has always been difficult. It was always assimilated to the letter that kills. And what is killed by the "letter," as we all know, is the living person, with his transience and his propensity to fickle change. Since *verbum caro factum est*, the Word was made flesh, the word as a supra-personal idea is suspect.

If rules are seen only as descriptions of acts that the dominant forces (i.e., groups of Masters) of society are desirous of having repeated because it is advantageous to their tranquillity or felicity, then it stands to reason that the authority behind the rules is only *masquerading* as generality or abstract entity (as in "the rule of law": *who* is law?) while it is in fact nothing else but the coordinated activity of a group with peculiar cultural characteristics ("legal culture," bureaucratic tradition," "the

ethic of the public servant,'' and the like). In the view of modern liberals and socialists, society has to be brought back to its very reality,
which is an association of persons, both incommensurable and equal in
dignity.[25] It must be a free association of persons, free, that is, of coercion (and political rules, statutes, laws, decrees, etc., are always backed
by coercion or the threat of it) and domination (and wherever there is a
state, roles are distributed unequally: persons will have to obey persons
even if the lawgiver believes himself to obey an ideal—both abstract
and ''objective''—authority). Only such a free association is not based
on power. Acts within it are chosen by the agents; prohibitions will only
protect persons (certainly not ideas: blasphemy laws are superfluous
where the idea of the sacred is replaced by the idea of the wholeness/
holiness of the corporeal-emotional person).

This is not to say that the free association of the liberal/socialist utopia is not ruled by anything. It is ruled, like all utopian communities
from the beginning of time, by love.

Again, this is not the term that is being used, but surely the symmetry
and mutuality of desire is properly called love. Kojève's *désir anthropogène* is defined as a desire of desire. If my desire of your desire is to be
reciprocated, two things are necessary. First, you must have a desire of
my desire (i.e., we do not desire each other in the sense that I can desire
a person without her knowing I would like a lamb chop: human desire
is made what it is by consciousness and self-consciousness—we do
desire one another as persons *in movement*, persons who feel, talk, act,
are conscious of themselves and of their finitude or transience). Second,
you must not be compelled by any external agency (not even by sexual-
ity as a general natural need or a non-specific, self-reflective stirring
within one's body) to desire me and your desire of me. And a prerequi-
site of these two conditions is no doubt the *intentionality* (in the scho-
lastic sense popularized by Husserl, i.e., being directed at, pointed at
something) of desire.

The liberal/socialist utopia is built upon this dialectic of desire. We
are expected to become citizens of a peculiar polity without city walls,
of what we might call a free association, where—and this is essential—
desire will always meet desire. There is no personhood available any
longer of a kind that might be ''cold,'' that is, unyielding to desire,
wanting obedience without wanting to be desired, which would mean
that he will be supposed to desire in turn. The impossibility of a Master
appearing on the socio-cultural scene is ascertained by the very character of a free association held together by the bonds of love. And what
saves this utopia from being an evangel is that it does not have to pro-

claim a change in human nature. Indeed, it will proclaim human nature as it is, wishing for recognition, wanting to be subject only in a realm of love where there is no king, no knight, no serf, no priest. We know what Nietzsche thought of this—and this offers the second main theme for Mr. Fukuyama, who sets out to illuminate our modern predicament with a pale, ironic hope. But Nietzsche too was a child of the liberal age, and when he fiercely defended hierarchy and strength, he thought it necessary to get rid of love. Hence his hatred of Christendom, hence his hatred of democracy. Hence his forgetting Plato.

What is curious about this peculiar moment in history that we witnessed (and some of us participated in it in the manner of the *Education sentimentale* or otherwise) is that when people rebelled against the socialist utopia that had led to an intolerable impasse, they did so inspired largely by the same utopia. Socialism promised the withering away of the state, and people wanted it to wither. Socialism promised a society that is entirely human, that is, a society governed by desire, and people wanted to remove the vestiges of authority standing in the way of a free association governed by desire. Socialism promised a state of affairs where conflict would be ruled out by the mutuality and reciprocity of desire, which was to prevent the emergence of heroes (strong Masters), and people objected to the heroism and tyranny of "real socialism" as opposed to socialist utopia.

And to give it a final twist, it seems certain that people in Eastern Europe rebelled not against socialism, but against the reform of socialism. When the first suspicion of a change in the ruling utopia had become known, a suspicion that the main idea was to be a republic of interests rather than the realm of perfect love, East Europeans rebelled. The "market reform" of socialism, as it was called, led to the suspicion that from now on there would be strong and weak people, that—worse still—privilege could solidify and be inherited. People who never experienced the mutuality and reciprocity of desire but who had been told that this was what was aimed at, feared to lose their idea of themselves, an idea that had been reinforced both by the dialectical utopia of desire and by the harsh dictatorship that sought to obliterate any idea of the common good which might have made the natives restless. Liberation was thought to consist in the re-establishment of the "empirical" person (corporeal, emotional, and transient); any pretension to the contrary, any pretension to a higher, impersonal version of the wretched humanity we know so well, was—and is—greeted with amused disbelief. The society created by the dream of anarchy (non-rule, non-government) was toppled in the name of an unspoken anarchic ideal of a society without authority, of a society without a state that is anything other than an agency protecting privacy.

Observers thought, and not without reason, that East Europeans wanted freedom. But this is exactly what they wanted in 1917 and 1919. Other observers thought, and again not without reason, that there was an authoritarian streak in the "change" of 1988–90: yes, East Europeans wanted a temporarily strong state which would rid them of their Masters, rid them of the strong. But was not this behind Lenin's and Trotsky's idea of a "dictatorship of the proletariat"?[26] Those seeking to introduce a modicum of suprapersonal order (constitutionalism, the rule of law, parliamentarism, the separation of powers, independent courts, civic patriotism, etc.) are got or will be got rid of. 1989 was a heresy rather than a revolution; it tried to restore, like all heresies, what had been lost by the corruption of the original idea. But this was history without speech: it appeared anti-socialist first, socialist later, yet it is both and neither. It is a revolt without an issue, a rebellion against a mere semblance of authority but a rebellion that wished away all authority, be it respectable or fraudulent.

A very similar thing happened in the case of the neo-conservative revolution in the West. Official liberalism had become statist, interfering, and moralistic. Neo-conservatives helped to restore the original utopia to its original libertarian grandeur. Of course the reader might say that he can find nothing particularly liberal *chez* the conservative "cultural warriors." I am not so sure. Traditionalism is a liberal attitude. The traditionalist will worship ancestral custom, old religion, or cultural canon not because they are universally good, but because he feels they are his. The adoration of what happens to be there (what is called today "cultural conservatism" but is nothing else but liberal traditionalism) cannot hurt the modernist glorification of the personal-in-its-finitude: traditionalism adores what is particular to a group of mortals, what has come down to them by a contingence of birth or dislocation. The unthinking love for "our way," while it is perhaps better than unadulterated nihilism, cannot be considered an antidote to liberal utopia—small wonder, since it is its direct consequence. With a peculiar coloring of traditionalism and a telling neo-Kantian and Weberian cult of "values" (for example, "family values") there is nothing to the new conservatism that was not a restoration of liberalism. Finally, when restoration happens according to "values," that is, revered preferences emphatically not grounded in what can be described in a universalistic manner, in a manner emphatically separated from existence (following the famous fact/value dichotomy[27]), one must wonder what has been restored here.

"Values," "tradition," and their cognates are indeed results of inferences from an inability or unwillingness to believe that there is something apart from individual will (or, if you wish, desire) that can or ought to regulate human behavior. When one chooses one's tradition, one chooses oneself. When one chooses someone else's tradition (e.g., out of revulsion for ethnocentrism or racism), one chooses oneself (one's autonomy) again. When one refuses to choose any tradition at all, one chooses oneself once more. The proponents of, say, "family values" do not say that the family is intrinsically superior to celibacy or promiscuity, but only that families are *our way*, that they are traditional to us (and thereby one chooses oneself) and that they are useful, a net societal gain (so one chooses one's advantage, thus oneself). The same goes for nationalism, which is a collective celebration of self-choice, at least nowadays.

A strange end to history! You could say that nothing happened—at any rate, nothing new. But this would be false. What happened is that history has become mute. Kings and rebels, tyrants and resisters subscribe to the same principle of mutual and symmetrical love. Everybody is dissatisfied, but nobody seems to want anything but desires fulfilled, desires desired.

The liberal/socialist utopia collapsed at the same time in the East and in the West, and it has been replaced by a mute replica of the liberal/socialist utopia. East and West are still different, but this is a difference due to accidental dissimilarities of tradition, which are not considered unique, only given and, in consequence, chosen. Blind hatreds are flaring up between people wrestling with the same inability to think anything, but *anything*, outside the liberal/socialist framework.[28]

I thought earlier that the ideas of representation in liberalism and communism were different. After all, liberals advocate representative government, a representation of will, of the *volonté de tous*.[29] The Bolshevik party, on the other hand, professed to represent not *will*, but *essence*: Through the epiphenomenal class interest of the proletariat it represented a universal need, a radical transcendence of the particular need, the need of becoming a well-rounded individual, not any longer reduced to the particularity of trade, estate, station. It was a reading of Kojève, prompted by Mr. Fukuyama's book, that made me understand that this well-rounded universal being, this hidden essence of History, to be created not by an act of will but by an inexorable Historical process, was none other than the man of the "anthropogenous desire." He is the man who is in search of recognition (of love), who is assured, irrationally, that he is certain to find what all moderns are thought to want: to be loved for himself alone, away from anything and everything impersonal or eternal. In a society where there is no "superstructure" any more, there is no possibility of moral compulsion. The Kantian contrast of legality and morality disappears, because there is no coercion. But you must not ask whether your love is good.[30]

Notes

1. Harold Brodkey, *The Runaway Soul* (London: Jonathan Cape, 1991), p. 505.
2. *The End of History and the Last Man.* Cf. Jeffrey Friedman, "The New Consensus: I. The Fukuyama Thesis," *Critical Review*, Vol. 3, numbers 3 and 4, pp. 373–410.
3. Jacques Derrida, *Spectres de Marx* (Paris: Galilée, 1993), pp. 97–127.
4. See Alasdair MacIntyre, *After Virtue*, 2nd ed. (Notre Dame: University of Notre Dame Press, 1984), pp. 36–78. Cf. Alasdair MacIntyre, *Three Rival Versions of Moral Inquiry*, chapter VIII (Notre Dame: University of Notre Dame Press, 1990), pp. 170–195.
5. Charles Taylor, *Sources of the Self: The Making of Modern Identity* (Cambridge: Cambridge University Press, 1989), pp. 382–83. Cf. Charles Taylor, *The Malaise of Modernity: The Massey Lectures* (Concord, Onatrio: Anansi, 1991). Taylor's and MacIntyre's view of modernity (together with that of Carl Schmitt, Leo Strauss, and others) is sharply criticized by Stephen Holmes in his *The Anatomy of Antiliberalism* (Cambridge: Harvard University Press, 1993).
6. G. W. F. Hegel, *System der Sittlichkeit*, chapter two: "Das Negative oder die Freiheit oder das Verbrechon," ed. Georg Lasson (Philosophische Bibliothek Bd. 144a, Hamburg: Meiner, 1967), pp. 38–51.
7. Cf. Charles Taylor, *Hegel* (Cambridge: Cambridge University Press, 1975), pp. 368–88. See also Jürgen Habermas, *The Philosophical Discourse of Modernity* (Cambridge: MIT Press, 1987), pp. 23–44, 60–69, and Jean Hyppolite, *Genesis and Structure of Hegel's Phenomenology of the Spirit* (Evanston, Illinois: Northwestern University Press, 1974), Part IV, chapters 3–5, pp. 259–318 and Part V, chapter 5, pp. 453–65.
8. G. W. F. Hegel, *Jenaer Realphilosophie*, B, IIb-c, ed. Johannes Hoffmeister (Philosophische Bibliothek Bd. 67, Hamburg: Meiner, 1967), pp. 217–25. On Hegel's early writings see Shlomo Avineri, *Hegel's Theory of the Modern State* (Cambridge: Cambridge University Press, 1972), pp. 13–32. On Hegel's idea of the particular, see Charles Taylor, *Hegel,* pp. 113–16. Cf. Taylor, "Hegel's Philosophy of Mind" in Taylor, *Human Agency and Language: Philosophical Papers 1* (Cambridge: Cambridge University Press, 1985), pp. 77–96.
9. Fukuyama, *The End of History and the Last Man*, pp. 181–91.
10. Cf. Peter Sloterdijk, *Critique of Cynical Reason* (London and New York:

Verso, 1988), esp. ch. 10: "Black Empiricism: Enlightenment as Organization of Polemical Knowledge" and ch. 11: "Transcendental Polemic: Heraclitian Meditations," pp. 329–56, 357–81. Compare G. M. Tamás, "Cenzúra" [Censorship], *Kritika*, 1994, No. 1, pp. 15–18 and No. 2, pp. 16–19.

11. Michael Oakeshott, *On Human Conduct* (Oxford: Clarendon Press, 1991), pp. 261–62.

12. Hans-Georg Gadamer, "Hegel's Inverted World" in Gadamer, *Hegel's Dialectic* (New Haven and London: Yale University Press, 1976), pp. 39, 41. Cf. G. W. F. Hegel, *Phänomenologie des Geistes*, ed. Georg Lasson (Philosophische Bibliothek Bd. 114, Leipzig: Meiner, 1928), *C* , VI, A, a, 2 a-b, pp. 323–27. See also Martin Heidegger, *Hegels Phänomenologie des Geistes,* Gesamtausgabe Abt. II., Bd. 32 (Frankfurt am Main: Vittorio Klostermann, 1980), pp. 162–216. Cf. Alexandre Kojève, *Introduction à la lecture de Hegel* (Paris: Gallimard, 1947), "En guise d'introduction," pp. 11–16, esp.: "L'homme s'avère humain en risquant sa vie pour satisfaire son Désir humain, c'est-à-dire: son Désir qui porte sur un autre Désir. Or, désirer un Désir c'est vouloir se subtituter soi-même à la valeur désirée par ce Désir" (p. 14). Cf. infra, passim. For an extremely useful dissection of the relevant texts, see Howard P. Kainz, *Hegel's Phenomenology, Part I: Analysis and Commentary* (Alabama: The University of Alabama Press, 1979).

13. See G. M. Tamás, "The Legacy of Dissent," *The Times Literary Supplement*, May 14, 1993. A fuller version of the same: G. M. Tamás, "Irony, Ambiguity and Duplicity: The Legacy of Dissent," *Uncaptive Minds,* Spring 1994 (forthcoming).

14. Alexandre Kojève, *Essai d'une histoire raisonée de la philosophie païenne* (Paris: Gallimard, 1968), pp. 86–7.

15. Cf. Hegel, *Phänomenologie, C, B*, c2-3, pp. 275–82. About speech as a constitutive element of modern commercial societies, see Donald McCloskey, "Bourgeois Virtue," *The American Scholar*, Spring 1994, pp. 177–91.

16. Hegel, *Phänomenologie, C*, VI, B: "Die Welt des sich entfremdeten Geistes," pp. 350–82.

17. Fukuyama, pp. 143–286.

18. Alexandre Kojève, *Esquisse d'une phénoménologie du droit* (Paris: Gallimard, 1981.) Cf. Jacques Derrida, *Spectres de Marx*, pp. 120–25. See also Allan Bloom, "Alexandre Kojève" in Bloom, *Giants and Dwarfs* (New York and London: Touchstone/Simon and Schuster, 1991), pp. 268–73. Bloom seems not to have read the *Essai* or the *Esquisse*.

19. Kojève, *Esquisse d'une phénoménologie du droit*, Part II, ch. 1, pp. 238–66. Cf. Kojève, *Introduction à la lecture de Hegel,* pp. 166–81. See also Jacques Derrida, "Le puit et la pyramide: Introduction à la sémiologie de Hegel" in *Hegel et la pensée moderne,* ed. Jean Hyppolite (Paris: Presses Universitaires de France, 1970), pp. 27–84, or Derrida, "The Pit and the Pyramid: Introduction to Hegel's Semiology" in Derrida, *Margins of Philosophy* (Chicago: The University of Chicago Press, 1982), pp. 69–108. The main source:

Hegel, *Phänomenologie, B* IV, pp. 133–72, and B VI, c, pp. 342–46. Gilles Deleuze, "What Is Desire?" in *The Deleuze Reader*, ed. Constantin V. Boundas (New York: Columbia University Press, 1993), pp. 136–42. Compare Roger Scruton, *Sexual Desire* (London: Weidenfeld & Nicolson, 1986), especially Appendices 1 and 2, pp. 364–91.

20. In the Presidential Address to the Hungarian Philosophical Society, 1992, published as G. M. Tamás, "Az engedelmesség indokai" [Reasons for Obedience], *Világosság*, vol. XXXIII, Nos. 8/9, September 1992, pp. 593–98. I have tried to give an account of authority, obedience, and suffering in an unpublished lecture delivered at Trent University (Peterborough, Ontario) in February 1994.

21. Etienne de la Boétie, *Le Discours de la servitude volontaire*, in *Oeuvres complètes*, ed. Louis Desgraves (Paris: William Blake, 1991), Vol. I, pp. 67–98. Cf. Peter Preuss, "Selfhood and the Battle: The Second Beginning of the *Phenomenology*," in *Method and Speculation in Hegel's Phenomenology*, ed. Merold Westphal (Atlantic Highlands, N. J. and Brighton, Sussex: Humanities Press/Harvester Press, 1982), pp. 71–84.

22. On La Boétie, see the beautiful chapter in Allan Bloom's *Love and Friendship* (New York and London: Simon and Schuster, 1993), pp. 399–428.

23. See Henri Lefebvre, *l'Etat. 2. Théorie marxiste de l'Etat de Hegel à Mao* ("10/18", Paris: Union Générale d'Editions, 1976), *passim. A contrario*, see Jürgen Habermas, *Zur Rekonstruktion des Historischen Materialismus* (Frankfurt am Main: Suhrkamp, 1977).

24. See Ernst Bloch, *Atheismus im Christentum: Zur Religion des Exodus und des Reiche* (Frankfurt am Main: Suhrkamp, 1977), esp. Part V, "Aut Caesar, aut Christus," pp. 135–203.

25. See Michael Oakeshott's limpid essay, "Talking Politics," in Oakeshott's *Rationalism in Politics and Other Essays*, new and expanded edition, ed. Timothy Fuller (Indianapolis: Liberty Press, 1991), pp. 438–61.

26. See Georg Lukács, *History and Class Consciousness* (London: Merlin Press, 1971). Cf. Lucien Goldman, *Lukács and Heidegger* (London and Boston: Routledge and Kegan Paul, 1977). For a critical inner view of socialism, see Cornelius Castoriadis, *Political and Social Writings*, 3 vols. (Minneapolis: University of Minnesota Press, 1988). See also *Situationist International Anthology*, ed. Ken Knabb (Berkeley: Bureau of Public Secrets, 1981), and René Viénet, *Enragés and Situationists in the Occupation Movement, France, May '68* (New York and London: Autonomedia/Rebel Press, 1992).

27. See Leo Strauss, *Natural Right and History* (Chicago and London: University of Chicago Press, 1953), chapter two, pp. 35–80. Cf. Leo Strauss, "On Classical Political Philosophy" and "The Three Waves of Modernity" in *An Introduction to Political Philosophy: Ten Essays by Leo Strauss*, ed. Hilail Gildin (Detroit: Wayne State University Press, 1989), pp. 59–80, 81–98; "Philosophy as Rigorous Science and Political Philosophy" in *Studies in Platonic Political Philosophy*, ed. Thomas L. Pangle (Chicago: University of Chicago Press, 1983), pp. 29–37. Compare Leo Strauss, "Relativism" in *The Rebirth of Clas-*

sical Political Rationalism, ed. Thomas L. Pangle (Chicago: University of Chicago Press, 1989), pp. 13–26.

28. An early premonition: Theodor W. Adorno, *Drei Studien zu Hegel* (Frankfurt am Main: Suhrkamp, 1971), or Adorno, *Hegel: Three Studies* (Cambridge and London: MIT Press, 1993). Compare Gianni Vattimo, *The End of Modernity: Nihilism and Hermeneutics in Postmodern Culture* (Baltimore: Johns Hopkins University Press, 1991), esp. part III, pp. 113–83.

29. See Erich Kaufmann, "Zur Problematik des Volkwillens" (1931), in *Grundprobleme der Demokratie*, ed. Ulrich Matz (Wege der Forschung Bd. CXLI, Darmstadt: Wissenschaftliche Buchgesellschaft, 1973), pp. 20–34.

30. In a sadly neglected essay, "Tradition and the Modern Age," Hannah Arendt gave us the definitive intellectual portrait of Marx, shedding a brilliant light on the nature of modern utopia. See her *Between Past and Future* (New York and London: Penguin Books, 1993), pp. 18–20, 23–24. In a remarkable series of lectures, published posthumously, Arendt tried to rehabilitate the idea of a political philosophy that will watch and judge rather than "act." See Hannah Arendt, *Lectures on Kant's Political Philosophy*, ed. Ronald Beiner (Chicago and London: University of Chicago Press, 1989). On a society without authority and without work, see Hannah Arendt, *The Human Condition* (Chicago: University of Chicago Press, 1958). Cf. Simone Weil, *Réflexions sur les causes de la liberté et de l'oppression sociale* (Paris: Idées/Gallimard, 1980).

8

The End of History?

Victor Gourevitch

The thesis of Francis Fukuyama's *The End of History and the Last Man* is simple and bold: modern liberal democracy, democracy as it has developed in the West, especially in the past two centuries, marks the end of history in the sense of being both its final stage and its final cause. The defining feature of "democracy," as he uses that term, is popular sovereignty (43). The defining feature of "political liberalism" is the formal guarantee and protection of basic individual rights (42). With liberal democracy so understood, humanity has attained the goals of its millennial struggle for the political order that is just, satisfying, and stable; and because it is, it tends to unite mankind, or at least to reduce the conflicts caused by geographical, national, and religious differences. There is therefore every reason to expect that it will be adopted the wide world over within the foreseeable future. Its superiority to the "historical alternatives available to us" is, at least in principle, universally acknowledged: even tyrants feel compelled to call their rule "democratic." With the collapse of Soviet Communism it faces no serious external threat. The most urgent question now is whether it is equally safe from internal threats. What are its problems and its prospects?

Fukuyama's argument is as bold as his thesis: Nature, and in particular human nature, is the standard of political action and judgment. Modern liberal democracy conforms to human nature as closely as a political order can conform to it; it is therefore just, satisfying, and stable, and therefore it is the completion and the fulfillment of history.

The two guiding premises of this argument are: that the account of the soul and of the just city which Plato has Socrates present in the *Republic* is essentially true (337), and that the whole of human history is the history of the actualization—and modification—of this Platonic

understanding of the soul and of the corresponding just political order
(138). In his view, the Idea of history as the gradual actualization of
man's humanity was first sketched by Kant, but it remained for Hegel
to work it out fully. His project is therefore perhaps best described as
an effort to reconcile Plato's understanding of the soul and of the just
city with Hegel's understanding of history as the actualization of man's
humanity, culminating in "the modern state"—Fukuyama's "liberal
democracy." What is most distinctive about his enterprise is, then, not
either his "Platonism" or his "Hegelianism," but his attempt to reconcile the teachings of Plato and of Hegel.

Fukuyama fully acknowledges, in his text as well as in his notes, that
his understanding of Plato and of the history of political philosophy is
in very large measure mediated by the teaching of Leo Strauss (and
more particularly of some of his students and students' students), and
that his understanding of Hegel is in very large measure mediated by the
teaching of Alexandre Kojève. He could not have chosen better guides.
Strauss and Kojève are the most outstanding and influential contemporary thinkers to have modeled their thinking on the thinking of Plato
and of Hegel respectively. Their classical debate, ostensibly about tyranny but in fact about the irreconcilable differences between the teachings of Plato and of Hegel regarding the relationship between philosophy and politics, serves as the immediate background for his
reflections.[1] Even the title of his book echoes that debate: on the one
hand Kojève vision of "the end of history," and on the other Strauss's
charge that there is no difference between that vision and Nietzsche's
harrowing evocation of the "last man."

In the *Republic,* Socrates initially distinguishes three parts of the
soul: desire *(epithymia),* spiritedness *(thymos),* and reason *(logistikon).*[2]
Desire manifests itself primarily as appetite and acquisitiveness. Its first
movement is to affirm, to approach, to appropriate. Spiritedness manifests itself primarily as anger, indignation, self-assertion, pride, and
shame, but also as vanity, vindictiveness, cruelty. Its first movement is
to deny, to recoil, to reject. Reason is both the end and the means of
rule over the other two parts. The primary object of desire may be said
to be the care and concern for bodily goods, security, and possessions;
and the primary object of spiritedness, the care and concern for non-
bodily goods, honor, and independence. When desire and spiritedness
so understood are compared, desire appears calculative, petty, slavish;
and spiritedness passionate, grand, noble. Dominance of one or another
part of the soul will make for a corresponding human type or political

regime: Achilles and Oedipus are embodiments of spiritedness, as are the Thracians, Scythians, and northern peoples generally.[3] On this account of the soul, being just is to have each part of one's soul doing its job well with a view to their common good; a just city is a city which provides suitable scope for the exercise of all three parts of the soul, and in which their corresponding human types do their jobs well with a view to their common good. Such a soul and such a city would be just "according to nature" because they conformed to what Socrates' interlocutors in a dialogue devoted to justice agreed is the nature of the soul. A moment's reflection suggests that this must be a provisional account of the soul, dictated by specifically—and narrowly—political considerations.[4]

It is in terms of a simplified version of this simple schema that Fukuyama organizes his argument and his account of history.

History is set and kept in motion by two "mechanisms," to use the term which he adapts from Kant (71 passim):[6] the "mechanism of desire," and the "mechanism of recognition" (144, 174–80, 189, 198, 204f); in other words, the desiring and the spirited parts of the soul are the moving principles of history. Although he claims to take the whole of history for his province, Fukuyama devotes most of his attention to modern times. For

> . . . it is precisely if we look not just at the past fifteen years, but at the *whole scope of history,* that liberal democracy begins to occupy a special kind of place. While there have been cycles in the worldwide fortunes of democracy, there has also been a pronounced secular trend in the democratic direction. . . . Indeed, the growth of liberal democracy, together with its companion, economic liberalism, has been the most remarkable macropolitical phenomenon of the last four hundred years. (47f)

The past four or so hundred years is also the period during which the "mechanism of desire" has come to assume unprecedented dominance. It owes that dominance in large measure to the power placed at its disposal by modern natural science. Modern science marks a turning point in the history of the race comparable only to the transition from the life of nomadic hunter-gatherers to the life of sedentary farmers. Modernity is irreversible (72f).

It is, of course, not so much modern science, "the discovery of the scientific method by men like Descartes, Bacon, and Spinoza in the sixteenth and seventeenth centuries" (72, 56f), that has transformed every aspect of human life, as it is the decision to enlist science in the relief of man's station and estate, in short, technology (131). Fukuyama virtually ignores the difference between science and technology throughout most of his argument. Perhaps one reason why he chooses to ignore it is that he wants to keep his discussion resolutely political. Indeed, regardless of what may be the status of science in and of itself, it plays a role in modern political society primarily in the form of technology (80f). In particular, modern society decisively depends on technology for military security (73–76, 127) and for the economic benefits that accrue to it from the conquest of nature (76–80). In short, it depends on technology for survival and for material well-being. Nations are therefore, so to speak, forced to submit to "the logic of modern advanced industrialization," which, in turn, forces them to adopt "economic liberalism" or capitalism. According to the dominant view, economic liberalism sooner or later forces them also to adopt at least a measure of "political liberalism"; by and by the "rational" structures and practices of economic and political liberalism weaken national, religious, and cultural divisions, and gradually but inexorably economic and political liberalism becomes a worldwide phenomenon. Fukuyama rejects this familiar account of the rise of liberal democracy. The "mechanism of desire" and the "economic rationality" or "rational choice" models of political conduct that are based on it fail to account even for capitalism (223–34), and they fail utterly to account for conduct and choices that are not strictly speaking economic, but political in nature (135). He goes to considerable lengths to show that economic liberalism is perfectly compatible with illiberal political structures, and that therefore considerations other than strictly economic ones must guide the political decision to establish democracy, or any other properly speaking political decisions.

Fukuyama holds Hobbes and Locke, "the founders of modern liberalism" (185f, 153, 154, 157, 159), directly responsible for the tendency to reduce political choices and conduct to the "mechanism of desire" or to economic rationality. Hobbes and Locke are the founders of modern liberalism in that they made equal natural rights the basis of the political association. Fukuyama adopts the interpretation of their natural rights teaching according to which they play on the fear of violent death to scare spiritedness into settling for mere equality of rights. On this interpretation, their teaching is based on little more than an appeal to "man's lowest common denominator—self-preservation" (157). This interpretation deliberately denigrates the nobility of the modern liberal project: to secure every human being's inherent dignity, and to provide a political bulwark against man's inhumanity to man (consider p. 261).

It denigrates it by systematically conflating the motives to which Hobbes appeals in his effort to persuade even the meanest capacity to do the right thing, with what he regards as the right reason for doing the right thing.[6] The device is transparent. It is not surprising to find critics of liberal democracy resort to it. It is surprising to find Fukuyama adopt it. For he proclaims himself a champion of liberal democracy— "the best possible solution to the human problem" (338)—and he nowhere so much as hints at how he thinks liberal democracy could have arisen independently of Hobbes's and Locke's natural rights teaching. Be that as it may. He concludes that the founders of "Anglo-Saxon liberalism" decisively tilted the balance between the desiring and the spirited parts of the soul in favor of the desiring part (185). They deliberately denatured the soul and its master passions, and constructed an entirely new human type, economic man or the bourgeois.[7]

Fukuyama has nothing but contempt for the bourgeois. The bourgeois is man with his spiritedness eviscerated, and rendered incapable of the passions, the needs, the aspirations, and the deeds that reach beyond material goods.

> The man of desire, Economic Man, the true *bourgeois,* will perform an internal "cost-benefit analysis" which will always give him reason to work "within the system." It is only thymotic [spirited] man, the man of anger who is jealous of his own dignity and of the dignity of his fellow citizens, the man who feels that his worth is constituted by something more than the complex set of desires that make up his physical existence— it is this man alone who is willing to walk in front of a tank or confront a line of soldiers. (180; cf.145, 160f)

But there is no turning back. Primitive forms of life "may in certain respects be more humanly satisfying" (77),[8] but the changes which modern science and technology have wrought in our lives and in our expectations are irreversible, if only because they have placed at our disposal riches beyond the dreams of avarice.

> . . . Few of those comfortable residents of developed democracies who scoff at the idea of historical progress in the abstract would be willing to make their lives in a backward, Third World country that represents, in effect, an earlier age of mankind. (130; cf. 85)[9]

The happy few who might be willing to make their lives in an earlier age of mankind would not affect the course of events. Even a nuclear war or a nuclear winter that spares any part of mankind must inevitably also spare at least the memory of modern science and of the promises of modern technology.

> And as long as a stake is not driven through that vampire's heart, it will reconstitute itself—with all of its social, economic, and political concomitants—within the space of a few generations. (127; cf.71f, 82–88, 336)

The outburst, with its comparison of modern science and technology to a vampire, is uncharacteristic of Fukuyama. As a rule he models his attitude toward liberal democracy on that of Tocqueville and of Kojève (310, 311) or, for that matter, of Hegel who, after all, borrowed the line "world history is the world court of judgment" which he made so famous, from a poem entitled *Resignation* (137).

By contrast, Nietzsche "rages" (311) at what he saw as the dehumanizing effects of liberalism and of the swelling tide of democracy. If early Anglo-Saxon liberalism may be said to favor desire to the virtual neglect of spiritedness and of all but a strictly instrumental reason, Nietzsche may be said to go to the other extreme, and to favor spiritedness to the virtual neglect of desire and of reason. He sweeps aside the claims of the body, of equality, of rights, and of the common good. Although Fukuyama's thinking is deeply influenced by Nietzsche's criticism of modernity, he rejects, "for now," Nietzsche's "hatred of liberal democracy" (314).

He turns instead to Hegel's political teaching. It provides the sober mean between the Anglo-Saxons' bourgeois and Nietzsche's over-man. Hegel's teaching, but especially that teaching viewed in the light of Kojève's brilliant and influential interpretation of the renowned "Master-Slave" struggle for recognition (*Anerkennung*),[10] can be seen as an attempt to restore the balance between the parts of the soul by returning spiritedness to its rightful place without denying desire its full due. Hegel-Kojève's teaching[11] thus provides a "deeper" and a "nobler" (145, 199f) moral-political psychology than the moral-political psychology of Anglo-Saxon liberalism. In Fukuyama's view, Hegel-Kojève's "struggle for recognition" so closely corresponds to Socrates' "spiritedness" that he frequently uses the two expressions interchangeably (165f, passim). In the struggle for recognition men assert and objectify their freedom, their "capacity for moral choice" and self-legislation, but also, in the final analysis, their being in every respect "radically *un*-determined by nature" (146, 149–52). The need and desire to assert and to objectify our freedom, and to have others freely recognize it, is constitutive of being human (152), and to be denied recognition, to be an Invisible Man (176), is to be denied one's human-ity. We need and desire not only security and material gratification; we also need and desire to assert our sense of our worth, and to have it recognized and confirmed by others (164–66, 167). That need and de-sire spur us to our greatest efforts and achievements. They override economic and all other considerations of narrow self-interest.

Fukuyama vividly conveys Hegel-Kojève's insistence that one is not properly human unless one risks one's life or is at least prepared to risk it, and that to try to save life and property at all costs is slavish. He repeatedly singles out for particular emphasis Kojève's remark that the struggle for recognition is a struggle for an idea or, as he puts it, "for pure prestige" (xvi, 143, 147, 148, 152, 155). To risk one's life for pure prestige is to assert oneself and to seek recognition as something more—or at least as something other—than exclusive concern with one's body, with avoiding death and gratifying one's appetites.

Kojève's account of the struggle for recognition owes much of its power to the fact that he moved it squarely to the center of political life. He holds that the struggle for recognition is the principle of all properly political choices and actions. It is re-enacted with every serious attempt to negate—or to preserve—a given state of affairs, and no such attempt can be regarded as serious if it does not involve at least the readiness to risk bloody battle and death in the name of an idea (or ideology), Ko-jève's "pure prestige." Fukuyama adopts Kojève's thesis: "the mecha-nism of recognition" is *the* mainspring of history. In particular, "the mechanism of recognition" accounts for the choice of equal rights, that is to say of political—as distinguished from economic—liberalism, in other words of liberal democracy properly so called.

Kojève's account of the struggle for recognition was transparently political in a more immediate sense as well. He left no doubt in his audience's mind that "now," in the mid-1930s when he was delivering his famous lectures on Hegel's *Phenomenology,* the man who most fully embodied humanity by risking his life for an idea was the revolu-tionary fighting for what he, Kojève, called the "universal and homoge-neous state." Regardless, now, of precisely how he conceived of this "universal and homogeneous state,"[12] he thought its actualization im-minent. And with its actualization history would end. The universal and homogeneous state would mark the end of history precisely because it would be "universal," everyone recognizing everyone, and hence everyone being, and being recognized as, free and "homogeneous," that is to say classless, and hence everyone being, and being recognized as also equal. For all practical purposes, "everyone's recognizing everyone as free and equal" is equivalent to the recognition of men's "natural rights." Fukuyama is therefore surely right to maintain that, at least on this decisive point, "Anglo-Saxon liberalism" and Hegel-Kojève's political teaching may, for all practical purposes, be said to agree (199–204).[13]

For Hegel, and for Kojève, "history," in the strong sense they attach to the term, refers to the millennial struggle to achieve political modes and orders that secure everyone's recognition as free and equal. Once such modes and orders have been instituted, history proper ends. There would be no political obstacles left to negate. And hence no more ideas (or ideologies) worth dying—or living—for. Everyone would be "satisfied." In a famous Note to the second, 1960, edition of his *Introduction,* Kojève described post-historical life as the global victory of consumerism—in other words of Fukuyama's "economic man" or "bourgeois"—conceivably "ennobled" by such strictly formal ceremonials of "pure prestige"—he now calls it "snobbishness"—as tea-ceremonies and ritual suicides.[14] For Kojève history ends as Hegel had said societies perish, for want of significant external threats or of internal contradictions to be overcome, in short from complacency and boredom.[15]

Fukuyama had argued that modern liberal democracy is best understood as Anglo-Saxon liberalism ennobled by German Idealism. That is, of course, what German Idealism had claimed for itself, and it is what accounts for much of the recent revival of interest in the moral-political teachings of Kant, Hegel, and even Fichte and Schelling. He had most particularly turned to Hegel-Kojève's "struggle for recognition" for help in restoring a passionate, public-spirited readiness to strive, to risk, and to sacrifice, as a counterpoise to what he considers Anglo-Saxon liberalism's pusillanimous self-seeking. Yet as his account unfolds, it appears that the outcome of the Hegel-Kojève reform falls far short of what he had expected of it. According to Kojève and, in Fukuyama's judgment, according to Hegel as well, the struggle for recognition ends with an *embourgeoisement* at least as dreary as that in Hobbes's or Locke's civil state. Fukuyama does not ask himself whether that outcome may not at least in part be due to some flaw in his schema: Hobbes/desire, Hegel/spiritedness. He does not ask himself whether the affinities between Hobbes's teaching and Hegel's may not reach much deeper than their differences. Although he notes that Hegel-Kojève's struggle unto death for recognition is a generalized version of Hobbes's state of nature as a state of war of all against all (146f, 154), he fails to note that the resolution of Hegel-Kojève's struggle, "recognition" of all by all, is a generalized version of the resolution of Hobbes's war of all against all, the social contract: both seek the grounds for intersubjective consensus.[16] And even assuming that Kojève's "pure prestige" really is nobler than Hobbes's "vanity" or "vainglory," and that Hegel's and perhaps even Kojève's liberalism really does ennoble Anglo-Saxon liberalism, the fact remains that it presupposes it.[17] Fukuyama's sharp contrast between Hobbes and Hegel, and with it his entire synoptic effort, is threatened by what might be called the Trojan Horse Effect: one throws open the gates to some few sparkling and apparently self-contained insights, only to find oneself surrounded by one's enemy's fully armed host.

Kojève's bleak view of the end—in the sense of the final cause and fulfillment–of history, led Strauss to challenge him to explain how it differs from Nietzsche's chilling evocation of the "last man" who "invented happiness and blinked."[18] Kojève declined the challenge. Fukuyama announces in the very title of his book that he takes it up. He proposes to show both that Kojève is right in asserting that we are at the end of history, and that he may be wrong in his bleak vision of it, that liberal democracy is the last stage of history, and that it *can be* its fulfillment. It can be its fulfillment only if "the end" does not entail the neglect and atrophy of spiritedness. It does not have to entail it. For virtually the only ambition liberal democracy does not tolerate is the ambition to be tyrant (320), and while Anglo-Saxon liberalism enervates spiritedness, Hegelian liberalism can energize it. Fukuyama believes that while on the Anglo-Saxons' account, rights and respect for dignity are simply given, "natural," on the Hegel-Kojève account of them, rights and respect for dignity might be said to be earned (e.g., 174, 294, 205).[19] The Hegel-Kojève account of earned recognition might therefore be said to allow for universal equal rights *and* unequal recognition of the spirited few more readily than does the Anglo-Saxons' teaching. It might thus be said to remain more faithful to the distinction between different human types and the different kinds of recognition which they seek and deserve. Hegel once illustrated that difference by glossing the old saying that no man is a hero to his valet, "not because the hero is not a hero, but because the valet is a valet." It would seem that in Fukuyama's judgment perhaps the greatest merit attaching to Hegel-Kojève's "recognition" is that it can also do justice to the morality of the "heroes," to their quest for earned recognition in proportion to desert.

In order to distinguish between the two kinds of recognition, Fukuyama adopts the Greek terms *isothymia* for the quest and the claim to equal recognition of equality, and *megalothymia* for the quest and the claim to unequal recognition of earned inequalities. When he criticizes Anglo-Saxon liberalism, he is criticizing what he regards as an excessive emphasis on "isothymia." And when he calls for a restoration of spiritedness to public life, he is calling for greater scope and rewards for "megalothymia," for fuller recognition that it is both noble and useful to strive to be a "hero," and to be recognized as one. Since the claims of the two forms of spiritedness cannot—and ought not—both be satisfied fully, the balance between them is always and necessarily unstable. How well that balance is maintained will ultimately determine the strength and stability of liberal democracy (292f). Fukuyama's book is dedicated to the proposition that nothing is more urgent than the effort to preserve or to restore that balance. For if that effort succeeds, liberal democracy will prove to be not only the last stage of history but also its fulfillment, and Strauss's—or Nietzsche's—challenge will have been met.

The gravest present threat to maintaining a satisfactory balance between "isothymia" and "megalothymia" is "relativism," the lack of a shared conception of human nature, or the outright denial that such a shared conception is possible or desirable. Relativism is most commonly justified by appeals to history, to the changes in our ways and our conceptions of ourselves from time to time and place to place. Fukuyama argues that such appeals owe what persuasiveness they may possess to the failure to understand that history is human nature actualizing itself, that its full actualization is modern liberal democracy, that, in other words, liberal democracy is "the end of history," and that "the end of history" clearly puts an end to (historical) relativism, leaving nature as the sole, universal standard (338). Or so it would seem. After all, according to the prevailing view, the distinctive excellence of liberal democracy is that it, better than any other regime, accommodates the endless variety of ways, attitudes, and beliefs, that this variety, and hence relativism, is of its very essence, and that its defining virtue is tolerance. According to this view, the appeal to human nature threatens at least in principle limits to tolerance, and would therefore be undemocratic. Fukuyama easily shows the incoherence of this view. Regardless of how tolerant a liberal democracy may be, it necessarily rests on some form of mutual "recognition," and hence on some shared conception of who properly qualifies as a partner in recognition. Beyond a certain point, disagreement about what it means to be a human being threatens even the most liberal of democracies (332).

Still, a political society's shared conception of human nature is one thing; human nature may be something else entirely.

The appeal to (human) nature, the attempt to restore (human) nature as *the* standard for political judgment and conduct (137–39, 288f), is without a doubt the most distinctive, the most ambitious, and the most difficult-to-understand feature of Fukuyama's argument. The most startling form which that attempt takes is the claim that modern liberal democracy actualizes in deed—"in reality" (337, 338)—as fully as it can be actualized in deed, Socrates' pattern "in speech" of the city that is just according to nature because it best conforms to the nature of the human soul (337). The claim is most immediately startling because one would not expect Socrates or Plato to rank modern liberal democracy high, let alone highest in the hierarchy of regimes. Nor is it a regime which anyone has ever deduced from their premises and principles. Most generally, in Socrates' just city the citizens are wise or virtuous; in modern liberal democracy the citizens' wisdom and virtue is replaced by institutions designed to make for wise and virtuous outcomes (e.g., 317). Fukuyama fully recognizes this shift, and he might argue that his efforts to rouse spiritedness to strive for earned recognition, honor, and at least a civic form of virtue are guided by Socrates's just city (304–7). How far do they really conform to it? Earned recognition is recognition in proportion to merit. Merit implies standards discovered or set by reason; or, as Socrates puts it, spiritedness ought to be subordinated to reason (164, 337). Fukuyama's effort to re-animate spiritedness might therefore appear also to be an effort to restore reason to a more authoritative ruling position. But he does not restore reason to a ruling position. Nor does he have spiritedness conform to standards discovered or set by reason. On the contrary. He holds that it is spiritedness, not reason, that sets the standards. Spiritedness "invests objects with value" (165; cf. 162f).[20] In other words, he goes far beyond simply insisting on the need for noble lies. He regards spiritedness as the cause not only of passionate attachment to "values," but of the "values" themselves. Spiritedness, and not reason, determines the rank of beings, goods, and goals. If that really is his settled view, then his efforts on behalf of spiritedness can only serve to promote the relativism and nihilism which it is his stated aim to combat.

Indeed, reason proper, noetic reason, plays no role in Fukuyama's account of the soul or of the city. He considers only two of the three parts of the Socratic soul, and he nowhere discusses their order or hierarchy.

In what sense, then, does Socrates' account of the soul and of the just city serve as Fukuyama's standard? Very near the end of the book, after briefly summarizing what Socrates says about the just soul and the just city, he observes:

By this standard, when compared to the historical alternatives available to us, it would seem that liberal democracy gives fullest scope to all three parts [of the soul]. (337)

The "historical alternatives available to us" appears to be a silent reference to the position adopted by Strauss:

It would not be difficult to show that liberal or constitutional democracy comes closer to what the classics demanded than any alternative that is viable in our age.[21]

Fukuyama's entire book is designed to refute that position.

Two short paragraphs later he states his own, definitive view without qualifications:

. . . liberal democracy in reality constitutes the best possible solution to the human problem. (338)

The blunt "in reality constitutes" has replaced the open-ended "the historical alternatives available to us, it would seem." When the two statements are set side by side, it is striking how categorically Fukuyama rejects the possibility that there might ever have existed in the past, or that there might ever exist in the future, a regime that corresponds more closely to the Socratic-Platonic standard which he claims as his own than does modern liberal or constitutional democracy. He gives no reasons for this sweeping judgment. One is therefore left to speculate about what they might be. The form in which he casts his entire argument would suggest that he rules out the possibility that a closer approximation to the Socratic-Platonic model might have existed at some time in the past because, before the introduction of technology, desire or appetition could not be fully satisfied; and that he rules out any closer approximation to the Socratic-Platonic model in the future because technology, once it has been introduced, will forever remain an unelimitable given (226f). In other words, virtue is ineffective. But then, technology minimizes the need for virtue, even if it does not altogether eliminate it.

The categorical

. . . liberal democracy in reality constitutes the best possible solution to the human problem (338)

is also striking for its unqualified assertion that "the human problem" admits of a single "best possible" solution, and that best possible solution is a political solution. It is hard to conceive how that assertion could be reconciled with the *Republic*'s analogy of the cave or, for that matter, with Hegel's quest for the "rose of reason in the cross of the present."

As Fukuyama frequently notes, modern liberal democracy stands or falls with universal equal rights or recognition, what he calls isothymia. Even granting that the quest for outstanding achievement and recognition, his megalothymia, somehow corresponds to what Socrates calls spiritedness (*thymos*), what does the liberal democratic recognition of equal rights (or the respect due to the inherent dignity of human beings qua human beings or qua "ends in themselves") correspond to in Socrates's account of the soul and of the just city? The very fact that Fukuyama felt compelled to introduce such a cumbersome un-Platonic term as isothymia indicates the problem clearly enough. And as he himself points out, neither the Anglo-Saxon liberals nor Hegel thought that Socrates-Plato had allowed for what they called rights and (subjective) freedom.[22] Now, Fukuyama, characteristically, wants to maintain both the Hegelian *and* the Socratic-Platonic positions. In agreement with Hegel, he asserts that Socrates-Plato failed fully to understand what they called "spiritedness," and that it remained for Rousseau and German Idealism to understand it, and to call it by its correct name, "freedom" or, in some of its manifestations, "history" (337, 149f, 152). In agreement with Socrates-Plato, he asserts that Rousseau and the German Idealists failed fully to understand that what they called "freedom" or, in some of its manifestations, "history," is really an aspect of (human) nature (207). In other words, he claims to understand Socrates-Plato and Hegel-Kojève better than they understood themselves. *What* he proposes to do is clear enough: to reconcile "nature" and "freedom" or "history," "Socrates-Plato" and "Hegel-Kojève." *How* he proposes to do so is rather less clear.

He comes closest to stating his argument in the following brief and obscure passage.

> The mere fact that human nature is not created "once and for all" but creates itself "in the course of *historical* time" does not spare us the need to speak of human nature, either as a structure within which man's self-creation occurs, or as an end-point or *telos* toward which human historical development appears to be moving. (138, cf. 207)

The two unidentified quotations in this passage are drawn from Kojève's review of Strauss's *On Tyranny*. Kojève does not speak, there or any-

where else, about "human nature." He speaks, rather, about a somewhat amorphous "human reality."[24] Still, Fukuyama charges, he simply cannot escape an at least tacit appeal to a determinate, enduring
human nature.

> While Kojève claimed he had no trans-historical standard by which to
> measure the adequacy of human institutions, the desire for recognition in
> fact constituted such a standard. *Thymos* [spiritedness] was in the end for
> Kojève a permanent part of human nature. The struggle for recognition
> arising out of *thymos* [spiritedness] may have required an historical march
> of ten thousand years or more, but it was no less a constitutive part of the
> soul for Hegel than for Plato. (207)

Kojève rejects that argument. The only criterion which recognition of
all by all needs to satisfy is the strictly formal criterion of noncontradic-
tion. Universal mutual recognition fully satisfies that internal—not
"trans-historical"—criterion. Universal mutual recognition is necessarily also equal recognition. Kojève therefore speaks of his end-state as
universal and *homogeneous*. His formula, "the universal and homogeneous state," can be understood as a variant of Kantian universalization. *Un*equal recognition, Fukuyama's megalothymia, cannot be similarly universalized, and hence cannot be reduced to a strictly formal
criterion, any more than—and for the same reason that—the justice of
Plato's *Republic* or any other form of distributive justice can be universalized. That is, of course, why Kojève's end-state is so vulnerable to
the charge that it is peopled by Nietzschean "last men." Be that as it
may. Fukuyama never directly considers Kojève's argument for a
strictly formal resolution of "internal contradictions." Instead, he consistently argues that "the-end-of-history" necessarily entails an appeal
to transhistorical human nature: A given political order may plausibly
be said to mark the end of history if (1) we cannot think of an essentially different and better political order; (2) the given political order is
free of essential internal contradictions, that is to say of contradictions
which it cannot resolve on its own terms; (3) it conforms to human
nature and satisfies all parts of it (46, 70; 136f, 290f). He fully recognizes that his first criterion, that we cannot think of a fundamentally
better political alternative, is inconclusive at best;[24] and he believes that
the second criterion, the absence of fundamental internal contradictions,
can only be satisfied by reference to the third criterion: the question
whether a given state of affairs is or is not rent by a contradiction between, say, the claims of equality and of freedom or of "isothymia"

and of "megalothymia," can only be answered by reference to "trans-historical"—"non-historicist"—"human nature" (136–39, 290).

How, precisely, does he understand these expressions? For the most part he holds that "nature," without qualifications, is what modern natural science says it is (72, 352f)—although he also makes the extraordinary claim that "nature is fully capable of biting back in the form of nuclear weapons or HIV viruses" (317, 324f, 298). Be that as it may. "Human" nature, by contrast to "nature" without qualifications, most emphatically is *not* what modern natural science says it is (296–98, et passim). Fukuyama never mentions, let alone discusses, his equivocal use of "nature" and the problems to which it gives rise, problems which led Kojève to eschew all references to "human nature" and to seek, instead, a strictly formal solution to the problem of recognition. He does, however, on one occasion offer a characterization of nature that eludes these difficulties: "nature" is the standard by which we decide what does and what does not count as "history" (138). On this view of it, "nature" is "trans-historical" by definition; and only by definition. For, as he immediately adds, it is a "variable" standard.[25] But if "nature" is a variable standard, then it is just as inconclusive a criterion for deciding that a given political order marks the end of history as is the fact that we, here and now, cannot think of an essentially better alternative. Indeed, both criteria are inconclusive for the same reason.

By and by Fukuyama tacitly—but none the less clearly—concedes as much. In his very last paragraphs he abandons his appeal to trans-historical human nature in favor of a strictly cis-historical, "provisional"— the earlier "variable"—consensus about human nature.[26] He is, as it were, forced to abandon it by his equation of Socrates-Plato's "spiritedness" with Hegel-Kojève's "recognition" (consider note 16 above). Yet by abandoning it, his version of the end-of-history argument—and hence his refutation of historicism—simply collapses. He had sought to overcome historicism by, as it were, capping history with trans-historical (human) nature. But a "trans-historical (human) nature" which proves to be no more than a provisional consensus cannot be invoked to resolve disagreements between competing provisionally plausible accounts, for example between his own conception of human nature and the feminists' conception of it (137f) or, for that matter, between Anglo-Saxon liberalism's conception of it and Hegel-Kojève's. It can therefore also not be invoked to dispose of historical relativism; nor to settle the question of which, if any, state of affairs marks "the end of history."

It should not really be surprising to find strains at various critical points of Fukuyama's theoretical construction. Most of them can be traced to his effort to reconcile positions which, once again, prove to be unreconcilable: "nature" and "history," "Plato" and "Hegel." What is surprising is that he should have thought it necessary to elaborate such an ambitious construction in the first place. It is not evident that he needs it in order to make his main theoretical point, that "desire," especially in the form of acquisitiveness, differs in nature from "spiritedness" or the quest for honor and for recognition. Nor is it evident that he needs it in order to explore his primary political concerns: how best to balance the competing claims of equality and liberty; and how to shift the emphasis from the dominant, Anglo-Saxon understanding of liberal democracy to his own, qualified Hegelian-Kojèvean understanding of it, in order to energize the public spiritedness which liberal democracy requires but for which it can, in his view, not make a sufficiently rousing case on the dominant Anglo-Saxon model (215; 148, 222, 316, 329, 332–34). His effort does, however, most impressively illustrate and embody the public-spiritedness, the intellectual and moral discipline and breadth which Hegel attributed to the public servants he called "the universal class" because of their devotion to the common good.

Notes

I wish to thank Professors Mark Lilla and Donald Moon for helpful comments on earlier versions of this essay. [Ed. note: This essay is reprinted from *Interpretation, A Journal of Political Philosophy*, 21, no. 2 (Winter 1993–94).]

1. Leo Strauss, *On Tyranny: Including the Strauss-Kojève Correspondence,* revised and expanded, eds. Victor Gourevitch and Michael S. Roth (New York: Free Press, 1991), pp. 88–94 (and see especially p. 125n59), 158–63, 189–92, 196–99.

2. Plato, *Republic* IV, 439D–441C; see also *Timaeus,* 69D–73A, *Laws* IX, 863B–869E, and XI, 935A–936B; contrast *Phaedrus,* 246A–B.

3. Plato, *Republic*, IV 435E; cf. Aristotle, *Politics*, V11.7, 1327b 23–1328a 7.

4. For Fukuyama's reading of Plato's political psychology, and most particularly of spiritedness, see Leo Strauss, *The City and Man* (Chicago: Rand McNally, 1964), pp. 110–12; and, among the growing number of subsequent studies of spiritedness, see especially Seth Benardete, "On Plato's *Timaeus* and

Timaeus' Science Fiction,'' *Interpretation,* 2 (1971):21–63, pp. 55f, "Leo Strauss' *The City and Man,''* *Political Science Reviewer* (1978):1–20, pp. 9–11, and *Socrates' Second Sailing* (Chicago: University of Chicago Press, 1989), pp. 55–58, 94, 98–102; Thomas Pangle in his edition of Plato's *Laws* (New York: Basic Books, 1980), pp. 452–57; see also Steward Umphrey, *"Eros* and *Thymos,''* *Interpretation,* 10 (1982):353–422; and Laurence Berns, "Spiritedness in Ethics and Politics: a Study in Aristotelian Psychology,'' *Interpretation,* 12 (1984):335–48. Fukuyama most frequently refers to essays in Catherine H. Zuckert, ed., *Understanding the Political Spirit: Philosophical Investigations from Socrates to Nietzsche* (New Haven: Yale Universily Press, 1988).

5. "The means [*das Mittel*] nature uses to achieve the development of all of its potentialities [*Anlagen*] is . . . men's asocial sociability [*ungesellige Geselligkeit*] . . .'' (*Idea for a Universal History from a Cosmopolitan Point of View,* Proposition Four; see also Proposition Seven). In this connection also consider the role Hegel assigns to self-interest and passion in historical development in particular and more generally in what he called "realization'' (*Verwirklichung*); e.g., *Vorlesungen über die Philosophie der Weltgeschichte,* vol. I, ed. Georg Lasson (München: Felix Meiner, 1930), pp. 59–66 (*Lectures on the Philosophy of History,* trans. Sibree [New York: Dover Publications 1956], pp. 20–26).

6. To take but one example, quite at random: According to Fukuyama, "Fundamental to Hobbes's social contract is an agreement that in return for the preservation of their physical existences, men will give up their unjust pride and vanity. . . . The side of man that seeks to show himself superior to other men, to dominate them on the basis of superior virtue, the noble character who struggles against his 'human all too human' limitations, is to be persuaded of the folly of his pride'' (pp. 156f). According to Hobbes, "[t]he force of Words, being . . . too weak to hold men to the performance of their Covenants; there are in mans nature, but two imaginable helps to strengthen it. And those are either a Feare of the consequence of breaking their word; or a Glory, or Pride in appearing not to need to break it. This later is a Generosity too rarely found to be presumed on, especially in the pursuers of Wealth, Command, or sensuall Pleasure; which are the greatest part of Mankind. The Passion to be reckoned upon, Is Fear'' (*Leviathan,* 14, *in fine,* Penguin ed., p. 200). Or again: "That which gives to humane Actions the relish of Justice, is a certain Noblencss or Gallantnesse of courage, (rarely found,) by which a man scorns to be beholding for the contentment of his life, to fraud, or breach of promise. This Justice of the Manners, is that which is meant, where Justice is called a Vertue; and Injustice a Vice'' (chap. 15, Penguin ed., p. 207). Hobbes nowhere concludes that, since righteous glory or pride, generosity, nobleness or gallantness of courage and justice are encountered but rarely, they represent "unjust pride and vanity'' or "folly, '' and should be overridden when and where they are encountered.

7. "The *bourgeois* was an entirely deliberate creation of early modern thought, an effort at social engineering that sought to create social peace by changing human nature itself'' (p. 185; cf. pp. 153–61 184–86, 222).

8. "Locke's observation that a king in America 'feeds, lodges and is clad worse than a day-laborer in England' neglects *thymos* and thus misses the point entirely. The king in America has a sense of dignity missing entirely from the English day-laborer, a dignity that is born of his freedom, self-sufficiency, and the respect and recognition he receives from the community around him" (p. 174; Locke *Second Treatise of Government*, sec. 41).

9. See for example Leo Strauss to Karl Löwith, August 20, 1945, in "Correspondence Concerning Modernity," transcribed and translated by Susanne Klein and George Elliott Tucker, *Independent Journal of Philosophy* 4 (1983), p. 113.

10. Alexandre Kojève, *Introduction à la lecture de Hegel* (Paris: Gallimard, 1947); *Introduction to the Reading of Hegel*, ed. A. Bloom, trans. J. H. Nichols Jr. (New York: Basic Books, 1969).

11. ". . . for the purposes of the present argument we are interested not in Hegel *per se* but in Hegel-as-interpreted-by-Kojève, or perhaps a new, synthetic philosopher named Hegel-Kojève" (p. 144).

12. See *On Tyranny,* Editors' Introduction, pp. xvi f.

13. E.g.: "*A human being counts as such because he is a human being,* not because he is a Jew, Catholic, Protestant, German, Italian, etc." (Hegel, *Elements of the Philosophy of Right,* ed. Allan W. Wood [Cambridge: Cambridge University Press 1991], sec. 209; see also sec. 66). However, "*[l]iberalism* [of the variety which Fukuyama calls "Anglo-Saxon liberalism"], not content with rational rights, with freedom of person and of property, with a political structure and its various civil institutions each of which performs a distinct function and with having the competent [*die Verständigen*] exercise influence over the people and enjoy their trust, opposes all this in the name of the principle of atomism, of particular wills: it would have everything be done by the people's express power, and with their express consent. With this formal freedom [*Formellen der Freiheit*], the people prevent any stable structures from getting established. Specific government actions are immediately opposed on the grounds that they are acts of particular wills, and hence arbitrary. The will of the Many topples the government, and what had been the Opposition now assumes power; but now that it is the Government, it is again opposed by the Many. As a result, agitation and unrest are perpetuated. This collision, this knot, this problem is the juncture at which history currently finds itself, and which it will have to resolve in the times to come" (Hegel, *Vorlesungen über die Philosophie der Weltgeschichte*, vol. IV, pp. 932f; for Sibree's translation, see *Lectures on the Philosophy of History* [New York: Dover Publications, 1956], p. 452).

14. Kojève, *Introduction à la lecture de Hegel*, 2nd ed. (Paris: Gallimard, 1960) pp. 436f; *Introduction to the Reading of Hegel*, pp. 150.; see also Kojève's lecture, "Marx est Dieu; Henry Ford est son Prophète," *Commentaire* (Printemps 1980), pp. 131–35.

15. *Vorlesungen über die Philosophie der Weltgeschichte, Einleitung: Die Vernunft in der Geschichte*, pp. 45f; Sibree translation, pp. 74f.

16. Yet he appears fully to accept Kojève's utterly anthropologized Hegel, his understanding of recognition as intersubjectivity, and of intersubjectivity as for all intents and purposes replacing reason and (human) nature; in quoting a passage in which Hegel speaks of "Spirit" [*Geist*], Fukuyama glosses: "i.e., collective human consciousness" (p. 60). In this context, consider also his acknowledgment and apparent dismissal of the decisive difference between Socrates-Plato's "spiritedness" and Hegel-Kojève's "recognition" (p. 165f), and the related discussion in endnote 7, p. 364; regarding Hobbes, consider *De Cive* II.1, Annotation.

17. "Hegel undoubtedly takes Hobbes as his point of departure. . . . Hegel consciously wants to 'return' to the Ancients ('dialectically,' that is to say by way of 'Hobbes')" (Kojève to Strauss, November 2, 1936, *On Tyranny*, p. 231). Or, as Fukuyama would have it, Hobbes and Locke ". . . anticipate many of Hegel's assumptions . . ." (p. 153).

18. *Thus Spoke Zarathustra*, Zarathustra's Prologue, sec. 5; see Strauss's letters to Kojève dated August 22, 1948, and September 11, 1957, *On Tyranny*, pp. 239, 291; "Restatement," p. 208.

19. ". . . individuals have duties towards the state in proportion as they have rights" (Hegel, *Elements of the Philosophy of Right*, sec. 261; cf. sec. 155).

20. Cf. "*Thymos* or the desire for recognition is thus the seat for what the social scientists call 'values' " (p. 213). Elsewhere he says that according to Socrates *thymos* is "an innately political virtue" (p. 183). It is not clear what that means: is *thymos* a virtue; where does Socrates speak of it as such; is it an innate virtue; again, where does Socrates speak of it as such; and what basis is there in the teaching of Socrates or of Plato for "innate virtue" of any kind? Alternatively, what might "innately political" mean? On another occasion Fukuyama asserts that ". . . Plato argued that *thymos* was the basis of the virtues . . ." (p. 337). Where does Plato argue that; of what virtues; of wisdom, of moderation; and how is Platonic justice or even courage intelligible without those two? Even granting that the virtue Aristotle calls *megalopsychia*— greatness of soul or "proper pride"—is "*thymotic*," he simply does not rank it as "the central human virtue" (p. 370n3); it is one of the two complete moral—not "human"—virtues, and for all of his praise of it, Aristotle does not go beyond saying that it seems to be a kind of crown of the virtues (*Nichomachean Ethics* 1124a 1f; and consider *Posterior Analytics* II, 13, 97b 15–25).

21. *On Tyranny*, p. 194; cf. *What Is Political Philosophy?* (Glencoe, Ill.: Free Press, 1989), pp. 306f.

22. E.g., Hegel, *Elements of the Philosophy of Right*, Preface, p. 20, and secs. 124, 185, 260 together with the Additions to them, as well as sec. 279, Addition *i.f.* "Whether any text that has come down to us from the Greco-Roman world (or any Biblical text) ever mentions what can properly be translated as 'human rights,' 'natural rights,' or 'the rights of man,' is doubtful (Thomas L. Pangle, "The Classical Challenge to the American Constitution," *Chicago-Kent Law Review*, [1990]:145–76, p. 153; *id.*, Thomas L. Pangle, *The*

Ennobling of Democracy [Baltimore: Johns Hopkins University Press, 1992],
p. 97).

23. The immediate context is Kojève's sharp criticism of Strauss's distinction between philosophy and politics. "The 'cloistered' life, while dangerous on any hypothesis, is strictly unacceptable for the philosopher who, with Hegel, acknowledges that reality (at least human reality), is not given once and for all, but creates itself in the course of time (at least in the course of historical time). For if that is the case, then the members of the 'cloister,' isolated from the rest of the world and not really taking part in public life in its historical evolution, will, sooner or later, be 'overtaken by events.' Indeed, even what at one time was 'true,' can later become 'false,' change into a 'prejudice,' and only the 'cloister' will fail to notice what has happened" ("Tyranny and Wisdom," in Strauss, *On Tyranny,* p. 155). Kojève states his objection to human "nature" most succinctly in his letter to Strauss of October 29, 1953, pp. 161f. Instead, he suggests, ". . . on pourrait définir l'homme comme une erreur qui se maintient dans l'existence, qui *dure* dans la réalité" (*Introduction à la lecture de Hegel,* p. 461; cf. p. 432).

24. ". . . Europe on the eve of the French Revolution looked to many observers like a successful and satisfying social order, as did that in Iran in the 1970s, or the countries of Eastern Europe in the 1980s" (p. 137; cf. 287–96).

25. "In the end, it would appear impossible to talk about 'history' . . . without reference to a permanent, trans-historical standard, i.e., without reference to nature. For 'history' is not a given, not merely a catalogue of everything that happened in the past, but a deliberate effort of abstraction in which we separate important from unimportant events. The standards on which this abstraction are based are variable. . . . But . . . [no] historian can evade the choice between important and unimportant, and hence reference to a standard that exists somewhere 'outside' of history . . ." (pp. 138f; cf. pp. 130, 189); see also Kant's regulative "Idea of man" in the Second Thesis of the *Idea for a Universal History.*

26. ". . . if, over time, more and more societies with diverse cultures and histories exhibit similar long-term patterns of development; if there is a continuing convergence in the types of institutions governing most advanced societies; and if the homogenization of mankind continues as a result of economic development, then the idea of relativism may seem much stranger than it does now" (p. 338). And after comparing history to a long wagon-train, he concludes: ". . . despite the recent world-wide liberal revolution, the evidence concerning the direction of the wagons' wanderings must remain provisionally inconclusive. Nor can we in the final analysis know . . . whether their occupants, having looked around a bit at their new surroundings, will not find them inadequate and set their eyes on a new and more distant journey" (p. 339).

9

Modernity's Irrationalism

Timothy Burns

> Kojève knows as well as anyone living that Hegel's funda-
> mental teaching regarding master and slave is based on
> Hobbes' doctrine of the state of nature. If Hobbes' doctrine
> of the state of nature is abandoned *en pleine connaissance de
> cause* (as indeed it should be abandoned), Hegel's fundamen-
> tal teaching will lose the evidence which it apparently still
> possesses for Kojève. Hegel's teaching is much more sophis-
> ticated than Hobbes', but it is as much a construction as the
> latter. Both doctrines construct human society by starting
> from the untrue assumption that man as man is thinkable as
> a being that lacks awareness of sacred restraints or as a being
> that is guided by nothing but a desire for recognition.
>
> Leo Strauss, *Restatement on Xenophon's Hiero*[1]

While the precipitous collapse of the Soviet Union has given rise to
innumerable articles on the end of the cold war and the dawn of a new
era in international affairs, none achieved the notoriety of Fukuyama's
"The End of History." Few pieces of scholarship could match, for the
sheer volume of response it provoked, Fukuyama's bold analysis of the
stunning events that have taken place in recent years and in our tumultu-
ous century as a whole. Needless to say, not all of the response was
favorable. Among other things, just when the Marxist-Leninist monster
had to almost everyone's relief finally breathed his last, Fukuyama, a
student of the Hegelian-Marxist Alexandre Kojève, appeared to be re-
viving the argument that we were in fact witnesses to the conclusion of
a dialectical process that had been at work in human history. Our vic-

tory in the cold war was, it seems, only "subjectively" a vindication
of Lockean liberal democracy over Marxism; "objectively" it was the
vindication of Hegelianism. We had won, but "we" were not what anyone had thought we were. For liberal democracy was, properly understood, the final synthesis of the master/slave dialectic, and Locke and
the American founders merely products, like us, of that dialectic. Victory parties—sober ones—ought, presumably, to celebrate the end of
History's march toward the realm of freedom, and posters of rationally
thymotic and homogeneous young professionals breaking their shackles
could now be unfurled on Wall Street and Pennsylvania Avenue. Fukuyama gave new meaning to the phrase that we had all along been our
own worst enemy. The miracle of historical dialectics had struck again.

Admiration for Fukuyama's subtlety and ingenuity would nonetheless cause thoughtful readers of his celebrated argument to turn eagerly
to its full elaboration in *The End of History and the Last Man,* the more
so in that the Nietzschean addition to the title of the argument could not
but pique one's curiosity. And those readers were by no means altogether disappointed. Fukuyama's extended analysis of contemporary
politics, both of the left and the right, is penetrating and insightful. To
the right, he reveals the groundless hopes of the neofunctionalists, who,
ignoring among other things the amazing success of authoritarian technological states, believe that free markets or postindustrial technology
will, by themselves and inevitably, result in a proliferation of democracies around the world (44–45, 109–30). He exposes the debilitating
failure of international relations "realists" to take into account the
human passion for dignity or sense of legitimacy, even and especially
among elites, who played so crucial a role in the collapse of communism (23–38, 245–65). He notes, similarly, the mistake of those who
viewed the Russian or Iberian people as inherently slavish (25–32, 50,
221). He reminds those overly cautious about prospects for an enduring
peace in the approaching post-communist world that there has never
been a war between liberal democratic states (262–63, 279). And he
points out at the same time that the much cherished "freedom" of liberal democracies has been purchased at the price of a narrowing of
political life, most visible in the restraining of ambition and the taming
of religious doctrines (308–12, 317–21, 325–27). To the left, he points
out the congenital blindness of socialists to the dynamic or fluid character of classes in a capitalist economy (290–91); the erosion of freedom
inevitably resulting from their demands for greater equality or "substantive democracy" (42–43, 292–96); the vacuity and self-deceit of
both the animal rights and self-esteem movements (297–98, 302–03;

332); the enduring need for both strong (if tame) religious faith and strong families in a regime that would sustain freedom (324–27); the necessity imposed on environmentalists to use technology, and hence capitalism, to overcome the damage done by technology (83–86); the inability of "dependency theory" to account for the extraordinary success of the newly industrialized economies of Asia (NIEs), or to recognize the feudal or socialist character of the Third World regimes whose evils it habitually blames on capitalism (41–42, 98–108, 118–19, 223); and the almost criminal failure of "convergence" theorists to recognize the lack of legitimacy and pluralism in the former Soviet Union or to admit to the horrors inflicted on the peoples living under communism (10–11). Finally, for those on the right or the left who have spent their adult lives in a cocoon, or who can't see the forest for the trees, or who believe that there is any attractive or "legitimate" political alternative to liberal democracy at the moment, Fukuyama delivers the morning news: fascism has been defeated, communism is in pell-mell retreat, many authoritarian regimes have fallen, and liberal democracy is on the rise in countries around the globe (12–22, 34–36, 39–51).

None of these points is in itself wide of the mark, but none depends on Hegelianism either. As Fukuyama knows, all of them can be made on the basis of a refined common sense; they are Aristotlean or Tocquevillean in character. Hence, while one can be grateful to Fukuyama for making them so forcefully, one can simultaneously regret that he has dressed them in neo-Hegelian clothing. And a similar objection can be raised against his deeper and more theoretical arguments concerning natural science and liberal democracy, the "twin pillars" of modernity, as well as his answer to the most profound critics of these twin pillars, Nietzsche and Heidegger. For Fukuyama's Hegelian account of modernity, an account that presents Hobbes and Locke as spokesmen for the "consciousness" of their times and as having a deficient grasp of human spiritedness or *thymos*, ignores or hides the fundamentally Hobbesian character of Hegel's own understanding of *thymos*. His Hegelian account of Nietzsche and Heidegger, on the other hand, wishes to obscure the fact that in their "radical historicism" we find an attempt to come to terms with both the logical conclusion and the self-destruction of Hegel's thought. This objection is not weakened but strengthened by the fact that, in the end, Fukuyama by and large abandons Hegel for Plato, "history" for "nature." For the circuitous route by which he leads his readers to this end is not a compelling one. And contrary to Fukuyama's intention, it tends to support not a genuine rationality but the ever increasing irrationalism of modern political life.

The Return to Hegel

The explicit purpose of Fukuyama's return to Hegel's Universal History is to assist the cause of liberal democracy by giving it a persuasive, noble account of itself (145, 199–200). Fukuyama attempts to show not only that liberal democracy is increasingly coming to be *seen* as the most satisfying regime, but that it *is* the most satisfying—that it alone best answers our deepest longings as human beings, especially the longing for dignity, and is therefore the most choiceworthy regime (200, 287–88). Just as Hegel had answered Kant's call for a Universal History that could "contribute to the achievement of universal republican government by giving man a clear view of his future," so Fukuyama, standing at the end of the twentieth century and assisted by Kojève and Hegel, will provide such a view (59, 70, 126, 135, 144, 281). We need it above all because, having neglected Hegel, we now lack a clear and ennobling understanding of "rights" in our regime. And this poses a global threat to liberal democracy, for as America goes, so goes the world. In particular, the Asian NIEs, who never understood themselves in the manner that we have, now await further evidence of America's decline into the morass of "egalitarian self-indulgence" in order to make their case for a new "beneficent" authoritarianism that would delay liberal democracy's ultimate triumph in the world (122–125, 241–43, 280–81). Fukuyama, who asserts that that triumph is *in the long run* inevitable, is nonetheless aware of how long and horrendous "the long run" can be. It is in this situation that he offers a return to the "nobler" argument for liberal democracy found in Hegel's Universal History.

The ennobling of our liberal democracy is in itself a daunting task; attempting to accomplish it on the basis of Hegel's Universal History could appear to be sheer folly. As Fukuyama states in his introduction, he is aware that the very notion of a Universal History has been discredited by the "most profound thinkers" of our century—Heidegger above all—who have attacked not only the possibility of discerning an intelligible History but the possibility of knowing *anything* to be true. There is moreover a popular prejudice against the notion of a directional history, a widespread "pessimism" born of the harsh disappointment of the hope in historical progress that had characterized turn-of-the-century thought. That pessimism is deepened by the fact that most of the horrors of our century have been caused by totalitarian regimes established on the basis of the very hope in historical progress (xiii).

Setting aside the deeper, Heideggerian objections to his enterprise in order to combat this popular prejudice, Fukuyama somewhat ironically[2] adopts the pose of a social scientist: he looks at the evidence from the "last four hundred years," which shows a "long-term pattern," a "trend," or "macropolitical phenomenon," evidence of a "fundamental process at work that dictates a common evolutionary pattern for *all* human societies" toward liberal democracy and capitalism (46–48). Having shown this megatrend, he is then able to introduce Hegel as the megasocial scientist who explained it: Hegel answered Kant's call for a "new Kepler or Newton who could explain the universal laws of human historical evolution," someone who could disclose the "meaningful pattern" that resides in this "overall development of societies generally," someone who could discern, in man's "slow and progressive evolution particularly in the development of man's reason, a final purpose," namely, "human freedom" embodied in republican government or liberal democracy, "which made the whole of history intelligible." Answering Kant's call, Hegel saw that through the "mechanism" of man's asocial sociability, or the "blind interplay of the passions" which had led to "conflict, revolution, and war" history had produced a noncontradictory system of government, that of liberal democracy, one that realizes at last human freedom because in it human beings become self-consciously aware of their freedom (55–60). And a version of the "mechanism" of asocial sociability that Hegel took over from Kant can be shown to be irreversibly at work today, and ever closer to the completion of its task. For an up-to-date modernization theory shows that technology—reason's attempt, through the application of the modern scientific method, to serve elastic human desires unleashed by free markets—has now spread almost everywhere, uprooting traditional ways of life and creating a homogeneous "consumer culture" that is conducive to liberal political institutions. Those countries that have attempted to resist this trend have either been charmed into joining it or have been compelled, by their need for defense against hostile technological societies, to emulate them. And since nothing short of a total cataclysm could wipe out the memory of the scientific method, the trend is permanently irreversible (71–108).

But as Fukuyama stresses, there are difficulties with such a strictly economic account of historical progress. It points at best to the inevitability of universal capitalism, not of liberal democracy. For while it shows us the operation of "reason and desire," that is, of calculation and bodily desire, it cannot explain the warfare or conflict that both characterizes most human history and is needed for the spread of modern natural science (88, 145). Moreover, it cannot answer the question "why modern natural science?" (80). And most importantly, the number of those with a consciousness of the freedom that democratic institutions embody is as yet too limited in scope not to be in need of propagation. The case for liberal democracy as the right regime for the end of history requires a compelling defense of the universal morality of "equal rights" that underlies that regime (117–122, 134). Fukuyama therefore returns to Hegel, or "Hegel-Kojève," in order to elaborate his teaching about "the desire for recognition." For that teaching, properly understood, shows us something "essential to man as man" which answers all of the problems left unanswered by economic modernization theory (138–39, 146). Hegel's master/slave dialectic reveals one part of a permanent, hierarchical human nature, *thymos*, to be both the true engine of the historical dialectic and a standard outside of history against which the results of history can be judged. Hegel's teaching provides us with the means to see the true moral ground of the liberal democracy and capitalism that had been invented by Machiavelli, Bacon, Hobbes, Locke, Rousseau, Adam Smith, and the American founders. It shows us that *thymos*, as well as the other two parts of the soul, reason and desire, find their fullest possible satisfaction in liberal democracy. Liberal democracy thus comes to be seen, through Hegelian eyes, as the closest possible equivalent to the best regime outlined by Plato in the *Republic* (334, 337).

No one can say that this Hegelianism is not highly original; Fukuyama himself indicates that it represents neither Hegel's own understanding of his thought nor Kojève's "peculiar" Hegelianism.[3] He is driven to elaborate it, we gather, by the following considerations. In the first place, Fukuyama knows that the rise of liberal democracy, and of its economic counterpart, capitalism, is explicable in a nonhistoricist manner. That is, the recent political moves toward liberal democracy may be *neither* wholly "accidental instances of good luck" *nor* manifestations of "some deeper connecting thread underlying them" (xiv), but the deliberate, intended result of the activities of modern political philosophers. Not the blind dialectic of history, but the deliberate work of modern political philosophers, from Machiavelli to Hegel, has shaped our consciousness.[4] Fukuyama speaks, and he speaks frequently, of "the modern project," to which both technology and modern liberal democracy owe their being, a project begun by Machiavelli.[5] He is aware that this alternative account of "the last four hundred years"[6] of history finds in the modern thinkers a radical *break* with all previous political philosophy, a break that represents both a conscious narrowing

(183–84, 317) and a lowering of political life. He himself goes so far as to say that, prior to the invention of modern natural science, history was *not* a dialectical process but was *cyclical*—with knowledge being gained and lost, and regimes moving from kingship to democracy and back again.[7] He further suggests that, since in the very long run there will be a cataclysm that will destroy us, "the end of history" is at best the end of a "cycle" of history.[8] Moreover, since Kant and Hegel are indebted to the early modern thinkers for their notion of man's asocial sociability, or the state of nature doctrine,[9] Hegelian thought may represent at best an attempt to make a silk purse out of a sow's ear, and at worst, a further narrowing of our political thought, a narrowing begun by Rousseau. So strong, in fact, is the evidence that Fukuyama presents, especially in his footnotes, *against* an Hegelian understanding of our situation that one is tempted to see his whole presentation of that understanding as playful or ironic, perhaps after the manner of Kojève (cf. 66).

Yet with each step back from Hegel, Fukuyama takes two steps forward, and in the end his account seems to remain Hegelian: thanks to the "laws of evolution" manifest in the master/slave dialectic, we have come to an awareness of rational, reciprocal recognition; we now inhabit, if not the perfectly satisfying social order, then its closest earthly equivalent, and it is only a matter of time before everyone on earth joins us.[10] The objections to his argument that one finds embedded in it are not, for him, decisive; they serve to refine rather than overthrow the true Universal History. Against the alternative understanding of modernity sketched above, Fukuyama presents the following arguments. First, that alternative understanding is manifestly deficient as a moral defense of liberal democracy; it supports rather than overcomes the widely felt dissatisfaction with liberal democracy's essentially "selfish" or bourgeois character. And the very existence of such dissatisfaction within liberal democracy means that the early modern thinkers were deficient in their understanding of human beings; their account of man neither satisfies the human concern for justice nor explains it adequately. Hegel, on the other hand, appears to differ from Hobbes and Locke precisely in his attention to justice, precisely in his attempt to show the consciousness of moral freedom as the heart of liberal democracy. Hegel placed the desire for recognition, or *thymos*, a "natural sense of justice," at the core of modern political life, whence Hobbes and Locke had mistakenly attempted to banish it (144–45). There is a "great ethical divide" among political philosophers (367n15), and the early moderns stand on the wrong side of it. Moreover, "neither the scientific method nor the liberation of human desire that drove subsequent efforts to conquer nature and bend it to human purposes sprang *ex nihilo* from the pens of Descartes or Bacon''; theirs was a ''discovery'' within a historical context (135; cf. 195). Had ''modern man''[11] not differed from the ancients before beginning the modern project, that project would never have been begun. The disagreement between the ancient and modern philosophers about human nature and about the kind of political and economic life that is best for us has to be explained. It cannot be explained in the vulgar manner of attributing all philosophic disagreements to the philosophers' allegiance to this or that political agenda, for a philosopher loves wisdom, not this or that particular group of human beings. He bends every fiber of his being to grasp ''clear and distinct ideas'' (386n4, 364n7). And the difference between classical and modern thought is attributable to the ''philosophic'' understanding possessed by the slave, to the *ideas* of the Christianity that had arisen between the time of the ancient Greeks and the time of modern philosophy—to the *idea* of freedom or universal equality that had emerged from this slave morality, and to the slave's *idea* of nature as something to be conquered through work (195–201; 365n5). Properly understood, Hegel's Universal History, which presents modern thought as a secularization of Christianity, of its *ideas* being made rational, can supply what is missing in the thought of early modern philosophers while doing full justice to their ''discoveries.''[12] History as it were gave rise to Hegel's comprehensive thought as the culmination of early modern thought and of the history of human thought simply. Hence, while our times have indeed been decisively affected by great thinkers, this simply means that the awareness of the full truth about man has not dawned on everyone simultaneously. It has required a gradual, thymotically driven ''discovery,'' and the dissemination of that discovery or the negation of all previous opinion about justice.

On the other hand, Hegelian thought has itself given rise to ''radical historicism,''[13] and this is the second consideration that moves Fukuyama to elaborate his highly original Hegelianism. Hegel, the ''first historicist philosopher,'' the first who ''believed in the essential historical relativity of truth,'' claimed no vantage point outside of history itself, but only an alleged final moment within history that provided full self-consciousness. Yet Marx subsequently claimed that Hegel's own thought still expressed the false consciousness of the ''realm of necessity,'' and this claim soon gave way to the attempt of ''radical historicism'' to come to terms with the growing, deadly awareness that *all* thought is relative to a specific historical horizon. Hence, while ''we owe to Hegel the most fundamental aspects of our present-day consciousness," it is also true that "the notion that history is . . . even comprehensible is very foreign to the main currents of thought of our time" (59, 69). The "relativism" that was both embraced and opposed by the radical historicism of Nietzsche permeates contemporary thought. For example, earlier versions of "modernization theory," the last attempt at a universal history, failed not merely because they offered an insufficient account of human beings as moral beings, but because they were unable to answer the charge of "ethnocentrism." For the proponents of modernization theory mistakenly "shared the relativistic assumptions of their critics," or had received instruction in "cultural relativism" (69, 352n41). Modernization theory self-destructed; its strongest argument was that advancing levels of higher education in countries with advanced industrialized economies would lead those countries to liberal democracy, but the content of contemporary higher education, being "historicist and relativist" (122; cf. 298, 306, 332), provides no solid support for the choice of liberal democracy. Historicist relativism has now spread to popular and crude historicist versions of modern natural science, and to the discipline of history, where it promotes the creation of self-serving myths.[14] It is, moreover, this final form of historicism which has given rise both to German fascism earlier in the century,[15] and to the growing fascism, or fanatical relativistic isothymia, of the left,[16] most evident in American universities and in some recent public policy. *The* present threat to liberal democracy, which is not at all a remote threat,[19] is in other words from a Nietzscheanized left, the final political product of Hegel's own historicist teaching.

Fukuyama's attempt to neutralize this challenge from radical historicism may be said to begin, paradoxically, with his initial presentation of Hegel as the first "*historicist* philosopher."[18] Following Kojève, Fukuyama gives us a Hegel in whom radical historicism is already present: there are no permanent "essential characteristics" to man; man is a creative and self-creative being, undetermined and open-ended. By this account, Hegel was aware that his own teaching could and would become merely "subjectively" true, or was only true until further notice.[19] As the first historicist philosopher, he was the first "relativist" philosopher. Fukuyama thus deprives Hegel of the full self-consciousness that obtains at history's absolute moment. This allows him, however, to take Hegel's statements about "man as man" as expressing not the rational self-consciousness of man at the end of History, but as pointing to man's "essential characteristics," to a fundamental, enduring nature that has, like a single human being, grown from its childhood to its wizened old age and finally achieved the means to satisfying itself in liberal democracy (136–139, 146). As Kojève had singled out "the desire for recognition" as the engine of history in Hegel, so too does Fukuyama, but on the basis of one of Leo Strauss's criticisms of Kojève (364n8; cf. 366n6)—his pointing to Kojève's need for a teleological understanding of nature—Fukuyama presents the desire for recognition, or *thymos*, as something "essential to man as man" and, as such, accessible in principle to all men at all times. *Thymos* is a concept "as old as political philosophy itself" (145, 162) but it was seen in its final, rational form by Hegel. In this way, Hegel is not only freed of the subsequent critique of his own thought on historicist grounds, but becomes a means of combating that critique, of combating the radical historicism of Nietzsche. "Nature" replaces the "rationality" of the absolute moment, but Hegel's master/slave dialectic is nonetheless preserved, allowing Fukuyama to present Nietzsche as "stuck in history," or as reacting violently and irrationally on behalf of an unregenerate master's megalothymia that is in the process of being negated by liberal democracy.

Finally, Fukuyama's Hegel, Hegel without the absolute moment, is able to avoid the charge of Emile Fackenheim and others that understanding history as "meaningful," as having an end that makes previous events "meaningful," leaves many victims the meaning of whose suffering is, to put it mildly, brutally explained by Kojève.[20] The new Hegel will avoid Kojève's "peculiarities," and in particular, his explanation and justification of the Nazis. Fukuyama's Universal History is therefore a more modest one; it is merely an "intellectual tool" (130) that can allow us to analyze our situation, and to judge particular historical events, including most events of the twentieth century, as wrong turns or historical "dead ends."

It is these considerations that lead Fukuyama to his novel account of Universal History, in which "the desire for recognition," or *thymos*, moves to its final, rational form through the historical master/slave dialectic. His is an account that acknowledges our indebtedness to early modern political philosophers, particularly Hobbes, but supplies what is lacking in their thought. It is free of succumbing to relativism, since it supplies not only a trans-historical ground for human freedom, but a means of understanding Nietzsche and his progeny on both the left and the right in a manner that neutralizes them. At the same time, it does not claim too much for itself, avoiding the claim of "rational self-consciousness" that would lend too much "meaning" to historical events and would be belied by both the obvious lack of rationality in contemporary political life and the need for some premodern or "irrational" supports for liberal democracy.

If this task were successfully accomplished, Hegel would indeed appear to be most helpful for understanding our world and for ennobling democracy. But whether anyone could succeed in such a task is doubtful. Fukuyama's attempt, it must be said, is a failure, but it is a particularly instructive and noble failure. For it allows us to see very clearly the inadequacy of the modern understanding of man in all its various presentations, from Machiavelli through Nietzsche, and to begin to understand the need to return to the understanding of man that is presented in classical political philosophy.

The Desire for Recognition

The new Universal History of "Hegel-Kojève" that is to supply us with guidance divides itself into four stages. The first of these is the "battle to the death" in an original state of nature. This state, which Hobbes had described in order to induce an awareness of our compelling need to find the best means to self-preservation, is for Hegel the location of the first stirrings of a distinctively human consciousness, a consciousness of freedom from nature's compulsions. For an initial "battle for recognition" or pure prestige is, according to Hegel's *Phenomenology*, the original affirmation by deed of our uniquely human capacity to choose *against* nature, against our natural fear; it is an affirmation of our freedom (146–156). The winner in this struggle won because he did not submit to the slavish desire to live, but proved himself superior to that (merely animal) desire. His submissive opponent, on the other hand, proved his slavishness to mere necessity by his submission. He was for this reason viewed by the victorious "master" as subhuman.

The second stage of history—the longest (372n2)—is characterized by the slave's development of a both a "work ethic" and a doctrine of equality before God. The slave, unsatisfied with his slavery, learns through his long, perpetual artful endeavors against the harsh natural world to value his work or to be proud of it, to seek recognition for a job well done; he comes to possess a "work ethic." At the same time, awareness of his capacity to conquer nature through his work causes him to posit his own moral freedom and hence the equal dignity of all human beings, slave and master alike, before God. The victor in the primordial struggle, on the other hand, cannot remain satisfied with the result of his victory, precisely because the esteem that he sought is now forthcoming only from a subhuman; this is his "dilemma."

The third, crucial stage is the "secularization" of both parts of the slave morality in the sixteenth century, beginning with Machiavelli's call for the conquest of nature and extending to Hobbes's argument for human equality based on our equal capacity to kill one another. The master for his part must eventually come to grant the human equality posited by this secularized slave morality in order to obtain the human recognition that he seeks, or to solve his dilemma in the only manner possible and hence rationally. The liberal democratic state, invented by Hobbes and Locke, which rests on the mutual recognition of the equal rights of all, is the "rational" solution to the struggle between master and slave that has been driving human history (200–208).

The final stage of history is "post-history," when the success of this "modern project" comes to sight as the inevitable culmination of the moral development of man. In it, all become conscious at last of their common humanity, and hence none can be fundamentally dissatisfied with the liberal democratic regime's official understanding of human worth, of its official sanction of mutual human recognition. The equal dignity of free, autonomous individuals that the modern liberal democratic state officially sanctions is the "meaning" of history.

Such then is the Universal History that is to supply us with the understanding of "man as man" that we need or, rather, that will allow us consciously to realize and articulate the understanding that we already possess. The inadequacy of that understanding begins to become clear, however, when we ask: when and how does the master begin to see the slave as *subhuman*? Certainly not before or during the primordial "struggle to the death," since the victor in that struggle desired the esteem of his opponent, and hence viewed him not as a duck or a bear but as an esteeming being like himself. And certainly not after his victory, for how could the victor view mere brachial or "physical" strength as the basis for superior worth, when his *thymos* is allegedly a passion that stands against what is merely physical? Yet the victor, according to Fukuyama, would condemn not the physical weakness, but the craven surrender of the vanquished. If so, what would cause him to spare the life of the vanquished? Not bodily desire, surely; he is above this. And might not the victor, if he is indeed a human being, be inclined to admire the prudence, the lack of boastfulness, or the absence of false hope, shown by the vanquished, who sensibly avoids the attempt to do what is impossible?[21] The victor might, to be sure, convince himself and others that the slave is unworthy of rule, but we do not *rule* over animals, and so to have such a conviction the master would have to view the slave as human but deficient in those human excellences that he regards as befitting a ruler. No fundamental change of "consciousness" can be seen to emerge, then, in and through a dialectic of recognition, since the dialectic presupposes that consciousness of a common humanity that is supposed to emerge only as the final product of the dialectic.

Granting this, one could still argue that the "master" would face a dilemma: he desires recognition of his superior worth, not from slaves, but from those human beings capable of bestowing it. And by Fukuyama's account, he could obtain the limited but available portion of such recognition only by lowering his estimate of his own worth and simultaneously raising that of the slave, that is, by coming to accept a fundamental and universal equality of dignity or worth. But could the master ever do so? Every honor entails an opinion of what is honorable, and the acceptance of that honor entails an acceptance of that opinion. Would it make sense to seek the honor of a society of cowards simply because they were the only ones who could bestow honor, if one held cowardice in contempt? Would a wise comic poet seek the applause of an audience of crude and stupid men, if he valued wisdom above all things? Could a reasonable man *become* superstitious in order to obtain the honor of his superstitious fellow citizens? Above all, would someone who desired, through noble acts of self-sacrifice, to achieve *immortal* glory for himself, that is, glory somehow sustained by an immortal being or beings, be satisfied with any strictly *human* recognition? Is there nothing rational in such a person's dissatisfaction with his mortal life, in his dissatisfaction with merely mortal goods like "recognition"? It is only by abstracting from the phenomena of honor and shame, by treating honor as devoid of any and all rational content, and as desired, not as a confirmation of one's genuine worth, but blindly, that is, by the animal passion that Hobbes called "vainglory,"[22] that one could arrive at Fukuyama's, or Hegel's, conclusion.

One might, finally, object that Fukuyama does present the desire for recognition as something that eventually comes not only to partake of reason but to be fully rational. If the master's decision to accept the equal dignity of all would not fully satisfy his desire to be deemed superior, it would nonetheless be the only genuine option open to his *thymos*, and hence he would be compelled by his reason to choose it. But this solution to the master's dilemma, his "rational" valuing or "rational" *thymos*, assuming that it were possible, would be no more than a calculated decision on the master's part to settle for half a loaf.

He would be submitting himself at the end of History to the State and to its doctrine of "equal rights" for the same reason that everyone is supposed to leave the Hobbesian state of nature and enter civil society: there is no other way to secure any portion of what one craves. Citizenship in the liberal state would, accordingly, be "rational" only in a Hobbesian sense: it would be what a purely calculative and subordinate reason hits upon as the best means to the satisfaction of one's blind but compelling desire to be esteemed, a means that is best or "rational" because all can agree to it. It would not be genuinely rational, since not only the opinion of what is estimable, but the goodness or worthwhile character of the very desire to be esteemed—of the desire to be thought *worthy* of a splendid, enduring good by virtue of one's devotion to the good of others, and the promise or hope that lies behind that desire—would not have come under reason's scrutiny.

There is, in short, something manifestly deficient in the understanding of *thymos* or "the desire for recognition" that Fukuyama presents as the engine of history and as the ground both for a fully human life and for a rational defense of liberal democracy. That understanding pretends that, achieving a full reconciliation with our mortality, we could attain a full satisfaction of our longings through the goods of this world, goods we can provide for ourselves. It assumes that our dissatisfaction with our mortal lives (and hence with mortal goods like reciprocal recognition) is simply irrational, something that is finally overcome or shed through the historical dialectic. But just as security from *violent* death promised by the Hobbesian state is not security from death, so "reciprocal recognition" cannot provide that immortal or complete good that is promised by the noble, or hoped for in the course of morally virtuous ("thymotic") actions, or in noble acts of love or devotion. In fine, this Hegelian view of *thymos,* (unlike, e.g., the classical view) neglects our inescapable, abiding desire for immortality, our inescapable concern for an eternal good for ourselves—a concern which finds expression in our admiration for the noble or just life, which stands above mere (perishable) creature comforts.

As the above considerations suggest, the understanding of *thymos* articulated by Fukuyama finds its original expression in the work of Hobbes. Fukuyama, however, presents his account of the Universal History as an alternative, *the* alternative, to the Hobbesian understanding of man upon which liberal democracy was originally founded. We must therefore briefly examine Hobbes's presentation of "natural man," particularly his presentation of vainglory or "the desire for recognition." This will enable us to see more fully the scope and bearing of the change in the understanding of human beings and of political life that was brought about by Hobbes, a change that was in fact accepted by Hegel—a change that has provided modern political thought with its most fundamental presuppositions. We will then be in a position to present a nonhistoricist account of modern political thought, one that will allow us in turn to see the rise of historicism out of the premises of early modern political thought.

Hegel and Hobbes

In order to predispose his readers to a consideration of Hegel's Universal History over and against the argument of Hegel's predecessors—of Hobbes, Locke, the American founders, and Adam Smith—Fukuyama initially suggests that the latter failed even to realize that there is an unconquerable *thymotic* side to man. To the early modern thinkers, man was essentially desire and reason alone; he was "Economic Man" whose *thymos* or vanity could and should be *eliminated* from political life (84, 150–54, 174, 185, 186, 206). This presentation allows Fukuyama to claim that whenever we speak about dignity, worth, or freedom we are using "Hegelian" as opposed to "Lockean" language (203–4). But Fukuyama knows that this is not true. He gradually discloses that Adam Smith, Machiavelli, the American founders, and finally, Locke, all recognized the need to preserve a place for *thymos* in modern political life.[23] He maintains to the end, however, that Hobbes had attempted to banish *thymos* from political life. Hobbes alone, then, by some strange quirk in the historical dialectic, appears to have been ignorant of the enduring power of *thymos* and of the need to tame it. For according to Fukuyama, while "vainglory" or *thymos* was indeed the central preoccupation of Hobbes's political philosophy (154f), it was for Hobbes simply a complicated, dangerous, and *unnecessary* form of animal desire, something to be *removed* from political life so that our desire for comfortable self-preservation could be satisfied. For Hegel, on the other hand, *thymos* was the ground of a genuinely human life. The issue then turns around Hobbes and Hegel: is Hegel's understanding of man "radically different" (152; cf. 149) from and superior to that of Hobbes?

The evidence suggests the contrary. Hegel's understanding of man is fundamentally Hobbesian on the very point where Fukuyama finds it different, namely, in the understanding of *thymos*. It is true, as Fukuyama argues, that Hobbes attempts to establish politics on the basis of the compelling fear of violent death, that he would have us use the power of a sovereign to lay low the pride of ambitious men. Hobbes does not, however, seek "to eradicate *thymos* from political life altogether, and to replace it with a combination of desire and reason" (185). For contrary to Fukuyama's claim, Hobbes's teaching about "'natural right'" is one which appeals to our *thymos*; it is a *moral* teaching.[24] Where there is no sovereign to decide controversies, Hobbes tells us, "to every man remaineth, from the naturall and necessary appetite of his own conservation, the *right* of protecting himselfe by his private strength."[25] In the state of nature, "[all] augmentation of dominion over men, being necessary to a mans conservation, it *ought* to be allowed him."[26] As Spinoza noted, natural right is for Hobbes not simply presented as coextensive with power—it is not what we are made by brute force to allow nor even what we "generally allow"—but is a liberty which *ought* to be allowed, in the circumstances of the state of nature. It assumes that the actions men take to preserve themselves in the state of nature are in themselves, or as a rule, *blameworthy*, but excused by the circumstances. The elimination of the "ill condition," of mere nature, of the "dissolute condition of masterlesse men,"[27] will free men from this circumstance, and hence remove the excuse of necessity that attends all of our actions. It will create the circumstances in which we ought not to allow men to do as their passions move them, but allow each the "rights" or claims that remain to us after our prudential, that is, necessary surrender of our right to all things through the social contract.

Hobbesian politics, liberal politics, rests then upon the belief, *the unexamined belief*, that we are free to be just or not, except in circumstances which can and ought to be overcome. Unlike Fukuyama, Hobbes never forgot that exculpation requires both the possibility of blameworthy actions, and a compulsion that denies blameability in a particular case. Hobbes knew, in other words, that it is only by being stated as a defense before political or moral men—before human beings who demand service to a perceived common good—that the appeal to necessity *justifies*, and only on the assumption that the behavior that is being exonerated is otherwise considered to be blameworthy. One doesn't excuse someone for wearing a hat on a cold day, or for having virtuous friends, however "rationally" one understands these activities, because one would never think of blaming anyone for them. Hobbes's argument for natural right depends, then, on our preexisting belief in the possibility of free choice—of a freedom to act against what our selfish interests dictate, in favor of a common good. Now it is true, as

Fukuyama argues, that there is in fact no *ground* for such a moral right in Hobbes, since according to Hobbes, all our actions are subject to mechanistic necessity, and hence "liberty" is simply a lack of bodily impediments.[28] It is true, in other words, that "the will" was for Hobbes simply one victorious passion or another in that perpetual struggle between passions that goes by the name of "deliberation."[29] But if Hobbes intended these arguments seriously, we have all the more reason to see that he was not unaware of the need to make a rhetorical appeal to our moral passions, or to ground the liberal state in *thymos*. The rhetorical character of Hobbes's natural right teaching is itself a measure of Hobbes's awareness of the permanent human love of freedom—of which Fukuyama finds him ignorant—and of Hobbes' recognition of the impossibility of rooting out that love by means of fear.[30] Hobbes' attempt to refound political life would never have succeeded, it would not have gotten off the ground, had he been unaware of the need to appeal to that thymotic sense of justice that is necessarily present in all political discourse.

Hobbes would not have *refounded* political life, on the other hand, had he not treated that sense of justice as devoid of any genuinely rational content. If his argument depends on a preexisting belief in the possibility of free choice, that is a belief that Hobbes wished to be *used* rather than explained or carefully examined. For Hobbes intended his teaching to foreclose all of the violent disputes about justice, and about the right way of life, that had unsettled politics in the past.[31] His doctrine of "natural rights" could and did displace competing notions of justice because it is both universal and minimalist; it assumes—as do all notions of justice—free human choice, while denying—as does no other notion of justice—the human capacity to arrive at an authoritative understanding of the best way of life. If all political life can come to be seen merely as the securing of as much of our equal, fundamental "natural right" as possible, then political life can be freed of all vainglorious, "thymotic" disputes about who is more or less worthy, superior and inferior, better and worse. Politics can cease being the arena in which human beings rule one another on the basis of an understanding of what way of life is best or most virtuous, and can become a matter of "governing" our various, blind passions—above all, our *thymos* or vanity.

It is here that the decisive break with premodern political philosophy is most visible, and it is on this point that Hegel follows Hobbes. To understand better this momentous change in the understanding of *thymos* effected by Hobbes, we must step back and note the truth of

Fukuyama's more limited claim that Hobbes successfully attempted to remove high political ambition, or megalothymia, from political life. For he aimed, as Fukuyama notes, to destroy the "religious fanaticism" that had rocked Europe for centuries. He aimed to make religion "tolerant" (255–60, 271), and this required a politics that could take from the vainglorious leaders of religious sects the opportunity to gain a following. But as Fukuyama also indicates, Hobbes's solution to the problem of religious warfare continued Machiavelli's "realist" project (246); it was part of the "social engineering" that "sought to create social peace by changing human nature itself" (185). Hobbes took up Machiavelli's proposal "that politics be liberated from the moral constraints of classical philosophy" (57). By following Machiavelli, Hobbes engaged in an activity fundamentally different from the attempt, characteristic of classical political philosophy, to give a prudent articulation and refinement of the commonsense opinions about justice or the moral life, an articulation that could both guide statesmen and (more importantly or primarily) lead potential philosophers, through careful and judicious indications of the serious problems with those opinions, to a different, a thoroughly and genuinely rational life. And Hobbes could abandon the classical "education of *thymos*" in favor of the Machiavellian project of counterpoising *thymos* with *thymos* (184) only on the basis of Machiavelli's moralistic rejection of our capacity to know the human good.

At the core of Machiavelli's "realism" is the teaching that there is no natural limit to the pursuit of our various desires, no discoverable need for a serene resignation to a world that cannot provide us with an immortal or perfect good, no intelligible human good that would allow one to argue that the life of tyranny, of unlimited pursuit of recognition or glory, is a mistaken life for a human being. All such limits are instead presented as the creations of "armed prophets," who have used both fear and the widespread human need for self-deception in order "to introduce whatever form they pleased" into the formless "matter" of human beings.[32] Hobbes wholly accepted Machiavelli's account of armed prophecy, of the use of the "seeds of religion," by the founders of commonwealths.[33] To be sure, while Machiavelli had held up such prophets for imitation, Hobbes presented them as the greatest obstacle to sound politics;[34] he sided with the diffident many against the ambitious few.[35] But Hobbes did so on the basis of Machiavelli's teaching about man and his place in the whole. For he not only accepted Machiavelli's argument that the love of freedom and the love of glory are two species of the same genus, belonging to the few strong and the many weak, respectively. Nor did he merely accept Machiavelli's teaching concerning the ability of a prince to reduce the expectations of subjects by means of fear; that ability had always been realized by astute political men. What was decisive, rather, was Hobbes' acceptance of Machiavelli's teaching concerning the lack of any genuine constraining reasons against doing so. He accepted Machiavelli's teaching concerning the universal necessity and hence unblameability of the unlimited "natural desire to acquire" and the relative abilities of the few and the many to accept and use this teaching.[36] He accepted, in other words, Machiavelli's rejection of the possibility of the theoretical life.

By presenting the desire for glory as universally compelling, Machiavelli had obliterated the distinction, central to classical political philosophy, between the theoretical life and the life of practice or action. He was at least not averse to presenting his own activity as fundamentally identical to that of the greatest political men, the "armed prophets" who, in order to "found their state and their security," or to obtain "glory," attempted like himself the difficult task of introducing "new orders and modes."[37] So that others could cease being cheated of the goods of this world, he aimed to destroy the reigning Christian order, and his critique of that order included a critique of reason's ability to know what is by nature good for a human being. We are as human beings a combination of "lion and fox";[38] our reason is a complex form of foxiness or adaptability; our laws are merely a complicated form of the warfare that we must wage in order to create an order out of the chaos that confronts us by nature.[39] In this way, human evil is reduced to animal evil, and all opinions about good and bad, just and unjust are denied any rational content. Reducing reason to decaying sense impressions regulated by a powerful animal passion,[40] Hobbes elaborated on this momentous Machiavellian teaching.

It was on the basis of this new understanding of human reason that Hobbes attempted to end religious fanaticism and to establish a stable, peaceful political life by means of his natural rights teaching. For that attempt required that the *truth* about God or gods, and hence about the right way of life, be made a matter of official indifference. As Hobbes indicates, his political teaching is meant to overcome the following difficulty: prophets claim to have an understanding of the way to human happiness, and "he that pretends to teach men the way of so great felicity, pretends . . . to rule, and reign over them; which is a thing that all men naturally desire."[41] Such pretensions lead inevitably to civil war; prophets have to have their quivers taken from them by the sovereign if there is to be peace, the more so as they offer gullible men the blandish-

ments of "greater punishments than death."[42] To leave prophecy un-
tamed would undermine the subject's obedience to the sovereign, which
depends strictly on fear.[43] Fear of violent death from the "Power of
men" can and must replace "Fear of Powers Invisible;"[44] a sovereign
can re-present to his citizens their compelling fear of violent death.[45]
With a sovereign power to keep them in awe, human beings can be
made to forsake vainglorious prophets and can become as cooperative
as other animals.[46] They can be made to see justice, hitherto grounded
in various and competing opinions of a divinely supported moral order,
as grounded in their blindly compelling, exculpatory fear of death. In
the light of these considerations we can understand Hobbes's claim that
even if one grants that everything the papists claim concerning the
Pope's direct descent from St. Peter is *true*, nay, even if we grant *that
the pope is infallible* in matters of faith and morals, this would say
nothing about his right to interpret Scripture for citizens, much less to
rule over them or to decide who should rule.[48] For the binding character
of a sovereign's laws about sacred Scripture, as about anything else,
owes nothing to their appeal to reason. To end religious strife, Hobbes
attempted, as it were, to dig an impassable chasm in political life between what is *true* and what is *obligatory*, to replace the force of argument with the argument of force.[49]

Not *thymos* per se, then, but the contentious opinions to which it
gives rise, were to be removed from political life, and these had to be
presented as groundless before *thymos* could be viewed as something
to be "tamed" rather than "educated." Educated *thymos*, that is, moral
virtue or righteousness, had to be understood as a manifestation of a
refined, blind animal passion—pride—before it could be rejected as a
means less "effective" than fear for securing a stable political order.[49]
Following Machiavelli, Hobbes abandoned or ignored the classical examination of the opinions of the righteous or pious citizen, the kind of
examination that could lead one, through careful dialectical argument,
to a compelling awareness of the right way of life, an awareness desired
and imperfectly grasped or divined by human beings engaged in political life. He became an advocate of the manipulation of human passions
that would cause opinions about superior and inferior worth to become
a private matter, or that would cause the content of speech to become a
matter of indifference to citizens, so that only the "right" to speech
would retain any importance for the citizen as citizen. It is this "taming
of *thymos*," made possible by a neglectful rejection of classical political
philosophy—by a neglect of its foundational, awakening intention—
which constitutes the "narrowing" of political life to which Fukuyama
alludes (317).

*   *   *

And it is this Hobbesian understanding of vainglory—a desire for recognition bereft of any rational content—that manifests itself throughout
Fukuyama's illuminating account of the Hegelian "desire for recognition." As we have seen, those who engaged in the "primordial struggle" are alleged to have done so not out of any notion of right and
wrong but out of a blind desire for recognition or honor; they looked
up to nothing, and had no inclination to persuade their respective opponents that they possessed those human excellences to which all ought
mutually to look up, and in which they could hope for salvation. As
Fukuyama states, the Hegelian notion of freedom "begins only where
nature ends" (152); it assumes that there is no natural rank ordering of
human beings, no natural human excellences that are discernible and
discerned by political men. Hence, Hegelian man is "moral" or manifests his humanity when he "makes and adheres to his *own* rules,"
when he *contradicts* his reason (150) or *defeats* his inclination to "sensibly back down at a challenge." The moral man is "willing to kill and
be killed over something of purely symbolic value, over prestige or
recognition" (148). And if this "moral" man's *thymos* is less blood-
thirsty at the end of history than at its beginning, it is not a whit more
rational. For the Hegelian dialectic toward the *rational* state is toward
a state the morality of which is as devoid of rational content as that
of Hobbes. The "freedom" that comes at the end of history consists,
according to Fukuyama, in the universally recognized, equal right of all
to exercise various "thymotic options"—for example, the equal right
to practice whatever religion one wishes (202, 216). But since all religion is "irrational," as Fukuyama boldly proclaims (222), the "rational
state" consists of the freedom to choose for oneself one or another
"irrational" manifestation of *thymos*. And it is not only religious opinion, but *all* speech, that is deprived of any claim to genuine rational
content in the "rational state." Speech is merely an expression of "thymotic points of view" (240); the founders of the American regime deliberately sought, in fact, merely to provide "outlets" for *thymos* when
they established freedom of opinion (270). What counts is not the truth
of the opinions—all of them are merely thymotic points of view—but
the mutual recognition by each speaker of his opponent's right to give
vent to them. Speech, accordingly, does not differ in kind from other
safe, universally tolerated "outlets" for thymos or "thymotic identification" (270) provided by the rational state—outlets like money-mak-
ing or conspicuous consumption. Finally, the allegedly rational state
also provides universally tolerated outlets for megalothymia, like "art,

literature, music, the intellectual life,'' mountain climbing, the ''pure snobbery'' of a tea ceremony, or playing on a soccer team (i.e., participation in what Fukuyama rightly calls a ''contentless'' activity). If one can't make it playing saxaphone on the jazz scene, the Oval Office remains a viable ''outlet'' for one's megalothymia. For the presidency, too, is one of the ''grounding wires that bleed off the excess energy'' of megalothymia in the rational state (315–19).

Hobbes's account of man was, clearly, never more mechanistic than this;[50] when both political and intellectual life are understood as products of ''energy'' and thereby made the equal of contentless activities, even the distinction between living and nonliving beings has been lost. Yet this is Fukuyama's serious—and very helpful—presentation of life at the end of history. He attempts indeed to hide the essential agreement between Hobbes and Hegel in this matter during the course of his explicit comparison of the two. Hegel, he argues, recognized the need to satisfy ''that side of man that seeks to show himself superior to other men, to dominate them on the basis of superior virtue, the noble character who is to be persuaded [by Hobbes] of the folly of his pride'' (157). But the very notion of ''superior virtue,'' or of ''society's best men,'' as well as any attempt to promote ''a particular way of life as superior or desirable to another'' (160), are at odds with liberal democracy; they have their place, as Fukuyama knows, in arguments for *rule*, not in arguments for the *government* of equally free and autonomous individuals (cf. 154, 317). If Hegel ''somehow'' attempted to ''preserve a certain moral dimension to human life,'' it was not by giving us ''something entirely missing in the society conceived of by Hobbes and Locke'' (161), but by elevating ''freedom,'' as they had done and as Rousseau and Kant did more vigorously, to an end in itself. In other words, ''tolerance'' only became ''the defining virtue'' of democratic societies (215), as Fukuyama wishes it to remain, when we adopted Hobbes's moralistic denial of the capacity of reason to discover what is by nature the best life for a human being.

The Emergence of Historicism

In the light of the peculiar moral appeal of the Hobbesian doctrine of natural right, we can understand the elevation of ''freedom'' in later modern political thought, as well as the liberal commercial republic advocated by that thought. The argument for the later stages of the Universal History then loses its force. Rather than the unintended result of the master/slave dialectic, those stages are exposed as nothing more than the gradual working out, and eventual radicalization, of Hobbes's premise. Above all, we are able to see what Fukuyama is very hesitant to expose: a non-historicist account of historicism.

As we have seen, the central event in the Hegelian Universal History is an alleged "secularization" of Christianity, the desacralizing of both the Christian slave's pride in the labor that frees him from a harsh nature, and of the consequent idea of his moral freedom and hence equality before God. It is the secularization of these "ideas," according to Fukuyama, that gave rise to liberal economics, or capitalism, and liberal democratic politics. Yet this alleged secularization is not only left unexplained by Fukuyama's dialectical History;[51] it is contradicted by his own argument. As he emphasizes, human beings are predisposed toward capitalism not only "to the extent that they can see their own economic self-interest clearly" (108), but to the extent that they feel *justified* in pursuing that interest, i.e., to the extent that profit-making has been made to appear "legitimate" (227; cf. 369n4, 377n9). And this justification requires, above all, that we accept the subordination of reason to the desire for money (77–81). But Christianity, far from justifying such a subordination, inhibits it. Such Christian notions as the "just price" (79), the sinfulness of usury, sumptuary laws, and "stewardship" of property constitute "moral and emotional barriers" to the acceptance of "economic growth," of increased productivity or profitability; they stand *against* the use of reason or science "to gratify [our] desire for security and for the limitless acquisition of material goods" (77, 80, 87). To destroy these "moral barriers" to economic liberalism, acquisitiveness had to be defended as *unblameable*, as necessary for our own collective well-being. Capitalism required the kind of moral defense that Hobbes, Locke, and Adam Smith gave it, the kind that replaced the "habits, customs, religions, and social structure" that had impeded or blocked it (94, 103).

Now, the required moral defense of capitalism could never have arisen *out of* Christianity. Like its political counterpart, economic liberalism represents not a secularized Christianity, but a "triumph over religion" (384n1; cf. 271). For the moral defense of "capitalism," as providing the means to the common betterment of mankind's material condition, required that our original condition be understood as one of *harsh penury*, improved only through man's greedy labor (366n13). The biblical doctrine of human responsibility, on the other hand—the doctrine of moral freedom—rests upon the assumption of a *perfect beginning* (cf. 376n5 with 377n9). Only a perfect beginning, an original state of grace, can guarantee that evil or suffering or harshness is due not to the harsh circumstances of nature but to human fault—that evil is not compelled but voluntary.[52] By guaranteeing a perfect beginning, the creative, provident God of Judaism and Christianity guarantees the sense of responsibility, or moral freedom, upon which the demand for justice—and all sense of gratitude, anger, remorse, and guilt— depends.[53]

Such is the God who, according to the teaching of Augustine and Thomas Aquinas, for example, has promulgated the natural law, according to which all human beings have knowledge of what is right by nature and will be punished for acting contrary to that knowledge. He is indeed the God before whom, as Fukuyama stresses, all human beings are equal. All the same, for Augustine and Thomas Aquinas, this equality of all human beings, our equal ability to act in accordance with justice, does not abolish natural inequality of intellectual capacity, or of human perfection in general, and hence does not establish an equal title of all to rule.[54] Quoting Martin Luther King Jr. as a representative of the "Christian" view on this matter, as Fukuyama does (196–97), is disingenuous: King was himself under the influence of modern, and even Hegelian, thought.[55] It is only with the modern abandonment of the strict moral demands of biblical faith that one could possibly entertain the notion that the freedom to choose is the "goal" (216; cf. 196), rather than the necessary condition, of the moral life.

Moreover, when we search in Fukuyama for the argument by which "freedom" became the goal of the moral life in modern political thought—by which virtue came to be seen as a mere means in the service of freedom—what we are led to is not Christianity, but the thought of Rousseau; it is in his thought that we first encounter a defense of moral freedom as an end in itself, or as a version of our original freedom "reacquired" at the end of history in a society directed by the general will. But Fukuyama conceals this from us. Just as he had originally withheld the early modern thinkers' attention to *thymos* in order to make his case for the superiority of Hegel's teaching, so he withholds from his account of the development of the notion of history the fact that not Hegel but Rousseau is the "first historicist,"[56] and relegates much of his presentation of Rousseau to the footnotes of his text. We are nonetheless able to discern the following crucial argument about Rousseau's role in the development of the notion of "rational freedom" and of the historicism upon which that notion depends.

According to Rousseau, a blind, mechanistic History[57] has given rise to human beings with *amour propre*, or a desire for recognition, a passion that causes human beings to love and defend their freedom in a manner that animals cannot. The question is, what is the status of the moral freedom that is assumed or posited by *amour propre*? By Fukuyama's own account, this freedom is, for Rousseau, groundless. For as he indicates, Rousseau was in fundamental agreement with the early moderns' teaching about natural man.[58] His state of nature is not a departure from but a radicalization of Hobbes's state of nature, or of Machiavelli's chaotic nature, which, as we have seen, required a reduction of human beings to animals. Lacking reason, possessing instead the unique faculty of perfectibility or adaptability, Rousseau's natural man lacked "the desire for recognition." *Amour propre*, from which man's love of freedom springs, is then not natural to man; it is *not* a "true human need" (83–84), nor are the opinions to which it gives rise supported by any moral order independent of human making. The "freedom" that is allegedly "reacquired" in the well-ordered civil society, the freedom that is allegedly a "social analogue" to natural freedom (371n13) is, then, groundless; "natural man" is man without reason, without an awareness of his mortality, and hence without the desire for recognition; far from loving and defending his "freedom," natural man would have exchanged it for a banana.[59]

Following these indications by Fukuyama, then, we arrive at the following conclusion. Rousseau, perhaps guided by Locke,[60] rejected Hobbes's natural right doctrine as too reliant upon fear-induced calculation to be practicable; it was insufficiently "realistic," or failed in its attempt to bring together the "is" and the "ought." While accepting the Hobbesian, mechanistic understanding of natural necessities in the physical world,[61] Rousseau indicated that the historical development of *amour propre* had given human beings a sense of worth or dignity so strong that it was impossible for them to practice a peaceful politics on the basis of fear of the sovereign alone. The Hobbesian doctrine of "rights" had to be more fully invested with moral content if *thymos* was to be controlled or tamed.[62] Yet the rehabilitation of *thymos* as a supplement to Hobbesian representative politics had to avoid the violent fights over justice and worthiness to rule to which *thymos* had always given rise. The rhetorical solution Rousseau proposed was "self-rule," an alleged analogue to the freedom of natural man, attainable by the formation of the "general will," by the transformation of one's own merely particular wishes into the form of a universal law. In this way, *thymos* could be turned against itself, or turned into isothymia. The freedom to make and submit oneself to universally acceptable laws was thus to be *rhetorically* presented as the end or purpose of political life,[63] (for the true end of representative government remains the same for Rousseau as for Hobbes and Locke: peace and stability[64]). Respect for equality of human "rights" became in this way a cause to which each citizen could dedicate himself. For a short time it even appeared right to say, with Voltaire, "I disagree with what you've said but am prepared to defend to the death your right to say it." This rehabilitated *amour propre* or *thymos*, and its attendant sense of dignity, proscribed any appeal to an end higher than "freedom" or self-rule. The new liberal citizen could be made willing to fight, and convinced of the justice of fighting, but only in order to defend the Hobbesian end of ending all disputes about rule. The Rousseauean citizen was proud to fight a war to end all wars, a war to end the suppression of equal freedom for all.

Modern liberal democracy was thus, for Hobbesian reasons, rhetorically presented as having "freedom" as its noble end. Kant, either out of genuine conviction or because, like Rousseau, he saw it as a means of "taming or harnessing" *thymos* for the sake of liberal democracy (163), attempted to present this freedom as the core of republican government. As Kant argued, the general will guarantees the goodness, that is, the universality, of one's wishes without recourse to any substantive consideration of man's *natural* perfection. In fact, all arguments made on the basis of man's nature, be they for or against the society characterized by the general will, are groundless. For the rational society, the society in which the general will exists and is known to exist, has been brought about not through man's intention, not through his attempt to establish the regime that accords with his specific natural needs and perfection, but by the process of human history first discerned by Rousseau. A full account of that history can show that History aimed all along at the creation of autonomous moral beings, at beings who had become conscious, in the "rational state," of their freedom from nature and nature's tutelage.[65] Reasoning that looked to "nature" rather than "History" could therefore provide no guidance for our life together as human beings. Only the universal moral laws willed by autonomous citizens at the end of History can do so.

But since these laws are "rational" in form only, that is, in their alleged universality, the historicist refinements of Hobbes's natural right doctrine cannot be said to have made it more "rational" in any substantive sense. The alleged final part of the historical dialectic, the coming into being of "rational" self-consciousness in the ideal state, looks instead like the final form of Machiavellian political thought, of the thought that begins with the self-imposed duty to satisfy our animal longings with the things of this world, and hence with the rejection of the only genuinely rational course available to us by nature. The true divide among political philosophers is thus not an "ethical" one but a philosophic one, and it concerns the status of reason. And as Fukuyama himself argues, the characteristically modern teaching about man has finally led to the wholesale rejection of "the possibility of a rational understanding of man;" the historicist belief that no understanding of the "nature of man" is possible constitutes the "deeper philosophic crisis" from which our current political crisis on the status of justice springs (296). Since Fukuyama is aware of this, we are led to wonder why he continues to cling to Hegel's historicism. The only intelligible reason seems to be that Hegel's master/slave dialectic allows him to attack the "radical historicism" of Nietzsche.

Confronting Radical Historicism

As we have seen, part of Fukuyama's intention from the start has been to neutralize the radical historicism that has grown out of Nietzsche's thought. Originally manifest on the right, radical historicism has now found a home on the left, where it has been put into the service of the left's moral crusades on behalf of the autonomous self. The result is a "fanatical isothymia" that demands respect for all "values," an end to all (necessarily arbitrary) rank orderings of human beings, and the "empowerment" of "oppressed" groups or "cultures." Fukuyama attempts to disarm this amazingly incoherent and politically disastrous thinking by first repositioning Nietzsche emphatically on the right, separating his thought from the fanatical isothymia of the left. He then argues that radical isothymia represents a threat to the end of History that "nature" will necessarily cry out against and destroy (314). This initial divorce of Nietzsche from the thought of the left permits Fukuyama to treat Nietzsche's doctrine of the Will to Power exclusively through an examination of the radically aristocratic, or right-wing, doctrine of the "overman." The overman, he argues, was a "prediction," a possible and indeed plausible threat to the end of History, but one which in fact represents the thought of a thymomaniac, of a man "stuck in History." For it is obvious that Nietzsche was merely reacting against the isothymia of the Hegelian slave in the name of megalothymia of the Hegelian master.[66] Rebelling against bourgeois man, Nietzsche was driven by his anger to misrepresent man as all *thymos*, all "anger," and nothing else (334); his historical situation had blinded him to the other two parts of the soul, reason and desire. And if "na-

ture'' will eventually overcome the left-wing threat of fanatical isothymia, the liberal democratic regime will take care of the right-wing
threat of the Nietzschean overman, of any and all rebellious megalothymia. For liberal democracy has rational ''outlets'' for megalothymia,
or at least for the tamed megalothymia that it still permits. Radical
historicists ought therefore to abandon Nietzsche's thought and em-
brace liberal democracy.

The initial difficulty with this presentation of Nietzsche is suggested
by Fukuyama's few statements on the understanding of the slave's nihilism, which Nietzsche aimed to overcome. According to Nietzsche,
that nihilism is *not* due to modern liberalism, a regime which is only
the latest manifestation of the slave morality. It is due rather to the
slave's ''historical sense,'' his ''awareness'' that there are no permanent truths. The ''true world'' has finally become a fable, and because
of this insight, the human spirit threatens to become enervated or thin.
Temporarily content with a Christian morality which, with the death
of God, has no longer any basis, the human spirit may soon become
consciously and passively nihilistic (306–07). It is against this possibility, the possibility of the last man, that Nietzsche presents his radical
aristocratic overman, the conscious, active nihilist who creates meaning
in the face of the meaninglessness that History has disclosed—in the
face of the awareness that all values or horizons have in the past been
creations of the will. The dawning crisis of nihilism thus understood
has indeed been created for us by the ''slave morality,'' the Christian
morality of guilt and bad conscience, but contrary to what Fukuyama
wishes to argue, Nietzsche has the greatest respect for this slave morality. If Hegel admired the superior humanity of the ''master,'' as Fukuyama claims (155–56), for Nietzsche the master was *subhuman*, bestial,
shallow, possessing a ''heart'' but no ''soul,'' like an eagle or a lion. It
is the slave who has given depth to the human soul or *created* the soul,
by internalizing his will to power.[67] Forced to turn against itself in the
form of resentment, the slave's secret will to power has made us human.
And it is the same ''ascetic'' slave's ''conscience'' that has finally
given rise to our intellectual ''probity,'' which compels us to see our
''values'' as nothing but creations.[68] For Nietzsche, it is the potentially
deadly ''relativism'' brought about by this intellectual probity that must
be counteracted by the conscious creator of values, the overman—not
out of anger, but out of love for man.[69] Nietzsche is indeed on the right,
then, but he is a radical *progressive* of the right. He is in no way reactionary or nostalgic; he does not call for a return to the master morality
of good and bad, but seeks a morality that is ''*Beyond* Good And Evil.''

Fukuyama would have us forget, in short, that Nietzsche's overman must resemble Napoleon in having not only the heart of Caesar but the soul of Christ as well.[70]

But what is most disappointing in Fukuyama's Hegelian critique of Nietzsche is that it manifests, rather than overcoming, the permanent danger of historicism: the foreclosure of argument. Nietzsche becomes a part, if an eloquent part, of the "lunatic fringe;" he is one of those who has either turned in the wrong historical "direction" or has set up a permanent camp on the road to the common destiny of mankind (337–38). The historical meaning of his work, which is determined by his historical situation, becomes more important than his own intention. As a result, no serious answer is given to Nietzsche's argument concerning our "historical sense," our nihilism. Certainly Fukuyama's claim that liberal democracy best satisfies the three parts of the soul outlined by Plato, rather than the one part that Nietzsche was allegedly driven to exult, fails to meet the issue. For assuming that this portrayal of Plato is accurate, how does it answer the Nietzschean claim that Plato's three-part soul was merely his *creation*? How does it prevent us from concluding that it is Fukuyama, not Nietzsche, who is "stuck in history," that his whole work is merely the last necessary effort of the last man to lock up the leader of the lunatic fringe for the sake of a society of last men, a society in which all members of the "lunatic fringe" will go voluntarily to the insane asylum? "Reason," he suggests, ought to content us with the "outlets" for *thymos* provided by our regime (313–21). But if, as Nietzsche claims, reason is incapable of learning the truth, especially about the "moral freedom" that is attributed to human beings by *thymos*, how could one ever be satisfied with liberal democracy?

If on the other hand Fukuyama wishes to say that there is a genuine ground for *thymos*, that its hitherto blind activity has now become rational in a dawning consciousness of the need for mutual recognition of equality, or isothymia, he must at least give a defense of the "free will" or "metaphysical freedom" that is, as he well knows, the linchpin of his argument.[71] Yet his promised defense of free will is never forthcoming. We are, it seems, to take it on the combined authority of Kant and Plato that human beings are free to make rational moral choices (296–97, 302–3). But even those who are inclined to bow to authority will have trouble accepting this new synthesis of Kant and Plato. For while Plato may indeed provide us with the means to understand genuine human excellence, it is all but a slogan that for Plato virtue is knowledge and hence vice is ignorance. As for Kant, Fukuyama himself had stressed that Kant denies that our (calculative) reason has anything to do with the specifically moral choice; Kantian freedom is altogether independent of nature and is not the freedom to live "according to nature" (149–152). In the end, Fukuyama simply relies upon the fact that all those who make thymotic judgments must *believe* in "moral choice or the autonomous use of reason" (298; cf. 150, 302–3). Unfortunately, it is just such *belief* which, Nietzsche alleges, was once the slave's creation, and is now lost to us.

The Classical Alternative

But does Fukuyama not indicate his true intention precisely in his appeal to Plato? Does he not attempt to move us from the Hegelian view that a transformation of human nature, an "evolutionary process," is at work in history, to the view that an apparently expelled nature "always returns" (288–96, 314–15)? A return to an understanding of "nature" is needed, according to Fukuyama, if liberal democracy is to regain its purpose and survive the threats it now faces. That understanding is available in the thought of Plato, who first set our sights on the end of history with his perfectly just city-in-speech. If full rational self-consciousness is not attained in the universal and homogeneous state, liberal democracy at least provides the closest possible approximation to a perfectly just satisfaction of the three parts of the soul that Plato adumbrated in the *Republic*.

To accept this final argument, however, we would once again have to accept what Fukuyama himself knows to be untrue. For he is aware of the following characteristics of the argument in the *Republic*. First, it is opinion, not reason, that rules in the city-in-speech; that city is and remains, like all political societies, a "cave." Second, "justice" in the ordinary sense has to do with one's relations to others; what the alleged "justice" of a well-ordered soul has to do with justice in this ordinary sense is not at all clear. For it is by no means clear what reason, the ruling part, will think of the self-sacrificing service to the good of others that is always demanded by justice. Third, and related to this, the city-in-speech is not presented as one that satisfies all three parts of the soul of each citizen; on the contrary, as Socrates twice states, none of the citizens of that city is satisfied—above all, not the philosophers who would be compelled to rule it. Finally, Socrates' tripartite division of the soul is deliberately and seriously flawed; it is presented with a view to the needs of his interlocuters and his diverse readers.[72]

Fukuyama's claim that liberalism satisfies all three parts of the soul requires in fact that Plato's tripartite division of the soul be turned into a Hobbesian division of the soul; liberalism satisfies a strictly calculative reason that is in the *service* of spiritedness and desire, of the kind of desire, moreover, that is to be found only in a "city of sows." If there is a permanent human nature, we cannot come to know it on the basis of this Hobbesian conception of man, of one that reduces all speech or reason to a calculating servant of animal passions. A more adequate understanding of man will have to begin by examining the Platonic argument that spiritedness is *at odds with* the genuinely rational life, or by recognizing the instructive joke contained in Plato's oxymoron of "the philosophic dog." For the Socratic dialogue is indeed, as Fukuyama states, "a conversation between two human beings on some important subject like the nature of the good or the meaning of justice" (61). And Plato doubtless expected and even counted on the admirable, commonsense assumption of the goodness of justice that most readers bring to his texts. But the successful defense of justice that we citizens of liberal democracy are expecting to find in a Platonic dialogue can blind us to its primary intention: the establishment of the possibility of philosophy, or the discovery, to be made by each of us, that the life led in accordance with reason is a necessary and desirable way of life, a discovery made by and through an examination of the *problem* of justice.[73]

The discovery of the life of reason to which we refer can perhaps be appropriately suggested by considering not Plato's thought, but that of Thucydides, with whom Plato is in fundamental agreement on this decisive issue. Fukuyama presents Thucydides as a classical "realist," and leads us to think that he, like contemporary students of international relations, was guilty of the "unreality of realism," that is, of having failed to take into account the power of *thymos*, of the desire for justice, in the lives of citizens and nations. In fact, he suggests, there were *never* any justifications of war or imperialism given in the past.[74]

But Fukuyama knows that none of Thucydides' characters ever dismisses or ignores justice in the way he suggests. For them, as for Aristotle,[75] the just and unjust, the good and bad, the noble and base, is what politics is all about. One exaggerates only slightly in saying that this is all they ever talk about. By examining their speeches and deeds, we are able to engage in the ascent from the pious, commonsense understanding of the citizen to the consistent understanding of human life that is possible, always and everywhere, on the basis of a full grasp of the problem of justice. The Athenian "realists" whom Thucydides presents to us, lacking this grasp, stop short on their ascent, failing as they mani-

festly do to accept their own argument concerning the compelling nature of the good. For this reason, they continue to pursue the eternal
glory that they anticipate will be theirs on the basis of their noble and
self-sacrificing exercise of imperial rule on behalf of their city—the
great or noble glory, in other words, that they believe will be theirs
because they deserve it. It is in fact precisely a thymotic resistance to
the argument about the compulsion to pursue what is good that characterizes those Thucydidean speakers who state the "realist" argument,
and that inhibits them, as it inhibits every other political man, from
accepting the truth that lies at the heart of their realist argument, or that
makes that truth painful or harsh for them. Moved by a love for the
noble or honorable, for what promises a deathless reward for self-sacri-
ficial deeds,[76]—by what Fukuyama calls *thymos*—the Athenian "realists" turned away from their own argument about the compelling nature
of the good, and continued to pursue the glory that dedication to their
city and to her empire promised.

Thucydides, for his part, did not resist the compulsion to know what
the good is for a human being, but beginning within the perspective of
citizens, he allowed his readers to see and take the argument of the
citizens to its logical conclusion. Perhaps for this reason, he was free of
the hopes that haunted his fellow Athenians, and free of those hopes for
a permanent human solution to the problem of political life that later
haunted Machiavelli and Hobbes. Above all, unlike modern "realists,"
he saw the need to address and overcome the claims made on behalf of
faith against reason's ability to know what is good for us, claims that
modern political philosophy, going on the offensive, made the unsuc-
cessful attempt to refute—an attempt that has now led to a peculiar,
fanatical, but confused attack on the pursuit of science or knowledge.

In short, Thucydides' thought, like classical political thought in general, leaves political life in its inherent dignity and offers sound advice
to political men, especially by its presentation of the need for moderation. It does not begin with an abstraction about thymotic or vainglorious man, and hence it is not led to proclaim, as contemporary Hobbes-
ians do, that religious faith or family attachments are "irrational." It
begins rather with common sense and, without doing violence to political life or to the opinions of political men, it facilitates an ascent from
political life to the life of reason. It is on the other hand, as we have
seen, one of the distinctive failures of Hobbesian thought that it precludes such an ascent. Beginning his analysis of political life with the
reduction of human evil to animal evil, Hobbes, and those who followed
him, thereby deprived political life of its peak.

By attempting to hide from us the distinctively human experiences of devotion to the noble and devotion to the divine, modern thought hides us from ourselves, and so hides the world's disclosure of itself from us. It exploits our need to think well of ourselves while encouraging us not to take justice or nobility fully seriously, and hence encourages us to thoughtlessly pursue low-grade versions of these. Unable to see our longings for what they are, we are unable to shed the delusions that sustain the inadequate, dehumanizing answers to them offered by modern life and modern thought. And now, having been disappointed by the failure of modern rationalism to provide the satisfaction that it promised, and horrified at the possible loss of our very humanity, which modern rationalism seems to be bringing about, we have begun turning away from reason altogether. And, not surprisingly, we hope for (and demand) the artful disclosure or "presencing" of the kind of absent, local god or gods who would support the "self-actualizing, autonomous" life that is the peculiarly modern (and allegedly *post*modern) version of justice.

Conclusion

The natural rights doctrine with which Hobbes attempted to refound politics was intended to promote above all an indifference to the truth, in order to end the disruptive and deadly strife into which genuine political debate is ever susceptible of falling, and allow us to secure by ourselves the blessings of peace and prosperity. It has succeeded, as Fukuyama knows, by narrowing political life, by eliminating from political life the kind of attachments and problems which can lead to the genuinely rational life. It has succeeded then, only by progressively obscuring from its citizens their deepest longings. Still, it was able for a time to give rise both to political greatness and to outstanding political analysis, and it had the advantage of promoting a political life that left philosophers alone. The same cannot be said of any regime in which historicism has become part of the reigning orthodoxy. For the refinements or adjustments of Hobbes's political thought, begun indeed by Rousseau and culminating in Hegel's philosophy of history, have eroded still further the potential of political life to give rise to an awareness of the need and possibility of knowledge of what is good for human beings. Those refinements or adjustments have simultaneously unleashed the disastrously hopeful prospect of a human end to all human troubles through a dialectic of history—one which allegedly gives rise to a new and advanced consciousness—and denied the existence of permanently intelligible necessities. Those who object to this thesis are, moreover, easily dismissed as the victims of false consciousness, fated ever to be "subjectively" correct and "objectively" wrong, expressing the interests of their class in their doomed historical epoch. When and as this happens, precious little room remains for the kind of political debate that provides the beginning of an ascent to knowledge, an ascent that has been shown by classical political philosophy to be available, in principle, to man as man.

Since our situation is threatened above all today by a dogmatic, historicist relativism, it would seem imperative that the means by which the ancients met the claim against the possibility of knowledge be made clear to those whose business it is to know. If, as the manifest difficulties with his argument have led us to suspect, Fukuyama intends to return us to Plato, through an ironic or playful presentation of Hegelian Universal History, he fails in that intention; his argument tends to reinforce rather than overthrow the stifling orthodoxies of late modern thought. Yet if his attempt is a failure, it is a failure to behold: it is at once monumental and graceful. It does not show us a rational self-consciousness at the end of History, nor does it provide the guidance that we need out of our situation. But it is of great assistance in showing both how we got here, and where we must go from here. By giving us the Hegelian understanding shorn of its absolute moment, Fukuyama reveals the inadequacy of the modern understanding of man, and points us back to the premodern rationalism that was rejected by the moderns. He shows us the abiding longing, which Plato presents as present in all human life, for that wisdom which alone can supply the guidance that we need.

Notes

1. *On Tyranny: Including the Strauss-Kojève Correspondence,* revised and expanded, eds. Victor Gourevitch and Michael S. Roth (New York: Free Press, 1991), p. 192. See also *What Is Political Philosophy?* (Glencoe: Free Press, 1959), p. 176n2, and "Comments On Carl Schmitt's *Der Begriff Des Politischen*" in *Spinoza's Critique of Religion* (New York: Schocken, 1965), pp. 344–45.

2. The irony appears perhaps most clearly in the fact that the table of democracies in the world (49–50) covers the past two hundred years, while Fukuyama argues as if it covers "four hundred" (48). The reason, as will soon become apparent, is that Fukuyama does not blindly view the "macropolitical

phenomenon'' as a mere trend but as the result of a deliberate modern ''project.'' See also the remarks on the deficiency of modern social science, 350n23 and 352n2.

3. See 62–3 with 136–39, 67 with 128, 144–46, 389n1.

4. ''The *bourgeois* was an entirely deliberate creation of early modern thought, an effort at social engineering that sought to create social peace by changing human nature itself'' (185); ''we modern bourgeois'' have been ''schooled by Hobbes and Locke'' (150); Rousseau's ''criticism of the Economic Man remains the basis of most present-day attacks on unlimited economic growth, and is the (oftentimes unconscious) intellectual basis for most contemporary environmentalism'' (84); the starting premise of the self-esteem movement ''is both Kantian and Christian (even if its promoters are unaware of their own intellectual roots)'' (302); ''Whether or not we acknowledge our debt to him, we owe to Hegel the most fundamental aspects of our present-day consciousness'' (59).

5. 57. Cf. 84, 130, 153–54, 355n3.

6. 48, 135, 355n3, etc.

7. See 88, bottom. Fukuyama's initial claim that ''before 1776 there was not a single [democracy] in existence anywhere in the world'' (48) is intended to support his case for historical progress, but he knows that this initial claim is spurious. That ''Periclean Athens did not systematically protect individual rights'' makes ''the democracy of Periclean Athens'' (48) a *nonliberal democracy* rather than a non-democracy. It was not, moreover, the only democracy to have existed prior to 1776. As Fukuyama himself states, ''. . . people *in all ages* have taken the non-economic step of risking their lives and their livelihoods to fight for democratic rights'' (134, emphasis added). See also the references to ''ancient republics'' and ''ancient democracies'' on 317 and 318, and cf. 305, 387n8.

8. See 87 (''or some other natural process that makes the earth completely uninhabitable by man'') with 356n4. Fukuyama is moreover aware of the fact that any ''meaningfulness'' in the progress of History is destroyed by our knowledge that the earth will, like all things, eventually decline. See Strauss, *On Tyranny* p. 224, and *The Rebirth of Classical Political Rationalism* (Chicago: University of Chicago Press, 1989), p. 238.

9. See 58-60, 146, 153.

10. 258, 265, 338-339, 382n13, 384n14.

11. See *On Tyranny: Including the Strauss-Kojève Correspondence,* revised and expanded, eds. Victor Gourevitch and Michael S. Roth (New York: Free Press, 1991), p. 210.

12. ''The success of democracy would suggest that the principles of liberty and equality on which they [*sic*] are based are in fact discoveries about the nature of man as man, whose truth does not diminish but grows more evident as one's point of view becomes more cosmopolitan'' (51).

13. 64, 314. The term is from Strauss: see *Natural Right and History* (Chi-

cago: University of Chicago Press, 1953), pp. 22–34; *The Rebirth of Classical Political Rationalism* (Chicago: University of Chicago Press, 1989), pp. 24–46.

14. See 352n2; 137 (bottom) and 139 (top) with 363n6. Cf. 237.

15. Fukuyama's original explanation of German fascism as a "unique evil and the product of historically unique circumstances" is deliberately weak and superficial. He refers to "the special intellectual and cultural traditions of Germany at the time, its anti-materialism and emphasis on struggle and sacrifice," claiming that these traditions "were in no way 'modern,'" and that "it is possible to understand nazism as another, albeit extreme, variant of the 'disease of the transition,' a byproduct of the modernization process that was by no means a necessary component of modernity itself" (129). The footnote to this statement (363n5) contradicts it; it refers to the Nazis' "nostalgia for an organic, pre-industrial society, and a broad unhappiness with the atomizing and alienating characteristics of economic modernity." It would be especially strange for a Hegelian not to realize that any opposition to modernity, particularly to its "alienation," presupposes modernity; even if we accept, e.g., that Nietzsche merely represents or gives expression to an eruption of premodern *megalothymia* (189, 301–308)—which is highly dubious—the fact that Nietzsche does so in terms of "master and slave moralities" indicates that he has been affected by Hegel. Moreover, Fukuyama knows that the German "intellectual and cultural traditions" to which he refers have both their origins and full expressions in modernity—in Rousseau, Kant, Hegel, Nietzsche, and Heidegger (146-152, 300-301, 333, 365n7, 389nn1,7, and the reference to Zarathustra's prologue contained in 302n9 with the statement on Hegel at 359n15)—or that thinkers like Carl Schmitt bear only the most superficial resemblance to proponents of "fundamentalist Shi'ism" (363n5; cf. 236). Fukuyama's initial, weak explanation is used, it seems, in order to maintain the case for historical progress and hence for liberal democracy.

16. See 296, 298, 337–38.

17. See 386n7 with 387nn 5, 6, 11, 13, and cf. the reference to "politically correct ideologues" of Maoist China on 95.

18. Hegel "was the first *historicist* philosopher—that is, a philosopher who believed in the essential historical relativity of truth" (62).

19. "Hegel maintained that *all* human consciousness was limited by the particular social and cultural conditions of man's surrounding environment" (62, emphasis added). "The *radicalness of Hegel's historicism* is evident in his very concept of man . . . Hegel . . . believed that in his most essential characteristics man was *undetermined* and therefore *free to create* his own nature" (63, some emphasis added). See also 146.

20. See 3 and 67 with 128, 144–46.

21. Consider, e.g., the advice of the "master" Athenians to the "slave" Melians in Thucydides, 5.111.3-4, or of Socrates to the Athenians in Plato's *Apology of Socrates*, 31d8-10, 32e.

22. See Hobbes, *De Cive*, I, 2; *Leviathan*, C. B. Macpherson, ed. (Middlesex: Pelican, 1971), p. 342.

23. For Smith, see 173–74; for Machiavelli, 184; for the American founders, 186–87; for Locke, 366n13.

24. Fukuyama's presentation of Hobbesian natural right and natural law (156) is confusing. The confusion stems from his claim that "self-preservation is the fundamental moral fact." An animal desire cannot be a "moral fact"; only a right can be a "moral fact."

25. *Leviathan*, p. 234.

26. *Leviathan*, pp. 184–85.

27. *Leviathan*, pp. 188, 238.

28. *Leviathan*, p. 261; see Fukuyama, 148–49.

29. *Leviathan*, pp. 127–28.

30. Just how rhetorical the argument is, is open to dispute. See e.g., *Leviathan*, p. 221: "If Nature therefore have made men equall, that equality is to be acknowledged: or if Nature have made men unequall; yet because men that think themselves equall, will not enter into conditions of peace, but upon Equall terms, such equalitie must be admitted."

31. Cf. *Leviathan*, pp. 165–166.

32. *The Prince*, trans. Harvey C. Mansfield Jr. (Chicago: University of Chicago Press, 1986), pp. 23–4, 101–2.

33. *Leviathan*, pp. 167–173.

34. *Leviathan*, pp. 164–68; cf. pp. 183, 203, 211.

35. *Leviathan*, p.185, with *The Prince*, pp. 39–40 and 76–77.

36. *The Prince*, p. 14. Acquisition is blamed by those who want to acquire but cannot; in truth it is necessary and therefore unblameable (p. 14 with p. 61). In accordance with this argument, Machiavelli continues to make a distinction between the few human beings who can see things for what they are and the many or the vulgar who are deceived by the appearances of things (p. 71) but the distinction is an attenuated one. It is not a distinction between the few "philosophic natures" and political men. Rather, it extends no further than that made by successful political men—by the Athenian ambassadors to Melos, for example (Thucydides 5.85, 103). The new distinction is between "the great" and "the people," between those who "desire to command and oppress" and those who "desire neither to be commanded nor oppressed" (p. 39).

37. *The Prince*, p. 23, with p. 61. The end that each man has before him, according to Machiavelli, is "glory and riches" (p. 99).

38. *The Prince*, chs. 18 and 19.

39. *The Prince*, ch. 12, beginning; ch. 18.

40. *Leviathan*, chs. 3–5.

41. *Leviathan*, p. 466.

42. *Leviathan*, p. 478.

43. *Leviathan*, pp. 588–89.

44. *Leviathan*, ch. 14, p. 200.

45. *Leviathan*, pp. 115, 118, 132f, 142, 144. On Hobbes's doctrine of representation, see Harvey C. Mansfield Jr., "Hobbes and the Science of Indirect

Government," *American Political Science Review*, Vol. 65, 97–110; Clifford Orwin, "On the Sovereign Authorization," *Political Theory*, Vol. 3, no. 1 (February 1975), 26–52.

46. *Leviathan*, pp. 225–26 with p. 100. Cf. Locke, *First Treatise*, secs. 56, 58, 60.

47. *Leviathan*, pp. 585–86.

48. The pre-Hobbesian understanding of reason as part of a soul that is driven to know, that rests unsatisfied with what is false, unclear, or uncertain, and which can therefore be said to be obligated by the known, is perhaps more visible today in the political discourse of nonliberal societies than in ours. One sees it, for example, in the remark of Czeslaw Milosz, that "the pressure of the state machine is nothing compared with the pressure of a convincing argument." Quoted in Jacques Rupnik, *The Other Europe* (New York: Pantheon Books, 1989), p. 213; cf. pp. 145–46.

49. *Leviathan*, pp. 200, 207.

50. The Hobbesian character of Fukuyama's *thymos* is equally evident in his attacks on contemporary international relations theorists. He blames "realists" for giving us a "billiard ball" understanding of international relations (248), but his account of *thymos* does little to correct this. What he says of the realists' definition of "power"—that it is so broad as to lose its descriptive or analytical power (257)—is true of his own description of *thymos*. When attempting to convince the "realists" that liberal democracy is the final product of history, on the other hand, Fukuyama does with Serbia and Bosnia what Kojève had done with Nazi Germany: the massacres in the former Yugoslavia are part of History's march toward freedom, "a necessary concomitant to spreading democratization" (272), "the birth pangs of a new and more democratic order" (274) taking place in the "historical world"; their meaning is grasped as such, objectively, by those of us who live in the post-historical world. Their Conestoga wagon is merely being temporarily waylaid on its way to Carson City (cf. 338-39). We who inhabit that city can either send out a posse to save them or play another round of golf, depending on which "outlet" our *thymos* takes or whether we are moved to satisfy some altogether different part of our soul.

51. A Marxian explanation appears on p. 61: the "classical example" of an internal contradiction in prerational societies was "the medieval city, which protected within it merchants and traders who constituted the germs of a capitalist economic order. Their superior economic efficiency eventually exposed the irrationality of moral constraints on economic productivity, and thereby abolished the very city that gave them birth." This begs the whole question of how Christians could come to see unlimited acquisition as *justified* (cf. Fukuyama's own criticism of Huntington's argument with respect to Catholicism at 374n8). Hence, relying on Weber, Fukuyama adds that Judaism and Christianity purged "class relations of magic and superstition" (375n18), and that Lutheran Protestantism abolished all official church hierarchy (374n8, 216). But neither of these could make greater economic efficiency *rational* to someone moved by the Christian Scriptures to *reject* unlimited acquisition.

52. Cf. Aristotle, *Nichomachean Ethics* 1114a15–20, 1114a31–b16.

53. I am indebted for these reflections to the following works by Leo Strauss: *City and Man*, esp. pp. 38–39 and 129; *Natural Right And History*, esp. pp. 83–84, 95–97, 150n24; "Jerusalem and Athens," *Studies In Platonic Political Philosophy*, esp. p. 155; "Progress or Return?" *The Rebirth of Classical Political Rationalism*; "Notes On Lucretius," *Liberalism Ancient And Modern*, esp. pp. 84, 86, 97, 100, 116–17, 122, 131; "The Law of Reason in the *Kuzari*," *Persecution and the Art of Writing*, esp. pp. 114, 139–41.

54. See Augustine, *De utilitate credendi*, 10.24. For the argument of Thomas Aquinas, see Strauss, *City and Man* (Chicago: University of Chicago Press, 1964), pp. 38–39.

55. This comes out especially in those sections of King's writings in which he speaks of *social progress*, a notion that takes the place held by the fall, redemption, and final judgment in Augustinian and Thomistic thought. See, e.g., Martin Luther King, Jr., "Letter From The Burmingham Jail" in Robert A. Goldwin, series editor, *On Civil Disobedience: American Essays Old and New* (Chicago: Rand McNally Public Affairs Series, 1968), pp. 65–69, 73, 75. Cf. *Why We Can't Wait* (New York: New American Library, 1963), p. 66. On the notion of historical progress and Christianity, see Ernest L. Fortin, "Augustine's City of God and the Modern Historical Consciousness," *Review of Politics* 41, no. 3 (July 1979), 323–343.

56. Cf. p. 63 "one important exception"; p. 83, "Rousseau understood before Hegel the essential historicity of human experience, and how human nature itself had been modified over time." Fukuyama tells us that Hegel's "first man," who began the historical dialectic, was for all intents and purposes taken over from the state of nature doctrine of "Hobbes, Locke, and Rousseau" (146); he repeats this on p. 288. Yet he explicitly compares and contrasts Hegel's state of nature doctrine only with that of Hobbes and Locke. In the body of the text, Rousseau's is presented only incidentally, first in the course of an argument against environmentalism (83–84) and then in the course of an argument against "realism" (255). The full and revealing argument concerning Rousseau and Hegel is presented only in the endnotes (365n10, 371n13, 373n7).

57. See 373n7: man's historical evolution is explained on the basis of the faculty of "perfectibility," a faculty compatible with a mechanistic physics, and not "free will," a faculty that depends on belief in god. Cf. J. J. Rousseau, *The First and Second Discourses*, ed. Roger D. Masters (New York: St. Martin's, 1964), pp. 113–14 with 103 and 167, top.

58. Cf. "Hobbes, Locke, and Rousseau," pp. 146, 288.

59. See Fukuyama, 147, top, with 83–84. Rousseau himself deliberately obscures this by using the ambivalent term "barbarous man" in the crucial part of the *Second Discourse* (Masters ed., pp. 164 ff.)

60. See Nathan Tarcov, "A 'Non-Lockean' Locke and the Character of Liberalism" in *Liberalism Reconsidered*, eds. D. MacLean and C. Mills (Rowman and Allanheld, 1983), pp. 130–40. Cited by Fukuyama, 367n13.

61. Rousseau, *First and Second Discourses*, pp. 103, 114. Consider also Rousseau's praise of Bacon, Descartes, and Newton in the *First Discourse,* 63.

62. See 355n2, 365n4 to ch. 14, and cf. Arthur M. Melzer, "Rousseau's Moral Realism: Replacing Natural Law with the General Will," *American Political Science Review*, LXXVII (1983), 633–51.

63. See Rousseau, *Discourses*, p. 167 and compare p. 114.

64. See Rousseau, *Discourses*, p. 174: "I would prove that agreement or conflict of these various forces is the surest indication of a well- or ill-constituted state."

65. See 57–64, 146–52, 192–202, 276–77, 296–303, 329–39; cf. Strauss, "The Three Waves of Modernity," *Political Philosophy, Six Essays by Leo Strauss*, ed. Hilail Gilden (New York: Bobbs-Merrill, 1975), pp. 90–92.

66. See esp. 189, and cf. 301, 304, 308, 314.

67. See *Genealogy of Morals*, trans. Walter Kaufmann and R. J. Hollingdale (New York: Random House, 1967), First Essay, aphorism 6, pp. 32–33.

68. *Genealogy of Morals*, Second Essay, aphorism 16, pp. 84, 85 (cf. aphorism 18, p. 87); Third Essay, aphorism 27, pp. 160–61 (cf. aphorisms 12 and 24).

69. See *Genealogy of Morals*, Preface, aphorism 3.

70. Cf. *Genealogy of Morals*, First Essay, aphorism 16, end (p. 54).

71. See 151, bottom, where Fukuyama puts the "tortured question" of the possibility of human free choice aside "for the moment."

72. The presentation of *thymos* in the story of Leontius, which Fukuyama presents as the most illuminating of Plato's presentations (163–66), is notoriously problematical, more so than Fukuyama's qualifying endnote (370n5) suggests. To begin with, that story shows *thymos* in the service, not of reason, but of opinion; Leontius is ashamed of his "desire to look," or his curiosity; he curses his eyes. Only by presenting reason in this context as "calculation" (*Republic* 439d5) is Socrates able to convince Glaucon that spiritedness is not opposed to reason in this case, and that there are three distinct parts of the soul. As Socrates explicitly indicates both before and after this story, however, reason has a desire of its own (*Republic* 435e7, 474c et seq.), and that desire must be satisfied, as it is in the philosophic life, in order for a human being to be happy. By Fukuyama's account, on the other hand, one would think that the *Republic* ends at the conclusion of Book Four. (See, however, 370n4.)

73. Contrast above, pp. xx. While there is no more pressing need than an examination of the fundamental questions concerning the nature of justice and the human good, such discussions must necessarily remain less than explicit; enlightenment is a modern mistake, one which would not have been attempted had its proponents engaged in the kind of examination we have in mind.

74. See especially 259, 267, and cf. 381n4, 379n1.

75. *Politics* 1253a1–9.

76. See e.g., Thucydides, V.105, 107, 109, 111, and see Christopher Bruell, "Thucydides' View of Athenian Imperialism," *American Political Science Review*, LXVIII, no. 1 (March 1974), 11–17; "Thucydides and Perikles," *St. John's Review*, XXXII, no. 3 (Summer 1981), 24–29.

10

The Ambiguity of the Hegelian End of History

David Walsh

The great merit of Fukuyama's provocative thesis, that the liberal democratic triumph represents the end of historical political development, is the quality of discussion it has provoked. It has compelled us to place political developments within the largest frame of reference, the horizon constituted by historical existence. We can no longer simply retrace the routinized questions of liberal justice or injustice, rights and their foundations, but now must take account of the more comprehensive question of the meaning of the liberal democratic construction within the final perspective of history. The effect, not too surprisingly, has been to direct our reflections back to the thinkers who in the past have most successfully and profoundly explored such a range of questions and, preeminently, to the work of Hegel. It was Hegel, as Fukuyama acknowledges, who most powerfully imposed the problematic of the end of history on modern consciousness. It is therefore with Hegel that any serious response to Fukuyama's contemporary reformulation of the end of history must begin. When that is undertaken, I believe, it can be shown that the construction of a historical terminus within time, even in the hands of its most brilliant exponent, rests on a fatal ambiguity, one that reveals the feet of clay of that last liberal empire as well.

A suspicion of the ambiguity of Hegel's political thought has been a theme since its inception. Almost from the very first Hegel felt compelled to defend his work against various misinterpretations. In the years following his death the ambiguity of the dialectical *Aufhebungen* gave rise to the radical split between right- and left-wing Hegelians, who unfolded the master's work in diametrically opposed directions. No more eloquent testimony to the uncertainty of his construction can be conceived than this divergence of intellectual and political movements extending down to our own day. Hegel's central philosophical dictum, "what is rational is actual and what is actual is rational," left itself open to both a conservative and a revolutionary construction.[1] By emphasizing the first half of the formula we arrive at the revolutionary proclamation that only what is rational is truly actual; the second half can then be revised to confirm that only what is actual in the revolutionary sense is really rational. The conservative or reactionary premise is obtained by insisting, with the latter half of the statement, that the status quo is rational; its justification is to be found in the preceding recognition that the rational has been incarnated in the existing state of affairs. Having focused on different principles within his thought, the various interpretations have reflected more the inner logic of their own starting points than the all-embracing wholeness of the original. Once broken the Hegelian synthesis cannot easily be put together again.[2]

This observation is borne out by the persistence of one-sided interpretations in the twentieth century. Besides the continuity of left-wing Hegelian criticism by Lukács, Kojève, Bloch, Marcuse, Adorno and others, and the even more grotesque spectacle of right-wing misuse of Hegel by the German and Italian fascists, there have also emerged the two centrist schools of his liberal critics and liberal defenders.[3] As illustrations of the problems of interpretation, these latter groups are highly instructive. Liberal criticism of Hegel has had a long history, reaching back especially to the work of Rudolf Haym, but more recently has emerged in reaction to the totalitarian manifestation of Hegel in the various communist and national socialist ideologies. This frequently polemical approach is best represented by Ernst Topitsch, E. F. Carritt, Sidney Hook, and most infamously, Karl Popper.[4] The charges advanced against Hegel—of advocating absolute power for the State, of exempting the State from moral obligations, of glorifying the idea of war, of toadying to Prussian reactionism, of nationalism, racism, and even anti-Semitism, in short, of providing "the fertilizer to which modern totalitarianism owes its rapid growth"[5]—are all well known. Almost as well established by now is the persuasive refutation developed by a generation of liberal defenders which, beginning with Franz Rosenzweig, also includes Eric Weil, T. M. Knox, Shlomo Avineri, Walter Kaufmann, Z. A. Pelczynski, Joachim Ritter, and many others.[6] Their invariably competent scholarship has all but rehabilitated Hegel as a bona fide member of the liberal constitutional tradition and virtually silenced the accusation of proto-totalitarianism.

Yet Hegel's liberal defenders, who today dominate the discussion, have not entirely escaped the objection of selectivity in their treatment.

For by and large they have read his political thought, as Pelczynski has recommended, in isolation from the rest of his philosophical system.[7] The picture of Hegel that emerges is of a moderate reformer who sought to promote individual freedom within the limits imposed by the requirements for a concrete political organization. Ritter expresses this best when he depicts Hegel as searching for a middle ground between Revolution and Restoration, the twin poles whose discontinuity with reality had become "the decisive problem of the age."[8] Viewed in this light, Hegel's Idea of the modern State became the definitive elaboration of universal human freedom, through its articulation of the essential institutional structures that make freedom possible. His achievement was to have developed "a legal order which accords with the freedom of selfhood and does it justice, and enables the individual to be himself and achieve his human determination."[9] Beyond this carefully balanced exegesis of the liberal Hegel, however, there still remain those dimensions of his thought that have given rise to less favorable interpretations. Missing from this account is any reference to that other side of Hegel that elevates the State above the requirements of "finite morality," endows the State with supreme right in relation to the individual,[10] and regards both States and individuals as merely "the unconscious tools and organs of the world Spirit at work within them."[11] Lack of comprehensiveness has been the rock on which more than a few interpretations of Hegel have foundered.

In an attempt to overcome this problem, other commentators appear to have simply abandoned the search for a consistent interpretation and have forthrightly acknowledged the presence of "tensions" within his thought. Ernst Cassirer in particular has drawn attention to the totalitarian elements within Hegel's construction, while steadfastly refusing to accuse Hegel of totalitarianism, on the grounds that "there is an unmistakable difference between his idealization of the power of the state and that sort of idolization that is the characteristic of our modern totalitarian systems."[12] Similarly ambivalent assessments may be found among Charles Taylor, Carl Friedrich, Dante Germino, John Plamenatz, and others, who struggle to reconcile the endlessly divergent tendencies of Hegel's speculation.[13] The resulting gain in accuracy is clear, but not much is obtained by way of explanation. How the conflicting implications of his thought were held together by Hegel still remains a puzzle. The root problem of how *he* could see the integration of the revolutionary, liberal, and conservative elements still stands in the way of a comprehensive interpretation of his political thought. For it is only by confronting this critical question that the study of Hegel can be placed on a sure foundation. Such is the object of the present essay. It begins with the hypothesis that the wide disparity of interpretations cannot be entirely blamed on the inadequacy of the interpreters; the cause must be attributed much more to the intentional ambiguity of the original. That is to say, that the ambiguity of Hegel's thought is itself the key to how he was able to "overcome" its opposing elements, and correlatively it is the failure to recognize the essential role of ambiguity that has given rise to so many one-sided or inconclusive interpretations. The argument is that ambiguity is no merely incidental dimension of Hegel's thought, but part of the deliberate strategy he employed in transcending the great oppositions of his own and all future ages. How else could the reconciliation take place? Sublating the differences between nature and spirit, faith and reason, individual and society, man and God, what is and what ought to be, required a radical transfiguration of reality. The tensions of existence could be removed only if reality itself had reached its self-reconciliation. This entails, if one is not God and not in possession of the divine transformative power, then at least the creation of the illusion of transfiguration through the manipulation of symbols that seem to achieve this magical effect. Other commentators who have remarked on this side of Hegel and even gone so far as to accuse him of a certain "dishonesty," of "fraud," or of an intellectual "sleight-of-hand," have not focused exclusively on the technique by which the equivocation is sustained.[14] It strikes me as imperative to first delineate carefully the nature of the ambiguity involved, before undertaking any discussion of the even more difficult questions of Hegel's intentions, what he hoped to accomplish by a linguistic distortion of reality, and so on. Space will unfortunately permit no more than a passing reference to these larger consequences at the close of the essay. For now, our purpose is confined to the more specific task of exposing the central ambiguity, first in his general resolution of the tensions of modernity through the *Phenomenology of Spirit*, then in its elaboration within the more strictly political arena of the *Philosophy of Right*.

I

Hegel's early development has by now received considerable attention. A succession of previously unpublished manuscripts and a wealth of expository analysis have revealed a young Hegel grappling with the very same problems as those of the Young Hegelians a generation later. Unknown to his left-wing followers, he not only shared their starting point—the problem of alienation—but had also explored the same variety of solutions within his early works. Hegel had identified the critical problem of the age as the overcoming of the series of oppositions now unloosed by the upheavals of the Protestant Reformation, the French Revolution, and the commercial-industrial rationalization that was just getting under way. While agreeing in each instance with the new achievement of individual freedom in these "world-historic" advances, he also recognized the abyss of isolation that thereby opened up between the individual and the larger social, political, and cosmic whole of which he is a part. If the Reformation were not to degenerate into the secular "boredom of the world,"[15] or the Revolution to debauch forever into the terror of abstract principle,[16] or the commercial-industrial liberation to give birth only to an impoverished urban rabble,[17] then some means of reconciliation between the abstract demands and the concrete exigencies must be found. He understood the contradictions of modernity at least as well as Marx or Kierkegaard: that an age that exults in individual freedom resorts to the most abject compulsion in its concrete economic and political existence.[18]

The problem, as Hegel recognized, was that enlightened rational critique could never replace the ethical substance of society it had undermined. Feudal custom, political privilege, religious dogmatism—all varieties of "positivity"—might disappear, but unless they were replaced by a new institutionalization of spirit the result would be even more destructive than before. He took as his goal, therefore, the articulation of the effective spiritual substance that would definitively resolve the tensions of man's historical existence. For this new ethico-religious dispensation would constitute the final realization of order within time. Hegel looked forward, as he expressed it in a manuscript of 1803, to the supersession of all oppositions when "spirit can venture to hallow itself as spirit in its own shape, and reestablish the original reconciliation with itself in a new religion, in which the infinite grief and the whole burden of its antithesis is taken up."[19] He wanted not only to become reconciled with reality, but to transfigure it—only later did he recognize these terms as identical.[20] At the same time he did not wish to abandon the newly won freedom of finite subjectivity; his object was to extend and advance freedom by providing it with a theologically and socially substantive foundation. Hegel set out to establish the reciprocal relationship between subjective freedom and the larger political and cosmic whole in which its manifestation takes place. In his struggle to articulate the mutual interdependence of substance and subject Hegel deserves to be regarded as the philosopher of freedom par excellence.

His first suggestion for unification of the individual with the universal process was the idea of a national religion (*Volksreligion*), inspired by the harmonious integration achieved by the Greek civic religions. He knew of course that no direct retrieval or simple reenactment of the Greek experience was any longer possible. If the "Teutons" were to have a "fatherland" it would have to be some form of rejuvenated Christianity, enkindled with the modern primacy of emphasis on individual freedom as the center of reality. The early theological writings show Hegel engaged in just this task of renewing Christianity with a view to its transformation into the religion of "universal reason." Indeed for a while Christianity could appear as the reconciliation of the extremes, since it comprised "no unity of the concept, but a unity of the spirit, divinity. To love God is to feel oneself in the 'all' of life, with no restrictions, in the infinite."[21] Inevitably, however, this union fell far short of the criterion Hegel had set himself: "Absolute freedom of all spirits who bear the intellectual world in themselves, and cannot seek either God or immortality outside themselves."[22] In a unity based on the feeling of love, the freedom of finite consciousness was necessarily submerged in an infinite that it could never fully comprehend. It was no better than that identification, professed by so many of his contemporaries, which Hegel sharply criticized as an attempt "to palm off its Absolute as the night in which, as the saying goes, all cows are black—this is cognition reduced to vacuity."[23] In contrast he maintained that the integration must remain fully transparent to finite experiencing consciousness.

To achieve this goal a crucial change of perspective was required. From a union that occurred through the annihilation of individual self-will in universal Love, Hegel now sought an integration that preserved subjective independence as its essential condition. Shortly after his arrival at Jena (1801) we find him working out the main lines of this conception. He no longer looked at the problem from the side of the individual, but much more from that of the totality of the unfolding world process—what he was already coming to denote by the term "Spirit" (*Geist*). "The individual as such is not the true but only the formal absolute: the truth is the system of ethical life."[24] Man's empirical being is essentially universal, for "it is not his individual aspect which acts but the universal absolute Spirit in him."[25] In this sense "the ethical life of the individual is one pulse beat of the whole system and is itself the whole system."[26]

Gradually Hegel elaborated the implications of this shift of viewpoint that made finite self-consciousness the essential medium through which

absolute Spirit arrives at knowledge of itself. Its most important consequence was that the reconciliation, since it occurs through a rational
apprehension of the necessity for transcending finite existence, preserves the full freedom of self-determination in the subjective pole of
the relation. Politically it implied that the regeneration of society was
not to be realized primarily through institutional transformation. For it
is not man but Spirit itself that accomplishes the transfiguration through
the contemplative self-actualization of the Absolute within history.

The first definitive expression of this new perspective appeared in
Hegel's *Phänomenologie des Geistes* (1807). The celebrated preface
summarizes the essential ideas of the work. "That the True is actual
only as a system, or that Substance is essentially Subject, is expressed
in the representation of the absolute as Spirit, the most sublime Notion
and the one which belongs to the modern age and its religion."[27] The
Phenomenology is the "ladder" Hegel provides finite consciousness to
lead it toward this "most sublime Notion," the recognition of its own
forms of consciousness and of self-consciousness as the indispensable
condition for the self-emergence of Spirit as Spirit. It begins with the
most elementary mode of consciousness in sense-certainty, the subject's certainty of possessing reality in sensation. From there it moves
dialectically through the forms of perception, understanding, desire,
reason, ethical life, and finite morality. At each stage it is the discontinuity between self-consciousness and consciousness, the conviction of
"being all truth,"[28] and the limited object of its knowledge, that promotes consciousness to the next level. The process is concluded only
when the "word of reconciliation" is reached in "the objectively exis-
tent Spirit, which beholds the pure knowledge of itself *qua universal*
essence, in its opposite, in the pure knowledge of itself *qua* absolutely
self-contained and exclusive *individuality*—a reciprocal recognition
which is *absolute* Spirit."[29] At this point the integration has been
reached in principle: the recognition of the necessity for self-transcending individual consciousness as the vehicle for the self-actualization of
universal Spirit.

All that remains is that this formally absolute unity might become
concretely absolute as well, that is, from the side of divine Spirit itself.
This is the final step in Hegel's shift of perspective. The point of Chapter VII of the *Phenomenology* is to demonstrate that this "universal
self-consciousness" is identical with the self-consciousness of God. In
Hegel's own admittedly dense description, Substance is thus finally revealed as Subject.

> Since self-consciousness surrenders itself consciously, it is preserved in
> its alienation and remains the Subject of substance, but since it is likewise
> *self*-alienated it still has the consciousness of the substance; or, since self-
> consciousness through its sacrifice *brings forth* substance as Subject, the
> substance remains self-consciousness's own Self.[30]

It is this insight that constitutes the simple content of revealed religion.
There, in Christ, for the first time "God is revealed as He is." Hegel
exults in the joy that seizes self-consciousness as it recognizes itself as
absolute Spirit, for "only when absolute being is beheld as an immediate self-consciousness is it known as Spirit."[31] The way lies open for
the supersession of the last element of externality in the Christian community's restricted identification of the divine self-consciousness with
the one historic individual, Christ. This must be removed in the recognition of the universal self-consciousness of Spirit so that the merely implicit unity might be realized and the world no longer have to "await
its transfiguration" in a beyond.[32] The process, already begun with the
death of the Mediator, "the death of the abstraction of divine Being
which is not posited as Self," must now be completed in the recognition
of its necessity so that Substance might "become *actual* and simple and
universal Self-consciousness."[33] The meaning of the entire sequence
traversed can at last be revealed as not only the individual's ascent
toward self-contemplation *in* the divine, but also the self-contemplation
of the divine in finite existence.[34]

When Spirit knows itself as actual in his self-consciousness, then
Hegel has reached the form of absolute knowledge—science or wisdom, no longer merely the love of it. It is that particular union of God
and man that has been able to avoid reducing the transcendence of one
or diminishing the freedom of the other. In absolute knowing the process by which consciousness progressively concretizes its object is seen
to be identical with the process of the object's self-concretization
through consciousness. All opposition between subject and object, self
and substance, has now been overcome in the recognition of their mutual necessity for the self-realization of Spirit as Spirit. The circle has
been closed, the end has found itself again in the beginning, once the
"in-itself" has become explicitly so "for-itself." That is, the work of
"actual history" is over now that the development of world-Spirit has
reached "its consummation as self-conscious Spirit."[35] Time itself has
in principle been completed, for Spirit "appears in Time just so long as
it has not *grasped* its pure Notion, i.e. has not annulled Time."[36] This
is the transfiguration achieved—and no longer merely anticipated in the

beyond of existence. Reality has been wholly spiritualized; there is no facet of our consciousness of the world that is not also consciousness of self. It is "the last shape of Spirit—the Spirit which at the same time gives its complete and true content the form of the Self and thereby realizes its Notion as remaining in its Notion in its realization—this is absolute knowing."[37]

The synthesis is indeed so complete that it is virtually impregnable, and we might even be tempted to accept its conclusion—were it not for its clash with our ordinary commonsense understanding of reality. A far-reaching revision of our conceptions of God and man, of reason and history is required to assent to Hegel's construction. It is surely an outrageous claim for human reason that it is capable of comprehending the entire historical course in which it is itself only a part, of thereby bringing history to its transfiguring culmination, and of constituting the essential medium for the self-realization of divine Spirit. The God of this speculation is clearly not the God of orthodox Christianity, who does not need the world in order to be God, and it is questionable whether it corresponds to any coherent conception of the Godhead other than Hegel's own.[38] But the assault on his construction from this standpoint is futile. Hegel can claim to have revealed the "truth" of such traditional notions by disclosing the inner necessity of the divine-human relationship. The thought of God existing apart from the world and our consciousness of him is merely an "abstraction."[39] We cannot concretely think of God except within such relationships and therefore it is obscurantist "picture-thinking" to maintain the transcendent being of God in himself. From a relation that is necessary in the order of knowledge we have been bamboozled into admitting its necessity in the order of reality—and no rational critique is possible from within the Hegelian System itself.

The crucial acknowledgment in the dialectical meditation is that the necessity of finite consciousness for the self-actualization of infinite self-consciousness is not merely a necessity from man's point of view: it is the necessity grasped by universal Spirit itself. When Hegel attains absolute knowledge at the close of the *Phenomenology*, this is no longer his individual self thinking about God. It *is* the self-consciousness of God because the realization constitutes "not only the intuition of the Divine but the Divine's intuition of itself."[40] Universal Spirit has arrived at its self-recognition within Hegel, and his apprehension of the necessity for his finite self-consciousness is simply the vehicle for the self-actualization of the universal self-consciousness of Spirit. This is why Hegel could believe that writing a book could bring history to its fulfillment. The recognition of the mutual necessity of man and God, particular and universal, individual and society was never merely a recognition from man's point of view; it was Spirit's own act of self-recognition and the reconciliation of the world of finite reality with itself. Hegel cannot be accused of divinizing the power of man or of reducing the divine to the level of human spirit. His arguments are perfectly coherent, more coherent in fact than those of any other messianic thinker, from within the terms of his own speculation. The difficulty lies, not with the elaboration of the System, but with the ambiguous presuppositions on which it is based, and it is to the exposure of this underlying ambiguity to which we must now turn. For it is Hegel's ability to win our assent to his starting point before we have fully recognized its implications that is the key to the consistency of his construction, and to the difficulties of interpreters that try to square it with our experience of the real world.

So far as I have been able to isolate them, the principles of ambiguity on which his speculative transfiguration of reality is based can be identified in two assumptions he asks us to make. First, reality is confined to what becomes an object of conscious experience. In order to transform "the object of consciousness into an object of self-consciousness," we must begin from the premise "that nothing is *known* that is not in *experience*, or as it is also expressed, that is not *felt to be true*, not given as an *inwardly revealed* eternal verity, as something sacred that is believed, or whatever other expressions have been used."[41] All that is known, in other words, is reduced to its content within consciousness. Even the known unknown, what is recognized as having an independent reality beyond consciousness, becomes identified with the dynamics of the knowledge of it within consciousness. Only on this basis could Hegel prevent us from insisting on the transcendent reality of God outside of the thought of him, or stifle our objections to his description of Christ's death as "the death of the *abstraction of the divine Being*," or finally dismiss all reservations in his complete identification of the divine Substance with "actual and simple and universal Self-consciousness."[42]

The second principle of ambiguity seeks to exploit the ambiguity created by this absorption of reality into the "medium" of consciousness. It consists of Hegel's rejection of all language depicting God, man, world, and society as separate entities and his insistence on employing the language that underlines their continuity. At the outset of the *Phenomenology*, for example, he declares that "it may be expedient, e.g., to avoid the name 'God' since this word is not immediately also a Notion, but rather the proper name, the fixed point of rest of the underlying Subject."[43] Instead of the language of entities Hegel prefers to use such intermediate terms as substance, subject, object, self, consciousness, becoming, self-consciousness, individual, universal, and so on. Once the parameters have thus been carefully defined in advance, effecting the reconciliation itself becomes a relatively easy operation.[44]

The procedure is illustrated well by the transition from revealed religion to absolute knowledge outlined above. Its critical point is the recognition that the only difference between religion and science is that

> what in religion was *content* or a form for presenting an *other*, is here the Self's own act; the Notion requires the *content* to be the *Self's* own *act*. For this Notion is, as we see, the knowledge of the Self's act within itself as all essentiality and all existence, the knowledge of this subject as substance and of the substance as this knowledge of its act.[45]

It is impossible to separate the exquisite confusion and profusion of meanings of "Self" in this passage. There is the divine Self that knows itself as "all essentiality and all existence"; the divine Self that knows its own essence as self-consciousness; the human self that knows the content of religion, God, to be immanent to its consciousness; and the human self that knows its own essence as self-consciousness. Hegel could maintain that he has not identified man and God, but only asserted that the "the divine nature is the same as the human"[46]—that both their natures are self-consciousness. Yet the result is clearly to endow man with the absolute knowledge that is equivalent to the Being of God. Once we accept the Hegelian *Geist*, the symbol in which all the ambiguity of the System is concentrated, we have no option but to follow the process of its self-externalization until it arrives at complete Self-actualization in the medium of "universal self-consciousness" belonging neither to God nor man—since they each constitute it by transcending their separate selfhoods.[47]

The failure to recognize this deliberate ambiguity at its core accounts for the wide disparity of constructions of Hegel's thought. Each interpretation can claim its own degree of justification, yet all exhibit a basic incompleteness in their refusal to adopt his original equivocal synthesis. Neither of the two fundamental alternatives, secularism or theism, can adequately capture the comprehensiveness of his speculative consummation of reality. They fail on Hegel's own criteria for reconciliation. The secularist reduction of Spirit to the universal human spirit (Kojève, Findlay, Kaufmann et al.) not only flies in the face of Hegel's explicit characterization of God—of his assertion that "He is Spirit,"[48] but is also inherently incapable of overcoming the great diremption of existence between what is and what ought to be. Only a Spirit beyond man can transform man, bringing nature, society, and history to their culmination within time. Equally defective is the theistic exposition (Lauer, Rohrmoser, Theunissen et al.), which falls both in the light of Hegel's repeated assertions that God or eternal Spirit "is no longer beyond the picturing consciousness or beyond the Self,"[49] and his consistent refusal to speak of God as a self-subsistent reality outside of our relationship to him. But most importantly, theism is impossible because a God beyond man's consciousness of him would impose an irreducible limit on man's self-determining freedom; eventually it would involve our surrender to the absolutely Other that we neither control nor comprehend. The ambiguity of his construction is therefore the key to Hegel's ability to reconcile the apparently irreconcilable. Only if we keep this ambiguity in mind can we make sense of his conviction that "the simple consciousness of the infinite is possible without the determinacy of the individual, independent, life."[50]

II

The same dialectical self-identity of finite and infinite Spirit is the principle that lies at the heart of Hegel's political thought. Rejecting the perspective of liberal individualism, which looks on "the will of a single person in his own private self-will"[51] as primary, and which sees the political order as a necessary reciprocal limitation of freedom, Hegel insists on regarding the substantive unity of the State as fundamental and as the positive expression of self-conscious freedom. That is, in place of opposition or tension between individual and society, he envisages perfect harmony. "The state is the actuality of concrete freedom." Through it, as Hegel goes on to explain,

> personal individuality and its particular interests not only achieve their *complete* development and gain explicit recognition for their right (as they do in the sphere of family and civil society) but, for one thing, they also pass over of their own accord into the interest of the universal, and, for another thing, they know and will the universal; they even recognize it as their own substantive Spirit (*Geist*); they take it as their end and aim and are active in its pursuit.[52]

The universal ethical substance of the State would have no existence apart from the individual members who bear it as the essence of their being, nor can the separated individuals find fulfillment outside of their self-transcending unity within the totality of the State. The recognition of their mutual necessity *is* the overcoming of their opposition.

The attainment of this final Idea of the State is, moreover, no mere idealization of a wholly nonexistent harmony. Hegel's intention, as he repeatedly emphasized, was "poles apart from an attempt to construct a state as it ought to be."[53] Rather it represented world-Spirit, which had now realized through his elaboration the form in which it must become actual, as Objective Spirit, in the organization of particular nations. He was the instrument because the historical process had now reached the point where Spirit could become known to itself through an individual who transcends his own finitude. It could not have occurred before the goal of world history had finally "been realized in a universally valid and conscious manner."[54] This makes possible not only the emergence of absolute Spirit in the universal self-consciousness of art, religion, and—above all—philosophy, but also the objective manifestation of Spirit as the ordering principle of the concrete political world. Since Hegel's construction is in this regard a reflection of the self-reconciliation of the moments within Spirit, it follows that his elaboration of the Idea of the State is itself the supersession of all political oppositions. His articulation constitutes in principal "the realm of freedom made actual."[55] The contemplative transfiguration of politics has already begun. As a comprehensive integration, it is the solution to Hegel's vexing problem of reconciling freedom and authority, avoiding the twin pitfalls of France and Germany, the terror of rational abstraction and the anarchy of nonrational particularism.[56] The identity of universality and concreteness is to be found only in the absolutely rational State. For this ultimate State alone is

> the actuality of the substantial will which it possesses in the particular self-consciousness once that consciousness has been raised to consciousness of its universality. This substantial unity is an absolute unmoved end in itself, in which freedom comes into its supreme right. On the other hand this final end has supreme right over against the individual, whose supreme duty is to be a member of the state.[57]

From the side of the individual, the laws and institutions no longer appear as something alien, but as an expression of that rational principle of freedom identical with his own being. From the side of the State, the individual no longer threatens the concrete order in the name of empty moral absolutes, but rather seeks to attain virtue through "simple conformity with the duties of the station to which he belongs."[58] In this perfect coalescence of rights and duties all alienation has disappeared, and "this very other [the State] is immediately not an other in my eyes, and in being conscious of this fact, I am free."[59]

The final self-actualizing State is, in Hegel's lyrical description in the conclusion of the *Philosophy of Right*, equivalent to the lowering of heaven to earth and the raising of the mundane realm to meet it. Its reconciliation is so complete that its separated moments constitute in effect a single "circle of necessity,"[60] invincible against all the partial objections that might be posed against it. For, once adopted, the perspective of the unfolding world-Spirit leads inexorably to the recognition of its self-objectification in the State as rational through and through. All that is missing is that actual states, in recognizing themselves therein, cause their independent powers to abandon their self-subsistence in order that they might "simply abide in their ideality and constitute nothing but a single individual whole."[61] Unfortunately this is the one eventuality that is still lacking. The failure of the anticipated transformation to occur is powerful evidence of the unreality of Hegel's construction, for true reconciliation cannot be achieved by glossing over the tensions of actual political existence within the framework of their ambiguous dialectical identification. Diremptions that had been so definitively transcended within the synthesis continue their unregenerate opposition when viewed from the perspective of reality.

First to fall apart in this sense is Hegel's unification of the ideal and the real, the "is" and the "ought." This most fundamental identity is, as we have seen, based on his conviction that the history of the world "is a rational process, the rational and necessary evolution of world-Spirit."[62] The exploration of the rational, of what ought to be, is "for that very reason the apprehension of the present and actual, not the erection of a beyond, supposed to exist, God knows where."[63] Reconciliation begins with the recognition that the ideal is itself part of the real, and is completed in the recognition of the necessity for its opposition to the merely empirical within the comprehensive world process. That is, the ideal must be denied any reality apart from its specific historical manifestation, so that it can be incorporated as a moment within the dialectical self-unfolding of Spirit. It is only if we are taken in by the first step, which plays on the ambiguity of the "reality" of the ideal (as a real standard or as having real existence within our conception of it), that we can be brought to the conclusion that the ideal has been realized in the encompassing emergence of Spirit as Objective and Absolute.

A more particular instance of this ambiguous reconciliation is Hegel's subsumption of morality into ethical life. Morality, he complains, arises from the perspective of finitude, of relation, and its contradictions can be transcended only by moving to the viewpoint of the infinite, the totality. The finite subject who wills what he ought to do claims to be exercising his freedom in choosing "duty for duty's sake." But the content of his will is something given by external circumstance or impulse, not something chosen; moreover, to be good, the action must be both opposed to self-interest and also in accord with self-interest; finally, the subject himself determines the consequences for which he will assume responsibility, as well as how the meaning of his intention is to be defined. All of these objections, which Hegel makes to Kantian morality, are focused on Kant's assertion of the absolute right of conscience, the right of subjective self-determination in isolation from the larger social and historical whole in which the individual exists. For the claim of conscience to be absolutely sacrosanct and yet wholly subjective removes the distinction between good and evil.[64] We are left, as a consequence, with the "absolute vanity" of the will—with "a goodness, which has no objectivity, but is only sure of itself, and a self-assurance which involves the nullification of the universal."[65] The abstract universal of the good and the abstract self of conscience must both be annulled and henceforth seen as moments within the totality of ethical life, that is, as "a subjective disposition, but one imbued with what is inherently right."[66]

The recognition of their mutual necessity preserves both free subjectivity and universal right within this higher unity. In actual practice this means that the individual's self-determination devolves into willing the objective laws and institutions that make his freedom possible. As Hegel explains, "an immanent and logical 'doctrine of duties' can be nothing except the serial exposition of the relationships which are necessitated by the Idea of freedom and are therefore actual in their entirety, to wit in the state."[67] The ambiguity is so well concealed that it is scarcely noticed that we have passed from a partial identity, well-grounded in experience, to a complete identity utterly without foundation in any source. Certainly, individual freedom can never be fully realized outside of the institutions and customs that make it possible, and clearly the isolated will moralizing in a vacuum can never escape the appearance of formalized subjectivism. But this is a far cry from reducing moral judgment to a particular set of ethical institutions, even to a set that maximizes individual freedom. In willing moral principles we will more than a specific political structure; we intend the eternal scale of values according to which all institutional articulations must be judged. Indeed, as Plato recognized, every concrete political structure will fall short of embodying this absolutely worthwhile end-in-itself. In contrast Hegel's speculation has conflated morality with ethical or customary life by means of the twin devices mentioned above: restricting the morally right to its expression by the autonomous free will, and then transforming it into a moment within the immanent objectification of universal Spirit. Reconciliation is effected through the ambiguity that wholly identifies moral principle with the universal self-consciousness of the modern state, a State no longer containing any institutions not willed by the Self.

We have arrived thus at the ambiguity that covers Hegel's ultimate political reconciliation between the individual and the universal, the subject and the State. The glowing language in which he fancies that "the self-will of the individual has vanished together with his private consciousness, which had claimed independence and opposed itself to the ethical substance,"[68] bears uncomfortable resemblance to the dreams of collectivist salvation soon to be developed by Marx, Comte, and others. Yet Hegel's transformation was of a different order, for it was to be accomplished not by revolution but by equivocation. Man is virtually reduced to being a member of the State because it is only through the State that his humanity is actualized.

> Since the state is Spirit objectified, it is only as one of its members that the individual has objectivity, genuine individuality, and an ethical life. Unification pure and simple is the true content and aim of the individual, and the individual's destiny is the living of a universal life. His further particular satisfaction, activity, and mode of conduct have this substantive and universally valid life as their starting point and their result.[69]

Now there is obviously an unexceptionable sense in which man develops fully only within a political community, but Hegel leaves no doubt that the recognition of mutual necessity between the individual and the State constitutes the transcendence of *all* opposition between them. As such it is credible only if we let their partial interdependence shade into complete integration. For the individual must be wholly identified with his self-articulation through the concrete ethical institutions, and the political structure must be wholly transparent to the self-transcending, finite wills that support it. No residuum of individuality or inner personal depth can exist any longer, for every dimension of the personality has found its expression in the manifest totality of the Idea now emergent within the historical process.[70] Even the sphere of egoistic wants, or the relationship to absolute Spirit, has its place within the fully reconciled State. By reducing all human experiences to moments of the Self, universal right and individual need, man and State, all have been transformed into the self-actualizing unity of Objective Spirit present within time.

The problem with which modern political theorists had grappled since Machiavelli—how to persuade self-interested individuals to identify their interest with that of the State—had now been resolved. Earlier thinkers had never been able to go beyond the articulation of a continuing tension between the individual and society, for while there is a very close congruence between the interests of *all* and the interest of the State, there can often be a very unsurprising lack of commonality between the well-being of a particular member and of the whole. What prevents the emergence of this anarchic, individualistic attitude within Hegel's State? The answer is of course that the individuals no longer look on the public realm as imposing a negative limitation on their freedom but, as exemplified by the universal class, "find their satisfaction in, but only in, the dutiful discharge of their public functions."[71] Such a transformation of human nature cannot be achieved by a traditional liberal appeal to enlightened self-interest. It occurs only when the individual has been subsumed within the unfolding of the universal, in the attainment of a goal that transcends his own finite purpose. That is, Hegel's political reconciliation is dependent on the larger spiritual unification of finite and infinite Being. He makes this evident by emphasizing the identity of principle pervading the State, religion, and philosophy. Describing the coincidence of structure between all three, he concludes: "Self-realizing subjectivity is in this case absolutely identical with substantial universality."[72] Without its theological underpinnings Hegel's Idea of the State would only be another liberal articulation of the tensions of politics, not their final supersession.

The coherence of the reconciliation, in other words, depends on maintaining the perspective of ambiguously complete Spirit. Once we shift to the view from the real political world the problems begin to appear. Thus no matter how convinced we may be of the perfect concordance of freedom and authority, we are bound to feel uneasy when Hegel talks, for example, of the necessity for war as "the power by which the particular independence of individuals, and their absorption in the external existence of possession and in natural life, is convicted of its own nullity."[73] Or, when the subordination of the individual to the unfolding process of world-Spirit is expressed in terms of even more total submission. For the "right of world-Spirit which is absolute without qualification" emerges from the dialectical conflict of history "as that which exercises its right—and its right is the highest of all—over these finite spirits in the 'history of the world which is the world's court of judgment.' "[74] But when he goes even further, in the *Philosophy of History*, to absolve world history from the judgment of morality and to declare that even though "the individual may be treated unjustly, it is a matter of indifference to world history for which the individual serves as the means of its development," no amount of protestation, that the individual finds his fulfillment within the universal process of Spirit, can make the reconciliation convincing.[75]

Moreover, even Hegel's own account in the *Philosophy of Right*, despite the surface of impenetrable consistency, contains two important sections where oppositions are exposed without ever being definitively overcome. The first is the problem that had long concerned him of the inability of civil society to remedy its own characteristic evil, which "consists precisely in an excess of production and in the lack of a proportionate number of consumers who are themselves also producers."[76] Apart from a few references to the desirability of welfare support by the Corporations, the necessity of a directive role by the State, and the possibility of emigration and colonization, nowhere is this problem ever resolved in principle. Equally curious is the undercurrent of unreconciled political oppositions one encounters in Hegel's description of the constitution of the State.[77] It contains many of the trademarks of a conventional "checks and balances" approach—the need for security "against the misuse of power by ministers and their officials," protections against the misguidance of the Estates and of public opinion, the introduction of bicameralism, and several other cautionary measures of a like frame of mind.[78] Such themes strike us as particularly odd within a constitution where each of the powers is "in itself the totality of the constitution" and which together form "a living unity."[79] These themes alert us to the point at which the encompassing reconciliation of Hegel's System encounters the unreconciled reality of our own experience. The threads of ambiguity that Hegel's dialectic had so masterfully knit together begin to part under the strain, and we are left to wonder about what remains of his great flawed project. Does it simply stand exposed as a grandiose exercise of speculative megalomania, as so many of his critics have charged?

This hardly seems a fitting conclusion for the greatest philosophical mind of the modern world. Yet even Hegel's staunchest defenders today cannot avoid an uncomfortable tinge of recognition in the charge. They gladly downplay some of their hero's more blatant outbursts of rhetorical excess. But they cannot wholly ignore, if they are honest, the comprehensive character of the reconciliation he proclaimed. Nor can we ignore the deepening fragmentation of social and historical reality over the past two centuries. Neither Hegel nor the legion of epigones has succeeded in putting an end to history, which persists in its incorrigible inconclusiveness up to our own day. At the same time the manifest failure of his construction should not be made the occasion for the kind of easy dismissal of his thought that has so frequently occurred in the English-speaking world. Such dismissals are all the more disingenuous insofar as they relieve the critics of the burden of struggling with the difficulties of Hegel's work.

The truth is that we cannot avoid grappling with the problems that he was among the first to recognize and preeminent in the line of response he pursued. The tragic utopian project of human self-perfection that has inspired so much of the modern world receives its definitive expression in the Hegelian System. He gave it the highest plausibility that was possible because he understood the impossible nature of the project. Man cannot perfect himself because he has no means of transformation except his present imperfect nature. Only if the order of reality as a whole, including divine reality, is already moving toward such a transfiguration is it possible. The process then ceases to be one in which human action is decisive; rather it is a process of infinite Spirit that is realizing itself within transfigured finite nature. Yet that construction, as we have seen, can be maintained only through the deliberate resort to ambiguity as the means of concealing the discontinuities.

The project of bringing history to its transfiguring fulfillment remains impossible, and in Hegel the impossibility is rendered transparent. At its deepest level his effort lays bare the tragic nature of the modern project. In full awareness of the patent impossibility of the modern aspiration—the aspiration to perfect ourselves, to provide ourselves with the objects of our deepest longings—he deliberately perseveres in the quest for even an ambiguous reconciliation. It is indeed one of the great tragic enterprises of the modern world, doomed to futility from the start. The transfiguring fulfillment of history cannot be attained through the ambiguity of a process that ignores all reality in depth beyond the dynamics of consciousness. Even Hegel's speculative genius does not contain enough of "the magical power (*Zauberkraft*) that converts it into being."[80] What it does contain is the fatality of the transfigurative impulse that can inspire such persistence even in the teeth of its impossibility.[81]

The Hegelian project bespeaks a depth that many of his contemporary admirers seem unwilling to acknowledge, especially those of a liberal persuasion who are only too ready to settle down among the fragments of the Hegelian system. We are naturally inclined to take up the insights and analyses that have survived the weathering of critique. But this would not be true to the deepest insight of Hegel—that truth cannot be obtained in discrete fragments. Only the effort to understand reality as a whole is worthy of the name *philosophy*. That includes the aspiration for transfiguring reconciliation of the tensions of reality, including those between God and man, time and eternity, good and evil, sin and redemption, individual and society. Without probing the depths of their unity we cannot claim to have really sought understanding of our situation. Hegel's philosophical achievement, which ranks him as one of the great synthetic thinkers, of the stature of an Aquinas or an Aristotle, is that he took up for the modern world the challenge of a comprehensive understanding. His deepest insight was that truth could not be partial. It must be understood as a movement that has no stopping point before it reaches an understanding that is adequate to the process of reality as a whole. There are no points at which dogma can be frozen as having been disclosed in privileged moments, without distorting the truth that dogma intends to defend.

"What is living in Hegel" is therefore the effort to follow out the living dynamic of reality, as in his illumination of the concrete interdependence of the individual and the State, of custom and morality, of particular and universal. What is dead is the conceit that the System has succeeded in comprehending the limits of reality, in a final dogma that renders the movement of the philosophic quest itself obsolete. The sleight of ambiguity that made this illegitimate extrapolation possible stands exposed. Yet its underlying principle, Hegel's aspiration toward the whole, remains intact. Philosophy is a movement that aims at truth as a whole, even though reality cannot be included in a System that concludes the quest.[82] If we are to avoid the great paradox of Hegel's philosophic supersession of philosophy, from the love of wisdom to its possession, then we will need more spiritual humility than he was able to muster. But we cannot avoid the conception of philosophy as a movement in search of an understanding of the whole that he recovered so well. The problem of balance is not to be eliminated by walking away from the tension of the love of wisdom, any more than it is to be removed by declaring the tension solved through the achievement of absolute knowledge. Even the more modest character of Fukuyama's liberal apocalypse does not quite escape the suspicion that attaches to all such claims to have reached the definitive structure of history.

Notes

I would like to express my gratitude to the Earhart Foundation for support provided during the period when this essay was in preparation.

1. G. W. F. Hegel, *Grundlinien des Philosophie des Rechts*, ed. Johannes Hoffmeister (Hamburg: Meiner, 1955), p. 14. Translated by T. M. Knox, *Hegel's Philosophy of Right* (Oxford: Oxford University Press, 1952), p. 10. Karl Löwith, *From Hegel to Nietzsche*, trans. David E. Green (New York: Doubleday, 1967), pp. 67–68.

2. An excellent survey of the diversity of interpretations of Hegel's political thought is available in Henning Ottman, *Individuum und Gemeinschaft bei Hegel* (Berlin/New York: De Gruyter, 1977).

3. Georg Lukács, *Der junge Hegel* (Vienna: Europa, 1948). Alexandre Kojève, *Introduction à la lecture de Hegel* (Paris: Gallimard, 1947). Herbert Marcuse, *Reason and Revolution* (New York: Oxford University Press, 1941). Ernst Bloch, *Subjekt-Objekt* (Frankfurt: Suhrkamp, 1962). Theodor Adorno, *Drei Studien zu Hegel* (Frankfurt: Suhrkamp, 1966).

4. Rudolf Haym, *Hegel und seine Zeit* (Hildesheim: Olms, 1962; originally 1857). Ernst Topitsch, *Die Sozial Philosophie Hegels als Heilslehre und Herrschaftsideologie* (Berlin: Luchterhand, 1967). E. F. Carritt, "Reply" and "Final Rejoinder" in Walter Kaufmann, ed., *Hegel's Political Philosophy* (New York: Atherton, 1970). Sidney Hook, *From Hegel to Marx* (Ann Arbor: University of Michigan Press, 1962); see also his "Hegel Rehabilitated?" and "Hegel and His Apologists" in Kaufmann, ed., 1970. Karl Popper, *The Open Society and Its Enemies* (Princeton: Princeton University Press, 1966).

5. Popper, *Open Society*, Vol. II, p. 59.

6. Franz Rosenzweig, *Hegel und der Staat* (Aalen: Scientia, 1962; originally 1920). T. M. Knox, "Hegel and Prussianism" in Kaufmann, ed., *Hegel's Political Philosophy*. Eric Weil, *Hegel et l'état* (Paris: Vrin, 1950). Shlomo Avineri, *Hegel's Theory of the Modern State* (New York: Cambridge University Press, 1972). Walter Kaufmann, "The Hegel Myth and Its Method," in Kaufmann, ed., *Hegel's Political Philosophy*. Z. A. Pelczynski, "Introductory Essay," *Hegel's Political Writings* (Oxford: Oxford University Press, 1964). Joachim Ritter, *Hegel and the French Revolution*, trans. R. Winfield (Cambridge: MIT Press, 1982). Steven B. Smith, *Hegel's Critique of Liberalism* (Chicago: University of Chicago Press, 1989).

7. Pelczynski, "Introductory Essay," p. 136.

8. Ritter, *Hegel and the French Revolution*, p. 62.

9. Ibid., pp. 49–50.

10. Hegel, *Philosophy of Right*, par. 258.

11. Ibid., par. 344. I am substituting "Spirit" here and throughout in preference to Knox's rendering of *Geist* as "mind," since "Spirit" seems to capture better Hegel's sense of *Geist* as a spiritual reality not strictly reducible to its human component.

12. Ernst Cassirer, *The Myth of the State* (New Haven: Yale University Press, 1946), p. 276.

13. Charles Taylor, *Hegel* (New York: Cambridge University Press, 1975), chs. XVI and XVII. Carl Friedrich, "Introduction," *The Philosophy of Hegel* (New York: Random House, 1953). Dante Germino, "Hegel as a Political Theorist," *Journal of Politics* 31 (1969), 885–912. John Plamenatz, *Man and Society*, Vol. II (New York: McGraw-Hill, 1963).

14. Löwith, *Hegel to Nietzsche*, p. 166. Carl Friedrich, "The Power of Negation: Hegels' Dialectic and Totalitarian Ideology," in D. C. Travis, ed., *A Hegel Symposium* (Austin: University of Texas Press, 1962), p. 34. Eric Voegelin, "On Hegel—A Study in Sorcery," *Studium Generale* 24 (1971), 343.

15. Karl Rosenkranz, *Georg Wilhelm Friedrich Hegels Leben* (Darmstadt: Wissenschaftliche Buchgesellschaft, 1963; reprint of 1844 edition), p. 135. Translation in Hegel, *System of Ethical Life and First Philosophy of Spirit*, trans. H. S. Harris (Albany: SUNY Press, 1979), p. 181.

16. Hegel, *Die Phänomenologie des Geistes*, ed. Johannes Hoffmeister (Hamburg: Meiner, 1952), pp. 414–22. Translation in Hegel, *Phenomenology of Spirit*, trans. A. V. Miller (Oxford: Oxford University Press, 1977), pp. 355–66.

17. Hegel, *Gesammelte Werke*, Bd. 6, eds. K. Düsing and H. Kimmerle (Hamburg: Meiner, 1975), pp. 320–24. Translation in *System of Ethical Life*, pp. 246–50.

18. See the masterful study of Hegel's relationship to his successors by Löwith, *From Hegel to Nietzsche*. On Hegel's conception of the problems see his essay on Natural Law, especially his criticisms of Fichte's advocacy of state power as the means of realizing freedom, a suggestion that Hegel rightly foresaw would lead to "the profoundest despotism." *Geammelte Werke*, Bd. 4, eds. H. Büchner and O. Pöggeler (Hamburg: Felix Meiner, 1968), p. 478. Translation in Hegel, *Natural Law,* trans. T. M Knox (Philadelphia: University of Pennsylvania Press, 1975), p. 124.

19. Rosenkranz, *Leben*, p. 141; *System of Ethical Life*, p. 185.

20. "Philosophy, therefore, is not really a means of consolation. It is more than that, for it transfigures reality with all its apparent injustices and reconciles it with the rational; it shows that it is based on the Idea itself and that reason is fulfilled in it." Hegel, *Vorlesungen über die Philosophie der Weltgeschichte*, Bd. I, *Die Vernunft in der Geschichte*, ed. Johannes Hoffmeister (Hamburg: Meiner, 1955), p. 78. Translation in Hegel, *Lectures on the Philosophy of World History, Introduction: Reason in History*, trans. H. B. Nisbet (Cambridge: Cambridge University Press, 1975), p. 67.

21. Hegel, *Theologische Jugendschriften*, ed. H. Nohl (Tübingen: Mohr, 1907), p. 297. Translation by T. M. Knox in Hegel, *Early Theological Writings* (Philadelphia: University of Pennsylvania Press, 1971), p. 247.

22. Hegel, "The 'earliest system-programme of German idealism,' " in H. S. Harris, *Hegel's Development Toward the Sunlight 1770-1801* (Oxford: Clarendon Press, 1972), p. 511.

23. Hegel, *Phänomenologie*, p. 18; *Phenomenology*, p. 9.
24. Hegel, *Schriften zur Politik und Rechtshilosophie*, ed. Georg Lasson (Leipzig: Meiner, 1923), p. 470. Translation in *System of Ethical Life*, p. 151.
25. *Schriften zur Politik*, p. 461; *System of Ethical Life*, p. 143.
26. Hegel, *Gesammelte Werke*, Bd. 4, eds. H. Büchner and O. Pöggeler (Hamburg: Meiner, 1968), p. 468. Translation by T. M. Knox in Hegel, *Natural Law* (Philadelphia: University of Pennsylvania Press, 1975), p. 112.
27. *Phänomenologie*, p. 24; *Phenomenology*, p. 14.
28. *Phänomenologie*, p. 479; *Phenomenology*, p. 415.
29. *Phänomenologie*, p. 471; *Phenomenology*, p. 408.
30. *Phänomenologie*, p. 522; *Phenomenology*, pp. 453–54.
31. *Phänomenologie*, p. 530; *Phenomenology*, p. 461.
32. *Phänomenologie*, p. 548; *Phenomenology*, p. 478.
33. *Phänomenologie*, p. 546; *Phenomenology*, p. 476.
34. *Phänomenologie*, p. 554; *Phenomenology*, p. 483.
35. *Phänomenologie*, p. 559; *Phenomenology*, p. 488.
36. *Phänomenologie*, p. 558; *Phenomenology*, p. 487.
37. *Phänomenologie*, p. 556; *Phenomenology*, p. 485.
38. The conception of God as the *ens manifestativum sui*, the being whose essence is to reveal itself, has its proximate origins in the theosophic mysticism of Jacob Boehme which played a critical role in the development of Hegel's speculation. Boehme, however, never denied the self-subsistent reality of God outside of the relationship with creation. See David Walsh, *The Mysticism of Innerworldly Fulfillment: A Study of Jacob Boehme* (Gainesville: University Presses of Florida, 1983), and *idem*, "The Historical Dialectic of Spirit: Jacob Boehme's Influence on Hegel," in *History and System: Hegel's Philosophy of History*, ed. Robert Perkins (Albany: SUNY Press, 1984), pp. 15–35.
39. *Phänomenologie*, p. 164; *Phenomenology*, p. 131, on the "unhappy consciousness" which is only aware of God as an other: "Where the 'other' is sought, it cannot be found, for it is supposed to be just a beyond, something that can *not* be found." On the same lines in the *Philosophy of Mind*, trans. W. Wallace (Oxford: Clarendon Press, 1971), par. 564, Hegel argues: "God is God only so far as he knows himself: his self-knowledge is, further, a self-consciousness in man and man's knowledge *of* God, which proceeds to man's self-knowledge *in* God."
40. *Phänomenologie*, p. 554; *Phenomenology*, p. 483.
41. *Phänomenologie*, p. 558; *Phenomenology*, p. 487.
42. *Phänomenologie*, p. 546; *Phenomenology*, p. 476.
43. *Phänomenologie*, p. 54; *Phenomenology*, p. 40.
44. Voegelin makes the same point more generally when he characterizes Hegel as constructing a "Second Reality" that would conceal the "First Reality" of experience. Its success depends on two conditions : "(1) The operation in Second Reality had to look as if it were an operation in First Reality. (2) The operation in Second Reality had to escape control and judgment by the criteria of First Reality." "On Hegel," p. 358.

45. *Phänomenologie*, p. 556; *Phenomenology*, p. 485.

46. *Phänomenologie*, p. 529; *Phenomenology*, p. 460.

47. Or as Voegelin puts it: "The 'death of God,' finally, is unintelligible without the 'death of Hegel.' " "On Hegel," p. 348.

48. *Phänomenologie*, p. 530; *Phenomenology*, p. 460.

49. *Phänomenologie*, p. 546; *Phenomenology*, p. 476.

50. Rosenkranz, *Leben*, p. 133; *System of Ethical Life*, p. 178.

51. Hegel, *Philosophie des Rechts; Philosophy of Right*, par. 29.

52. Ibid., par. 260.

53. *Philosophie des Rechts*, pp. 15–16; *Philosophy of Right*, p. 11.

54. Hegel, *Die Vernunft in der Geschichte*, p. 45; *Reason in History*, p. 40.

55. *Philosophie des Rechts*, par. 4.

56. *Schriften zur Politik*, pp. 198–200; *Hegel's Political Writings,* trans. Z. A. Pelczynski (Oxford: Oxford University Press, 1964), pp. 281–83.

57. *Philosophie des Rechts*, par. 258.

58. *Philosophie des Rechts*, par. 150; cf. also par. 147.

59. *Philosophie des Rechts*, par. 268.

60. *Philosophie des Rechts*, par. 145.

61. *Philosophie des Rechts*, par. 272.

62. *Vernunft in der Geschichte*, p. 30; *Reason in History,* p. 29.

63. *Philosophie des Rechts*, p. 14; *Philosophy of Right*, p. 10.

64. *Philosophie des Rechts*, pars. 138–40.

65. Hegel, *Enzyklopädie der philosophischen Wissenschaften*, ed. F. Nicolin and O. Pöggeler (Hamburg: Meiner, 1959); *Philosophy of Mind*, trans. W. Wallace (Oxford: Clarendon Press, 1971), par. 512.

66. *Philosophie des Rechts*, par. 141.

67. *Philosophie des Rechts*, par. 148; see also *Vernunft in der Geschichte*, pp. 93–94.

68. *Philosophie des Rechts*, par. 152.

69. Ibid., par. 258.

70. Hegel's System does not permit any conception of personal immortality. Death accomplishes nothing for, as he explains, "consciousness does not survive the renunciation. Consequently the true sacrifice of being-for-self is solely that in which it surrenders itself as completely as in death, yet in this renunciation no less preserves itself." *Phänomenologie*, p. 362; *Phenomenology*, p. 308.

71. *Philosophie des Rechts*, par. 294.

72. *Enzyklopädie; Philosophy of Mind*, par. 552.

73. *Enzyklopädie; Philosophy of Mind*, par. 546.

74. *Philosophie des Rechts*, pars. 30, 33, 340.

75. *Vernunft in der Geschichte*, pp. 98, 171, 76.

76. *Philosophie des Rechts*, par. 245.

77. Peter J. Steinberger, "Hegel's Occasional Writings: State and Individual," *Review of Politics* 45 (1983), 188–208.

78. *Philosophie des Rechts*, pars. 295, 301, 318, 312.

79. *Philosophie des Rechts*, par. 272.

80. *Phänomenologie*, p. 30; *Phenomenology*, p. 19. See also Tom Darby, *The Feast: Meditations on Politics and Time* (Toronto: University of Toronto Press, 1982), ch. 6, on the magical element in Hegel.

81. For a meditation on the process by which that fatality is broken see David Walsh, *After Ideology: Recovering the Spiritual Foundations of Freedom* (San Francisco: HarperCollins, 1990).

82. Voegelin's often harsh remarks, he insists in his last work, are not to be taken "as a critique of Hegel but, on the contrary, as an attempt to clarify and stress his achievement. His rediscovery of the experiential source of symbolization, as well as his identification of the fundamental problems in the structure of consciousness, is irreversible. What must be reversed is his deformation of the problems identified." *In Search of Order, Order and History*, Vol. V (Baton Rouge: Louisiana State University Press, 1987).

11

Technology, Christianity, and the Universal and Homogeneous State

Tom Darby

In 1806, on the eve of the battle of Jena, Hegel revealed the significance of what he called, in the *Phenomenology of Spirit*, the "outline" of a "New World." Later Hegel went to Berlin and there described the regime fit for such a world. In Paris during the years leading to World War II, Kojève concluded that in order for it to have been possible for Hegel to have revealed the significance of this new world and the political order appropriate to it, history, in principle, had to have been over. Later, when Kojève grew tired of elaborating the implications of Hegel's revelations, he spent some time in Japan and then went on to Brussels where, elaborating the principles of the "New World," he helped to realize the EEC. Most recently, in America, just prior to the fall of the Soviet Union, Fukuyama looked at the world, applied Kojève's conclusions, and said that our world was the one Hegel had described. Fukuyama wrote this in an article which was read, chattered about, criticized, and applauded by academics, pundits, and those who walk the corridors of power. Then Fukuyama's picture even appeared on the cover of the *New York Times Magazine*. And soon after, Fukuyama wrote a book giving a fuller account of his thoughts about Kojève's thoughts about Hegel's thoughts about what Hegel had called the "New World."

Fukuyama's *The End of History and the Last Man,* as a reflection on Kojève's and Hegel's thought, is not unusual, for philosophy has always been a dialogue between those alive and those dead. Philosophy always has been first a description and then an interpretation of that description. But description and interpretation cannot be the same for the live thinker and the dead one, for the interpretation, and hence the description, are rooted both in the experience of the thinker whose thoughts

197

are interpretations and in the interpreter himself. Perhaps this is why Hegel's experience of what he took to be the end of history in 1806 was never understood in its profound concreteness until the next century. Perhaps, after the meaning of the end of history was adumbrated by Nietzsche, it had to rise out of the horrific brutality of twentieth-century experience before it could be clearly and boldly stated by Kojève.

Thus Fukuyama's fascinating book is not unusual because of what one might call its highly derivative character, for reflection on experience—both live and dead—and the subsequent animation of thought through a reflection, and hence interpretation of it, has always been the defining characteristic of philosophy. What is unusual is the amount of attention Fukuyama's book has attracted—attention of people who never have attempted to read a word of Hegel, who previously never even had heard of Kojève, people who—one might guess—would have scoffed at Francis Fukuyama's accretions as altogether mad.

Furthermore, the fact that *The End of History and the Last Man* has attracted so much attention not only makes the book more fascinating, but perhaps tells us much that is not so apparent about the book itself. What is there about this book that so many have found attractive? Oddly enough, the most apparent thing about the book is what one might have taken to be its most esoteric element, the thesis itself—found to be the very title—that history has ended. So what one otherwise may have expected to be the least accessible aspect of the book is indeed the most apparent and most attractive. Why? The answer is to be found in Fukuyama's conclusion that history culminates in liberal democracy as manifest in America or Britain today, and that the democratic liberal regime of this type is the very globe-transforming whirlwind of freedom tantamount to the Universal and Homogeneous State (UHS) so named by Kojève. It is this optimistic conclusion that many have found so attractive.

I will not argue that the democratic liberalism as outlined by Fukuyama is what one ought not to prefer, for I too share the prejudices of those who prefer it and am quite glad to live in that part of the UHS called Canada. But I will argue that the connection between Fukuyama's conclusions and the varied and great number of people who have been attracted to what is found in Fukuyama's book has profound implications. Furthermore, I contend that neither from Hegel nor from Kojève can conclusions such as Fukuyama's be drawn. My own conclusions likcly will be found less optimistic and less attractive. But ironically, these pessimistic and unattractive conclusions may prove more satisfying.

So with the phenomenon of satisfaction we will begin and end. We will do so because by the accounts of Hegel, Kojève, and even Fukuyama—despite their differences—the UHS must be satisfying. In Hegel's account of history and its end there are two kinds of satisfaction: the satisfaction of desire, and the (distinctly human) satisfaction of the desire for recognition. The latter desire is a negation and elevation of the former. The first is animal; the second, human. This is drawn upon, explained, and elaborated by Fukuyama by reference to Plato's tripartite soul, with its appetitive, reasoning, and *thymotic* divisions. The *thymotic* portion pertains to the desire for recognition, and the reasoning part, through its alliance with the *thymotic* and appetitive parts, yields degrees of satisfaction bound by and limited to the nature of the soul. But when radically historicized by Hegel, human and nonhuman nature are transformed into history, and satisfaction—in both forms—is progressively increased. Thus, if history has ended, then the UHS—in all three parts of man's historicized tripartite soul—must be completely satisfying. So, to what extent, if at all, does the UHS meet this requirement? And to what extent, if at all, does the kind of UHS necessary for meeting these requirements resemble democratic liberalism?

Since Fukuyama has made a celebrated endorsement of Kojève's claim that history has ended, and because I have no substantial disagreements with Fukuyama's endorsement, we begin by examining the final conditions which must be satisfied in order for the end of history to be realized. Thus we begin with Hegel's revelation of the significance of Napoleon's historic action, which, in principle, marks the realization of the UHS. Next we will examine what is meant by Hegel's revelation of the significance of Napoleon's actions and the establishment of the principles of the UHS. Last, after having examined the appearance and meaning of the final conditions that must be satisfied for the concrete appearance of the UHS, we will see what the UHS must look like in order to satisfy these conditions.

Wisdom and Power

> The state is the divine idea as it exists on earth.
>
> —Hegel

At the end of history is the final regime, but this state is not the final goal of history, for the goal of history is wisdom. Kojève says that wisdom is achieved by the satisfaction of the conditions of what he calls a "double criterion." He reasons that the one who has wisdom, or absolute knowledge, "must be a citizen of the universal and homogeneous state," because the knowledge he has, in order to be complete, must be circular. He concludes from this that "the wisdom he has can be realized . . . only at the end of history."[1] Thus power, in the form of the State, must bring an end to history, before wisdom, the goal of history, can be reached. The key to what Kojève means is to remember that this man who possesses wisdom, complete knowledge—or what Hegel calls the system of science—is a citizen of this "Universal (i.e., non-expandable) and Homogeneous (i.e., nontransformable) State," for this state is the "basis for the circularity of the system."[2] Now the meaning of the "double criterion" and the conditions that must be satisfied emerge clearly: (1) the current state of this actually must correspond to what for Hegel is the Perfect State and the end of History, and (2) Hegel's knowledge must be truly circular.[3]

Kojève's "double criterion" contains two kinds of truth, preceded by another kind of truth that serves a condition for the "double criterion." The preceding truth pertains to the end of history. I refer to truth that is *developmental* or *progressive*. It is teleological or consequential in that each developing moment is seen to be true only in *relation* to its completion. But the first kind of truth of the "double criterion" is a derivation of *corresponding truth* in that it consists of an identity of life and knowledge, fact and belief, desire and satisfaction. It is descriptive, hence *realized* or empirical. The second kind of truth of the "double criterion" is just as Kojève says it is: deductive, circular, and taking the form of the syllogism. It is *revealed*.

It would appear that these two types of truths are altogether incomparable, yet this is what the double criterion requires for history to have culminated in the UHS. But Kojève says that what is important about the end of history is whether the double criterion is possible "in principle." However, because a possibility can be neither proved nor disproved (can be neither true nor false), the State exists as an "ideal." And ideals can be transformed into action through which those "facts" about the world that do not correspond to the ideal can be negated—that is, transformed or eradicated. Here is the connection between wisdom and power, knowledge and action, and the relation between these two opposite pairs and these two kinds of seemingly incompatible truths.

These connections are further illuminated by focusing on the relation between Hegel and Napoleon. Kojève reminds us that the historical facts contained in Hegel's *Phenomenology* are important for an understanding of that book, and that the existence of Napoleon is one of those historical facts. But without a context Napoleon's empirical or historical or factual existence would be insignificant, and it is the *Phenomenology* that provides such a context, thereby revealing the meaning or essence of Napoleon's existence to us. But before Hegel's book could have been written, and before the essence of Napoleon's existence could have been revealed to us, this fact, among others, must exist. From this it must be concluded that just as it is necessary for Napoleon, the realizer, to have preceded Hegel, the revealer of Napoleon's significance, action precedes knowledge. But Napoleon merely acts and Hegel merely thinks. Without Hegel the significance of Napoleon's action would not have been revealed, and without Napoleon's factual, empirical, or historical realization Hegel's book would be but a story—a fiction at best and at worst a perverse desire, an ideology. Kojève calls this link between action and knowledge the "dyad" of Napoleon-Hegel. It is this dyad that constitutes the completely satisfied, that is, completely self-conscious and therefore wise and perfect man. But as Kojève notes, Napoleon is unable to reveal this, for it is Hegel's role to do so. Thus, Kojève concludes, "Hegel is somehow Napoleon's self-consciousness."[4]

What does this mean? How can one man be the self-consciousness of another? Hegel is now dead, and when one is dead one is neither conscious nor self-conscious, but Hegel's thoughts about the fact of Napoleon's existence are preserved in Hegel's book. Hegel's book not only contains the answer to this question but connects this *relation* of Napoleon and Hegel to the end of history and the advent of the Universal and Homogeneous State. But just as the essence of Napoleon is linked to the revelation of Hegel and the revelation is linked to the existence of Napoleon, the State (or power) and the advent of wisdom (or the system of science) are also linked. And this link is a circular one. It is circular first because it is not relative and second, because it is not relative, it is complete. Action results in the process called history, which results in the UHS and wisdom. The UHS is, in principle, complete power, that is, uncontested power. And wisdom is complete, nonrelative truth or absolute truth.

The link between the two moments in the dyad also is circular because both Hegel and Napoleon were men and the *Phenomenology* is also about the essence of man. And just as Hegel's revelation is linked to Napoleon's realization and ultimately the end of his actions, the *Phenomenology* is a revelation of the essence of man revealed by a dead man known as Hegel.

If wisdom has appeared in the form of Hegel's book, then so have the Universal and Homogeneous State and the completely satisfied and perfect man. For this to be so, wisdom would have to be a complete account of the essence of the existence of man. Kojève's explanation is that Hegel radically denies transcendence of the finite. He says that man is time, time is history, and that time *as* history, and therefore *as* man, is eternal only in the form of the thoughts of a dead man called Hegel elevated to and preserved in a book called the *Phenomenology*. But if the book is eternal and complete, man's infinitude is a revelation that man's essence culminates in his own realization of his own finitude. This is to speak circular truth, circular because it is related only to itself. But because this truth can be spoken, it is spoken in time, as Hegel spoke it in 1806. However, circular, complete truth revealed through speech is an eternal truth: the word of God. Yet this God is both finite (dead) and infinite (eternal). He is the God incarnate in the existence of the dyad Napoleon-Hegel who reveals himself as conscious of himself in the form of Hegel's book containing the System of Science.

Yet we must note that this dyad of Napoleon-Hegel and, by extension, man-God, would mark the completed goal of history, the advent of the UHS and wisdom, were it not for one unsatisfied condition. It is this fact: a dyad is a dualism, and in order for the UHS to appear, for history to end and wisdom to be realized, disparate moments of the dualism will have to become synthesized. In other words, the two moments in the dyad will have to be transformed into a monad. Without this transformation, action and knowledge remain only partial or relative.

Put another way, Hegel realizes the significance of Napoleon's actions but does nothing, and Napoleon acts but does not know the significance of what he does. But to do something, while it entails consciousness, is not necessarily self-conscious doing, for in order for this "doing" to constitute self-consciousness, it must be related back to the doer through reflection. In self-reflection the facts about the world are not transformed, yet the consciousness of the one who does the reflecting is transformed. It is this consciousness-reflecting-itself-into-itself that is transformed into self-consciousness. This is why Kojève has said that "somehow Hegel is Napoleon's self-consciousness."

If the Napoleon-Hegel dyad is but the man-God dyad writ small, corresponding conclusions must be drawn. Man, by negating the given—by negating nature qua nature and the nature of his own soul—progressively frees himself from nature. In doing so man comes to realize himself as a mortal (historical) being. His realization is a condition of his freedom, for until he recognizes himself as mortal he does not free himself from the infinity of the given. To be human is to oppose the given, to be free. And in the end it is to accept death as the condition of humanity. This realization can only come with man's willingness to risk his life in the final fight for recognition, the historical form of which is the French revolution—a complete turn, a new beginning, a new world. "In the beginning was the word and the word became flesh."

Kojève has even gone so far as to identify Napoleon as the epitome of this incarnation of the word. He calls Napoleon the "*Logos* become flesh." This is said because Napoleon exemplifies the man who embodies the ideals of the French Revolution, and takes the final risk of life on behalf of these principles. This final action is a sacrifice of life so that individual men can be recognized universally, not by some transcendent God but by *other men*. It is through Napoleon, the embodiment of man-as-death, that man finds life. But man's life, life through death, is not life in some beyond. It is life on earth—life in the Universal and Homogeneous State.

But to repeat what was noted above, in order for this to have happened, this dyad must have been transformed into a monad. Although Kojève is not explicit in his description of just how the metastasis of Napoleon-Hegel occurs, what he says about this transformation allows one to draw a revealing conclusion.

> Napoleon is turned toward the external world (social and natural): he understands it because he acts successfully. But he does not understand himself (he does not know that he is God). Hegel is turned toward Napoleon but Napoleon is a Man, he is perfect man by his total integration of history: to understand this is to understand man, to be understood oneself. By understanding (= justifying) Napoleon, Hegel achieves, therefore, his consciousness of *self*. Thus he became a Sage, a complete philosopher. If Napoleon is revealed God (*Der arscheinede Gott*), it is Hegel who reveals him. Absolute Spirit . . . that is of the real (natural) world implies the Universal and Homogeneous State, realized by Napoleon and revealed by Hegel.[5]

Hegel has recognized Napoleon, but the problem is that Napoleon has not recognized Hegel. Thus the dyad remains a dyad rather than transforming into a monad. For the metastasis to be complete, Napoleon—who represents complete power or the UHS—would have to recognize Hegel—who represents complete knowledge or wisdom.

But an implication does not the *truth* make, certainly not the truth that is nonrelative or circular. For the *truth* to appear, the principles of

Hegel's System of Science (wisdom) must be recognized, or accepted as wisdom by the power of the UHS.

Eternity, Time, and the System of Science

> Man indeed does not desire another nature, but only the perfection of his own.
>
> —Nicholas of Cusa

Kojève tells us that Hegel's "Science is the eternity which reveals itself to itself."[6] But men do not exist in eternity, unless, of course they are in heaven. However, if they were in heaven, they would be angels perhaps, but they would not be men. Men have bodies; bodies have selves, and bodies and selves exist in time. So how can one say that this self-consciousness derived from the metastasis of the two men—Napoleon and Hegel—exists in eternity? The enigmatic Kojève has an answer.

> The result of the action (realization) of the Wise-man is . . . perfect. It does not change and it cannot be gone beyond or exceeded: briefly, it has no future properly so called. Consequently, this action is not an historical event properly speaking, it is not a true moment in time. And to say so is to say that it is no longer a human reality. Once again, the empirical existence of science in the world is not man but *Book* (the *Phenomenology of Spirit*). . . . The *Book* endures itself; it deteriorates, it is reprinted, etc. But the tenth edition in no way differs from the first edition: one can modify nothing in it, one can add nothing to it. All the while the *Book* remains identical to itself.[7]

If the metastasis of the dyad Napoleon-Hegel does not occur in the world of selves and bodies, where then does it occur? Hegel himself provides this answer: "Spirit, which, when thus developed, knows itself to be Spirit, is science. Science is its realization, and the kingdom it sets up for itself in its own native element." In whatever this "native element" may be, we may be sure that this is where the metastasis occurs. Hegel is emphatic. "A self having knowledge purely of itself in the absolute antithesis of itself, this pure ether as such, is the very soil where science flourishes, is knowledge in the universal form."[8]

Where is this "native element" that Hegel identifies as "the pure ether as such?" Is Hegel referring to *aither*, that substance thought by the ancients to occupy the space beyond the moon, the space occupied by the stars? Does "knowledge in the universal form" exist in some heaven, in some beyond?

In order to answer this question yet another riddle must be solved. If the metastasis takes place in the *Book*, and the *Book* is in "eternity," and if, as Kojève claims, this solves the mystery of the metastasis of the physical bodies and selves of Napoleon and Hegel, then to whom does this self-consciousness belong? It can belong to neither Napoleon nor Hegel, for both are dead. And Kojève never tires of telling us that Hegel meant that when you are dead, you are dead, so to speak. So Napoleon, and man in general, in the final act of risking his life, gives up his dream of eternal life—life in a beyond. But the *Book* has eternal life. Thus the self-consciousness belongs to no one but does belong to the "System of Science" that exists eternally in the ether. So the ether is not that upper region of space imagined by the ancients, nor is it some heaven believed to exist by Christians. It is that hypothetical substance supposed by eighteenth- and nineteenth-century natural science to occupy *all* nature or space. Thus this ether is universal and homogeneous, it is that "kingdom that [Spirit] set up for itself in its own native element." But Spirit is time and time is man, thus this kingdom is the UHS manifest through the elaboration of the principles of the system on earth.

Kojève has told us that if the system can be proved to be circular, then it is in *principle* true. But principles—abstract ideas—are like that self-consciousness of Napoleon-Hegel. They do not exist in time. But when Hegelian science is *recognized*, that is, conceptualized, grasped, accepted by the actual empirical world, the principles of the System of Science, which previously belonged to no one, will belong to everyone. Principles when recognized cease to exist in a timeless beyond. They cease to be mere abstract ideas because they are seen as relative to temporal reality and are transformed into ideals or values. And while principles can be proved neither true nor false, ideals or values are true to the extent they can transform temporal, empirical existence in conformity with the *principles* of the *system of science*. "Time is the Concept." And when time is grasped conceptually, the "facts" of social and political life can be transformed into the new world: the universal community of Hegelian science—the UHS.

Kojève contends that Hegel is the man who reveals Napoleon as the realized God (*der erscheinende Gott*). In other words, Hegel reveals (justifies) Napoleon through explaining that the essence of Napoleon's action (freedom) redeems the suffering of man. But if this is established only in *principle*—or established in the ether of the system—then who is Hegel? The answer would have to be that Hegel (God the Father) reveals the essence of the empirical existence of Napoleon (God the Son). But Hegel too is dead and, since the System of Science is eternal because its Spirit will live forever in the *Book*, the *recognition* of the System is tantamount to the establishment of the spiritual community— the UHS (the mystical body of Christ-Napoleon). At the same time, the dead dyad Napoleon-Hegel is ''resurrected'' and is united in the System of Science (the Holy Spirit) located in the eternal ether. But the ether, as we have noted, is not the space beyond the earth as envisaged by the ancients; rather, it is that hypothetical substance which was thought to occupy *all* of nature (space). Thus the eternal System is not just of the earth; since it is located in the ether and the ether is everywhere, the System is the Spirit that joins earth and heaven.

The New World of the UHS

> He [Hegel] did not know the extent to which he was right.
>
> —Georges Bataille

It was first noted by Feuerbach and then by Marx that Hegel's God was but a projection of what man valued as his best assets. Since God is but a *projection* of man, investing in man yields both credit for the present and dividends for the future. But Kojève showed us that even if Hegel had not realized it, the implications of Hegel's thought make Feuerbach appear as if he was merely trying to take credit for what Hegel already had said, and they make Marx look like someone who took the tip from a crooked broker. So much for Feuerbachian naturalism, or as we used to say, international socialism. Let us return to Hegel and then, regrettably, to other vulgarities.

Feuerbach and Marx notwithstanding, Hegel tells us in the preface to his *Phenomenology* of just what his project consists.

> The systematic development of truth in scientific form can alone be the true shape in which truth exists. To help bring philosophy nearer to the form of science—that goal where it can lay aside the *love* of knowledge and be actual *knowledge*—that is what I have set before me.[9]

What we have come to call philosophy since the time of Plato's Socrates is love of knowledge, and this love of knowledge arises out of our ignorance. We desire knowledge because we are not wise. And were we wise, had we complete knowledge, or knowledge of the whole, or systematic knowledge, we too would be complete and therefore would desire nothing. In Plato's *Apology*, Socrates is charged with being a "Wise-man" who "delves into things above and below the earth." Reluctantly Socrates finally admits that indeed he is wise "but in a limited sense" (*Apology of Socrates*, 20d–e). Socrates calls this *limited* wisdom "human wisdom" and goes on to say that human wisdom is conditioned by our awareness of our ignorance.

Because he is a man, Socrates, like other men, is *limited* in both body and mind. Because he has a body Socrates is positioned in space and time and encounters the cosmos or the whole and his place within it from where he stands during his mortal life. This is not to say that Socrates' knowledge is merely a reflection of his standpoint in space and time. Philosophy is a speech about man as a creature who can know, yet whose knowledge transcends—albeit in a limited way—the standpoint of particular men bound by birth and death—space and time. Thus, as seen in Book VII of the *Republic*, man, when ascending from the cave into the light, cannot look directly into the sun, and after his sojourn above, must return to the cave—his home of opinion, shadows, and images.

Hegel's task, as stated above, is to do away with the limits of merely knowing; it is to possess wisdom or science. But to do so is tantamount to arriving at a standpoint that is bound neither by space nor by time. Hegel does not do this, as do Plato and other philosophers, by transcending the bounds of space and time within the limits of their humanity. In fact, as Kojève says, Hegel does nothing; he merely describes and deduces the meaning of what he "sees." And what he sees and the meaning he deduces is a humanly created absolute. The humanly created absolute is the whole, the world projected as a system: a universe. The whole is the System of Science and it is not only Hegel's "task" to attain it, but man's project as well, for this whole is a system related everywhere and for all time to man. It is the UHS projected in the image of man.

But how is it possible for Hegel, who is a man, to have this view of the whole? In order to have such a view, Hegel's perspective would have to be from everywhere at once and for all time. His perspective would have to be *without standpoint*. He would have to be God. But Hegel's standpoint is from "the ether of the concept" and since the concept is time and man "has time in him," man, like the ether, the concept, and time, is seen by man to be at all places at all times.

So here we come full circle, back to those historical footnotes to

Hegel—to Feuerbach and Marx. Although they criticized Hegel for not saying what he actually said, in a curious way they were correct. They were correct in seeing that for the System of Science to be true, it has to be created by men. But until the twentieth century no one except ideologues of various stripes took Hegel's profound atheism seriously. It is this atheism that is the centerpiece of Kojève's Hegel.[10]

Kojève, in an article published in a collection honoring Alexandre Koyré, makes the connection between Hegel's atheism and modern science. Here he sharply distinguishes between "pagan" science and modern science, and not only identifies the latter as "Christian" but tells us that modern science derives specifically from the nonpagan, altogether Christian notion of the Incarnation.[11]

> What, in fact, is the Incarnation, if not the possibility for eternal God to be actually present in the temporal world where we, ourselves, live, without, at the same time, descending from his position of absolute perfection? But if this presence in the sensible world does not detract from his perfection, it is because the world itself is (or will be) perfect. At least to a certain extent (an extent furthermore that can be measured with precision).[12]

Kojève then goes on to say that modern science is a "projection." And it was "into the heavens" that modern man "projected the body of the resuscitated Christ followed by the entire earthly world where he was born and died." With this projection modern science was born four centuries ago. It was, says Kojève, "equivalent to inviting the scientists to apply themselves without delay to the gigantic task of elaborating mathematical physics."[13]

I am asserting that the link is none other than the curious metastasis of the dyad Napoleon-Hegel, realizer and revealer, between power and wisdom, life and death, eternity and time. It is the link which allows us to see how the double criterion for the end of history and the appearance the UHS is satisfied. This metastasis is Hegel's "link in the chain," his "magic word" (*Zauberwort*).[14] This link—the metastasis, the "magic word"—is modern science or technology.

* * *

Prior to the modern world there were techniques, but there was no technology. The word technology is comprised by coupling the words *techné* (art) and *logos* (reason). This coupling of *techné* with *logos* makes explicit the *gathering together* and the *relating* of techniques in a reasoned or purposeful way. Hence our English word technology, in coupling *making* and *knowing*, speaks of a production that is purposive and rational and therefore the best available means to some specified end. This rational characteristic involves *some* knowledge of the relation between the *means* and *ends*, between *realizing* and *revealing*. Briefly, let us contrast technology to *mere* production in order that we might see that while related, it is distinct from it.

Mere production is like reproduction in that it is tied to the biological cycle of nature. But the cycle of nature is broken when the *relation* of the *difference* between desire and satisfaction is conceptualized. Conceptualization entails *reflection*, hence *relating* a *present* desire to a *past* satisfaction, thus *memory*; and at the same time, a *self-conscious projection* of the desire into the *future*. With this conceptualizing—with this relating, remembering and projection—mere production is transformed into the ''logic'' of *use*. Mere production becomes useful or purposeful. This purpose-able or linear ''logic'' of use is the basis of *technique* in that technique is bound to specific means and ends arising out of the conceptualization of the relations of desire and satisfaction.

When, in the early modern period, we first brought together or related or generalized an ensemble of techniques, *technology* appeared. With technology the ''logic'' of use is transformed into the ''logic'' of *efficiency*. Thus the ''logic'' of efficiency is the ''logic'' of technology. Efficiency is a *ratio* between means and ends, between the *realizer* and the *revealed*, and the measure of efficiency is the calculated *difference* between them. Thus the smaller the ratio the greater the identity, and the greater the efficiency in any given space at any given moment in time. Technology is like technique in that it is reflective, but it is like mere production in that its ''logic'' is *internal* to it. And because it refers only to itself, it is self-governing. Thus technology determines its own ends, alters its own limits, and in this sense, is *autonomous*. All technologies are self-adjusting *systems*—mechanical, electronic, economic, social, political—that generate their own laws through their reflections on their own *internal* relations. This internal, self-referring, self-generating, and self-adjusting aspect of technology we call *process*. And *externally*, process is manifest as *development*. This is why technology is called progressive and is cybernetic.

The essence of technology lies in its progressive revelation to man that both the nonhuman and human world consist of quantifiable, calculable, manipulatable *stuff*, the primary value of which can only be understood or appreciated in relation to an increase of human power. Everything increasingly becomes caught up in technology's circular, ''self''-referring process, losing its objectivity and dissolving into malleable raw material to be shaped by man's will, made to satisfy his desires and longings. So just as it was once said that "God is everywhere," today man looks across the planet and into the stars and sees *himself* everywhere.

Action, which, until the end of history, engendered the historical process, has now been revealed by Hegel and realized by those today who value the principles of the System of Science. The realization is tantamount to the universal transformation of both nature and human nature into human usefulness. Nature and man have both become "a technical problem," the solution of which is the proof of man's and nature's use. The logic is circular. Technology thus combines the linear and thereby *discontinuous truth as development* or correspondence, and the circular, that is *continuous, truth as proof*, the two aspects of Kojève's double criterion, into a *logic of efficiency*. This "logic" is the logic of identity and difference, the logic that renders the unequal equal. Heidegger has described it as follows:

> Projection and rigor, methodology and ongoing activity, mutually requiring one another, constitute the essence of modern science, transforming science into research.[15]

In that the UHS is the embodiment of the System of Science on earth and in the heavens, and the system of science is the Holy Spirit, the UHS also is the incarnation of God's desire. "God is love." But man is God. He is a god whose longings are in principle satisfied through the increasingly efficient elaboration of technology.

Kojève speaks of "the 'gift' of the Holy Spirit." This is the way most people today view technology, as a "gift" of natural science, in that for most people technology is seen as applied natural science. Most are grateful for what is taken as a "gift" and do not question the authority of the perceived bestower of the gift. And this is why for most people today science is holy, as is its spirit, technology, which most people today regard with a combination of fear and wonder. But in the revealing there is a concealing. Technology is *not* applied science. Actually, it is just the other way around: from the earth to the heavens, just as Kojève has said. Thus it is through the realization of technology— through research—that modern science is revealed. Technology is not "value free," and the goodness or evil of it does not depend on the goodness or evil to which some human might apply it. It depends on and is measured by the degree to which it satisfies desire and is, therefore, efficient.

Conclusion

According to Hegel, Kojève, and Fukuyama, the UHS is the perfect regime. Hegel's regime appears in outline when he sees Napoleon under his window astride a white horse. Kojève's regime, mediated by the cataclysmic twentieth century and the thoughts of Marx, Nietzsche, and Heidegger, proved true to him in Paris, and perhaps was confirmed later as he sipped a fine Bordeaux and puffed on a Havana cigar in the Tokyo Hilton. Kojève elaborated the principles of this regime in Brussels, and today it appears to be with us in the form of the EU, NAFTA and GATT, CNN, the IMF, and however many acronyms letters of the English alphabet will yield.[16] While there is something both radical and disturbing in Kojève's and even Hegel's vision of the perfect regime, some have taken comfort in Fukuyama's optimistic vision. And one can understand why one may have drawn such a conclusion and certainly why so many have found this comforting conclusion attractive. Those were heady days. Communism was on the wane and finally collapsed. In the West, people spoke of the "peace dividend" and in the lands of former enemies there was a swelling tide of enthusiasm for liberty and democracy. Yes, it appeared that we had won. Fukuyama even provides us with the score card in the form of graphs to illustrate the extent of our victory. Today the notion of the end of history has become a popular myth, an amusement. And Tocqueville long ago noted how seriously Americans take their amusements.[17]

Although these happy events took place only a few years ago, much has changed, but it is not necessary to list facts, for data is both treacherous and malleable *stuff*. But fundamentally, is our victory based on some "ontologically" superior difference? Did we "win" because our values are superior? Perhaps we were "victorious" because what we now call democratic liberalism has proved to be more efficient than the technological tyranny—the totalitarianism—that ruled Russia for three-quarters of this century. Perhaps "ontologically" we liberal democrats and those now dead communists were the same. Perhaps, as the ironic Kojève says, we are but rich Russians and they poor Americans.[18]

I must repeat that I will not quibble with Fukuyama's preference for a regime as described in the initial pages of his book: a regime based on the principles of the rule of law, rights, and liberty. I too prefer this and cannot imagine, much less offer a theoretical defense of, any order that I would consider more desirable given our circumstances at the close of this century.

But without technology the realization of democratic liberalism—and other less desirable forms of rule—is but a fantasy. And our failure to recognize this poses a danger to what today is likely our *best possible* regime. Yet, as far as I can see, Fukuyama's description of the democratic liberal regime and what appears to me to be the UHS do not fit. Fukuyama does not deny the technological character of this "perfect" regime, but he does view technology as both *applied natural science* and, thereby, neutral or value free.[19] This is perhaps a result of what I would call his preoccupation with what he takes to be the *fixed nature* of the soul, with its appetitive, reasoning, and spirited divisions. While Fukuyama nowhere denies change in our human lot, nor that we transform nature and that spirit-as-history is the result, he does seem to think that at the end of the long battle of history somehow the soul remains intact. Now we must return to Hegel.

Hegel's "perfect" regime is described only after history is "in principle" ended. His *Philosophy of Right* attests to a form of order that one might call the best liberal constitutional monarchy that could have been realized in Hegel's time. Herein a civil society mediates between the private and public realms and is the theater for the satisfaction of the varied desires of the Estates (classes) within the political unit. Although it differs from the regime described by other "contractarian" thinkers, such as Locke and Kant, without a social sphere in this regime there would be no apparatus to stand between the State and the private sphere, and no apparatus in which the complex diversity of desires could be adjudicated and administered. But it is one thing to balance the desires and longings of a people of a nation-state the political culture of which is shaped *by* and *in* history. It is quite another to sort out and satisfy the desires and longings of a population as diverse as the globe itself. And this, of course, is where the universalizing and homogenizing aspect of our technology comes in.

While technology is the common denominator of the population of the planet, it is also that which divides us most. It is the negative freedom of our reified and ever increasing animal desires, which binds us as reanimalized man. It is also our positive freedom translated into our longing, which allows us to rise to what we think we ought to be, thereby giving us the satisfaction of self-esteem. But it also is our *thymotic* part of the soul that rips us apart—"japanizing" us, as it were, into ever-fragmented groups, translated not only into bungy jumpers and skydivers but also into our now "postmodern" nationalists and practitioners of so-called "identity politics." I refer here to our new politicized fundamentalists and their "politics of private desire" based on race, sex, sexual preference, or whatever titilation one chooses. As

Hegel said, the frivolous love the New World, while others are bored with it.[20]

But worse, because our ideals, which constitute the satisfaction of our greatest longings, have become relativized into values that cannot be sustained by the exhausted historical culture upon which depend our democratic liberalism and other political communities, that which we hold most dear and that to which we aspire becomes no longer sustainable. For some postmoderns there is no author, hence authority, to any book; no essential truth, therefore no philosophy; no fixity to politics, and so right becomes naked power; law is translated into a mere instrument of power, which blazes the path to the satisfaction of desires the worth of which is relative. For these "japanized" *active* or *self-conscious* nihilists, there is no fixity to the past. And history, to the extent that it is willed even to have existed, is whatever the "historian" desires it to be. While this self-conscious nihilist called "japanized man" is just as much a citizen of the UHS as his reanimalized counterpart, he is a greater danger to democratic liberalism in particular and to civic culture in general. Reanimalized man merely blinks, chews his cud, and marvels as he takes his local mall for the whole of the UHS, while the self-conscious nihilist smugly congratulates himself as he plots to blow the place up, reveling, as he does so, in the absurdity of our times. The former are but the soul-less bodies who happily dwelt in Plato's cave, but the latter are the unhappy souls without bodies let loose from Homer's Hades.

It is a fact that many everywhere today profess to being liberal democrats without taking into consideration that democratic liberalism cannot be understood apart from late Christianity and modern science. Surely it is no accident that the once devout now vote and that the liberal democratic experiment resembles the experimental method, and this leaves one with the suspicion that this before which so many on the planet genuflect is but a *magic word*, the meaning of which can be whatever one desires it to mean. But because the UHS is technological, desire, in order to be sustainable, must be *efficient*. Efficient desire is just desire. Thus efficiency is the form justice takes in the UHS.

We humans who, by definition, are uncompleteable creatures will always resist the closure of total discourse or the complete charm of the "magic word." Thus we are left with an old question. How ought one live in the UHS? Ought we to accept efficiency as our fate and delight in the variety of this Disneyworld of virtual reality? Or ought we to be fired by resentment and take revenge on the UHS and go for its technological jugular vein? To do the first is to be an unselfconscious last man, while to do the second is to be a selfconscious nihilist. But there is a third way. We can question our fate. For man is not, as Fukuyama says, a "problem;" rather, he is a question. The question is not "what" we are but "who" we are.[21] And this, as long as we are men, remains the question.

Notes

1. Alexandre Kojève, *Introduction to the Reading of Hegel*, ed. A. Bloom, trans. J. H. Nichols (Ithaca: Cornell University Press, 1968), p. 95.
2. *Introduction to the Reading of Hegel*, p. 95.
3. *Introduction to the Reading of Hegel*, p. 95.
4. *Introduction to the Reading of Hegel*, p. 70.
5. A. Kojève, *Introduction à la lecture de Hegel* (Paris: Gallimard, 1947), p. 153.
6. *Introduction à la lecture de Hegel*, pp. 574–75.
7. *Introduction à la lecture de Hegel*, p. 385.
8. G. W. F. Hegel, *The Phenomenology of Mind*, trans. J. B. Baillie (New York: Harper and Row, 1967), p. 86.
9. *The Phenomenology of Mind*, trans. J. B. Baillie, p. 70.
10. Tom Darby, *The Feast: Meditations in Politics and Time* (Toronto: University of Toronto Press, 2nd ed., 1990), pp. 107–14. I am indebted to the insights afforded me by Hugh Gillis in his manuscript in progress, "Kojève's Atheism."
11. Alexandre Kojève, "L'Origine Chrétienne de la Science Moderne," in *Mélanges Alexandre Koyré*, Vol. II (Paris: 1964), p. 303. Also see Alexandre Koyré, *From Closed World to the Infinite Universe* (Baltimore: Johns Hopkins University Press, 1957). Koyré makes a similar point but in quite a different context. See especially his section on Nicholas of Cusa, who, Koyré says, denies the imperfect position of the earth in respect to the heavens (pp. 19–23).
12. Ibid.
13. Ibid., pp. 303–304. Also see Kojève, "Hegel, Marx et Christianisme," in *Critique* No. 3–4 (Paris, 1946), pp. 365–66. ". . . The Hegelian philosophy is not a truth in the proper sense of the term: it is less the discursive revelation adequate to reality than an idea about an ideal, that is to say a 'project' which concerns itself with being realized, and therefore to be established by action."
14. Hegel, *System of Ethical Life*, trans. H. S. Harris, unpublished version, Appendix, p. 11. Also see Eric Voegelin, "On Hegel—A study in sorcery" (*Studium Generale* 24C, Paris, 1971), 341.
15. Martin Heidegger, "The Age of the World Picture," in *The Question Concerning Technology and Other Essays*, trans. William Lovitt (New York: Harper and Row, 1977), p. 126.
16. Concerning the relationship between Kojève's philosophy and his role

in the establishment and development of the EEC, see Dominique Auffret, *Alexandre Kojève: la Philosophie, l'Etat, fin de l'historie* (Paris: Grassec, 1990).

17. Alexis de Tocqueville, *Democracy in America*, tr. George Lawrence (New York: Doubleday, 1966), pp. 609–11.

18. Kojève, *Introduction à la lecture de Hegel*, p. 436.

19. Francis Fukuyama, *The End of History and The Last Man* (Toronto: Maxwell Macmillan, 1992), pp. 1–4, 83–87, 89–93. For the relation between "technology," modern natural science, and global economics, see especially pp. 202–5. "But communications technology itself is value-neutral" (p. 7). "Human beings are *free* to pursue certain branches of science rather than others, and they can obviously *apply* the results as they please . . ." (p. 72, the italics are mine). But then: "Any state that hopes to maintain its political autonomy is *forced* to adopt the technology of its enemies and rivals" (p. 73). "Modern natural science *forces itself* on man, whether he cares for it or not . . ." (p. 76, again the italics are mine). Fukuyama is not alone in thinking technology to be value free, "applied" natural science. Most people do. To think otherwise would be altogether inefficient.

20. Kojève says that "japanized man" is a snob. "By nature snobbery is the prerogative of a *small minority*. Now, what we learn from Japan is that it is possible to democratize snobbery. Japan is eighty million snobs. After the Japanese people, English high society is a bunch of drunken sailors." Kojève, "Entretien avec Gilles Lapouge," *La quinzaine littéaire* 53 (Paris: 1968), pp. 18–19. See also Darby, *The Feast: Meditations on Politics and Time*, ch. 5. For the connections between snobbery in the West and politicized fundamentalism, see Marion Montgomery, *The Trouble With You Innnerlekchuls* (Front Royal: Christendom College Press, 1988). For Hegel on frivolity, boredom and the New World, see *Phenomenology of Mind*, p. 75.

21. Fukuyama, pp. 337–38. Fukuyama says that while the UHS might not be the best regime "in speech," it might turn out to be the best "in reality" (p. 337). This reminds one of that other best regime "in speech" *reluctantly* described by Socrates in Book V of Plato's *Republic*. Were this best regime realized it would, in *reality*, turn out to be the *worst*. For the UHS, does the "third wave" come "when experts become kings and kings become experts"? Is the wave technology? Maybe, after all, Fukuyama too is being ironic.

12

The Tower of Babel Rebuilt: Some Remarks on "The End of History"

Peter Fenves

Announcements of the end of history are of course nothing new. Announcements of this sort can even be said to keep history going until the end does come and there is nothing more, or nothing new, to announce. Histories of these announcements can be written, and an end to these histories can then be announced, which in turn can generate a history of the announcements that histories of the end have come to an end. And a new announcement can thereafter be made to the effect that histories of the announcement that history has come the end have come to an end. . . .

Very soon the seriousness of all these endeavors comes into question. The ambiguity of the word *history*—one of those marvelous ambiguities that, according to Hegel, makes us aware of the dialectical character of certain languages—gives the question of seriousness its urgency, for this question concerns nothing so much as the relation of language to reality or, in other words, the relation of history as narrative and history as the events narrated. An announcement is serious only as long as it is "really" meant, and an announcement counts as history, or as part of a serious history, only if what is really meant is, of course, historical reality. When the end of history is announced, the question of seriousness becomes all the more serious, for this announcement not only must be really meant but also presupposes a decision on the nature of historical reality, if not a decision on the nature of reality itself: How does the announcement of the end relate to the end itself? What does such speech have to do with the occurrences of which it speaks? Why speak at all? Why not remain speechless, when, after all, the end has come? Speechlessness is attractive in this context for the simple reason that it maintains a certain solemnity, a seriousness that few discourses, not even funeral orations, can match.

But talk of funeral orations is not always appropriate when the "end of history" is under discussion. It is not only possible not to lament this end but, like Kojève and Hegel, to celebrate the end of history as the fulfillment of a *telos* or the satisfaction of desire. Declines, fall, catastrophes, and disasters may all be endings but they are not necessarily ends, *teloi*, purposes, or objects of desire. Even if the end of history is haunted by the specter of Nietzsche's "last men," the emergence of such ghostly figures during twilight hours need not count as a reason to mourn. It takes little effort, then, to see why one would desire to announce the end of history: the end of history is itself desirable. The announcement of the end of history not only declares something to be the case, it also, and perhaps more importantly, expresses a desire for the purpose of history, its end, to be realized. Yet the announcement of this end, especially when it takes place in the context of a "universal history," can do even more: it can contribute to the fulfillment of the desire it expresses; it can help to bring about what it announces, namely the end. The equivocation of the word *end*, as in "purpose" and "conclusion," redeems the word *history* of its ambiguity, since the announcement of the end of history in the course of a "universal history" can itself become a historical event. It is even possible that the end of history cannot come to pass without a prior announcement that the end has come. The effectiveness of this announcement is then a properly historical problem, perhaps the last historical problem and, if so, an unavoidable one for any "universal history" that wants to present itself as serious.

The announcement of the end of history can itself be historical. This possibility gives rise to a conflict between the desire to make this announcement and the seriousness of the desired announcement: if the announcement of the end of history is a serious one, history should have come to an end, since this is what has been declared, but the very desire to make this announcement indicates that there is still a place not only for desires but for new desires—for historical desires, for those desires that give rise to what counts as history. And yet, if every historical desire has not yet been fulfilled, the end of history has not yet come, and the seriousness of any announcement to this effect is, to say the least, questionable. Seriously announcing the end of history is therefore no mean accomplishment, and if it cannot be done, if every announcement of the end of history that does not arise from revelation and does not herald apocalypse is condemned to a certain irony, then the question of the relation of historical language to historical reality becomes considerably more difficult. The desire to make the announcement that history has come to an end is already a sign that there remains something in history to desire, and it is not altogether certain that this "something" is the completion of the process through which history has come so far; it could be for an end to all this talk of ends.

I

These remarks are motivated by a reading of Fukuyama's *The End of History and the Last Man*. But the problem to which they are addressed—the problem of announcing "the end of history" without being able to base this announcement on a divine revelation—is by no means limited to his book. Indeed, this problem occupies the attention of every one of the modern philosophers Fukuyama cites, and nowhere are the parameters of this problem more clearly articulated than in the philosopher who first pursued the kind of history Fukuyama seeks to accomplish, Immanuel Kant. Fukuyama sees his project as the fulfillment of a desire for world-history that Kant first expressed in "An Idea for a Universal History with a Cosmopolitan Intention" and then renewed in "An Old Question Asked Anew." Both of these titles reappear in *The End of History and the Last Man* and in their own way show how the end of history comes about: just as historically relevant desires are supposed to find the most adequate satisfaction in liberal democracy, so the desire on the part of liberal philosophers for an account of universal history finds its satisfaction in Fukuyama's formulations. But borrowing titles is not always an innocent practice, and it is of interest to see what happens between the expression of a desire for a universal historian and its fulfillment; it might even say something about the interest in history itself.

Whereas Kant emphasizes that the "idea of universal history" he proposes takes root only within the context of a specific intention—a cosmopolitan one, an intention therefore to free oneself from regional particularities and local languages—Fukuyama pays scant attention to the intention of the historian who "asks anew" the old question, and one reason for this is readily apparent: he has been misled by a mistranslation of Kant's title. Fukuyama claims that his universal history will take "a point of view far more cosmopolitan than was possible in Kant's day" (70), but Kant was never much concerned with points of view; he wanted a universal history written *in weltbürgerlicher Absicht*, "with a cosmopolitan intention." This error in translation indicates at the very least the difficulty of achieving this intention, particularly when it is directed toward translating one vocabulary of volition into another one. It is, however, the intention—or better still, the desire—of those who speak of world-history, according to Kant, that stamps the character of *historiam rerum gestarum* for the simple reason that it is impossible to speak of world-history without announcing in some way or other "the end of history," the purpose and goal of the apparently endless series of disasters that make up "the great stage of the world."[1] This is, for Kant, precisely the problem: the "objective validity" of historical language is implicated in the validity—or probity—of the subject who makes a claim about history, and for this reason every such claim poses the question of its motivating desires. Answering this question precedes any genuinely philosophical renewal of the "old question"—and so it does with Kant.

Kant discovers something when he examines the desire to answer the "old question" concerning the purpose and direction of world-history. It appears that the very desire to answer this question is somehow harmful. Whereas Fukuyama begins *The End of History and the Last Man* with a short discussion of what he sees as the only alternative to his position—what he calls "pessimism," a highly ambiguous word to which we will return—Kant opens his "Renewed Question" with three possible responses to the "old question." Each response to this question, each "prognosis," turns out to be detrimental to human history, which Kant figures as a suffering patient, and the root of the harmful effect of prognostic discourse lies precisely in the treatment of history as passive, hence as a patient on which a doctor, or anyone in authority, can operate. If, for example, someone in authority says that history has no end, purpose, or goal, this statement contributes to the manifest randomness of events on the world stage. If, by contrast, an authoritarian voice says history will come to an end in some fiery apocalypse—what Kant calls the "terroristic mode of representing history" and attributes less to sanguine physicians than to choleric priests—it thereby contributes to the terror of history and guarantees that things will get worse. If, however, the prognosis is more favorable, if an authoritative voice announces that the end of history, understood as its purpose, is within sight, another kind of risk arises: once there is any break in the continuity of progress—and there are bound to be breaks since otherwise the "old question" would never have arisen—the promise of improvement is likewise broken, and the breach of this promise will make talk of the future ever more unpromising and will, in turn, make efforts at improvement ever more suspect.

Direct pronouncements on the end of history are questionable not only because the ones who make them are unable to secure adequate knowledge but, more importantly, because such pronouncements from those who are in a position of authority are far from innocent: they either help bring about an undesirable ending or make the very notion of historical ends suspect. Announcing the end of history doubtless contributes to some end, but the end to which it contributes is never the object of desire. Direct responses to the "Renewed Question" only make things worse.

II

"Things are getting worse"—this is the dictum of "pessimism" against which *The End of History* is written. Kant's "Renewed Question" does not in fact announce that things are getting worse; quite the opposite, and yet the conclusions of the "Renewed Question" have nothing in common with the announcement of the end of history. For Kant reaches his conclusions about the continuity of progress toward an unreachable Idea by an entirely indirect route: he reads what he calls a "historical sign." The indirection of this reading leaves its mark in his answer to the "old question": a certain discontinuity is made the very condition for the announcement of continual progress. Speaking of historical progress in a direct manner, by contrast, holds historical discourse hostage to every sort of discontinuity, and since discontinuities of some sort are bound to emerge, such speech undoes its own promise: history does not become more comprehensible; rather, the terms in which this comprehensibility have been cast are emptied of their significance. Announcing not merely the continuity of historical progress but its end makes this situation even more precarious, for every subsequent historical altercation must be understood, or explained away, as one more regression. Consistent appeals to the concept of regression have an effect on the announcement of "the end of history": it, too, must regress. Unexpectedly, history takes a turn toward its beginnings, and so it does in *The End of History*. Its opening sentence asks us to renounce "'our pessimism,'" but in the course of Fukuyama's exposition we soon learn how very much the *desire* to make an optimistic announcement runs counter to its message: the desire to make us renounce "our pessimism" is a regression *at the level of historiography* to the beginning of history, to the struggles of the "first man."

"The twentieth century, it is safe to say, has made all of us into deep historical pessimists" (3). Thus Fukuyama opens his book and distinguishes himself from "us" and "our pessimism." His optimism thereafter seeks support for its claims in Hegel's famous law of desire: the object of desire is the desire of the other. Desire can only satisfy itself in a distinctiveness that must be "recognized" as such; full satisfaction of desire would involve mutual recognition of an otherness of which we are part and that in turn recognizes each of us as distinct, as independent, as free. The first clause of this law brings history into motion; the last clause brings it to completion. Fukuyama does not simply describe the workings of this law but acts its first clause out—in the very first sentence. The desire to announce that history has come to a desirable end is a historical desire, a desire to distinguish oneself if not in history, then at least in historiography, but *this* latter distinction, like all historically relevant distinctions, cannot escape the Hegelian law of desire. The renewal of a certain historiography, which is after all Fukuyama's expressed desire, makes the renewal of history itself desirable, and since history can be renewed only if it has not yet come to an end—or this apparent end is no longer seen as desirable and therefore no longer seen as an end in the first place—the renewal of historiography under the dictum "the end of history" contributes to the undoing of the very end it proposes. Coming to an end thus becomes an interminable and inconsistent process, a process Kant gives the rather silly name "Abderitism" in order to capture its lack of seriousness.

The author of *The End of History and the Last Man* distinguishes himself in historiography in precisely the same way that the "first man" distinguished himself in history. Both Fukuyama and this "first man" distinguish themselves by taking certain risks. An analysis of the different risks each takes does more to explain the difference between the beginning and end of history than does a lengthy discussion of what Fukuyama calls "the empirical flow of events" (70). Whereas the "first man" risks his life for honor, Fukuyama risks his honor alone, not his life. For, as he makes clear in the chapter on the "Idea for a Universal History," his optimism exposes him to the accusation that he is a fool: "We need to ask whether our pessimism is not becoming something of a pose, adopted as lightly as was the optimism of the nineteenth century. For a naive optimist whose expectations are belied appears foolish, while a pessimist proven wrong maintains an aura of profundity and seriousness. It is therefore safer to follow the second course" (70).

Optimism in this sense is the great historiographical risk, the only risk contemporary world-historians can run, and it is a risk in a very specific sense: if one appears "foolish," one loses not only distinction and "depth" but also "seriousness." The words the optimist speaks no longer have a relation to historical reality. And it is the risk of appearing silly that Fukuyama claims to take when, by announcing the end of history, he begins historiography anew. Unlike "the first man," he does not risk his life for the sake of prestige; rather, he risks nothing but his prestige—and this change is just more evidence for, and a direct outcome of, the end of history. By contrast, "our pessimism" runs no risks. If things get worse, the pessimists can still claim to be right; if things get better, the pessimist can nevertheless claim another type of authority—not, to be sure, the authority that accrues to those who make their pronouncements come true, nor to those whose predications turn out to be accurate, but the authority of subjective "depth" and sagelike "seriousness." Such authority may be even more desirable than that of mere correctness, for in the face of "the empirical flow of events" it can claim to divine those things that do not appear as such and are, to this extent, metaphysical.

Fukuyama is, of course, completely wrong when he presents the nineteenth century as a hundred years of optimism and the twentieth century as so many years of pessimism. One need only recall how strongly the thought of pessimism's inventor, Arthur Schopenhauer, held sway over the latter half of the nineteenth century, and the movements for which the twentieth century will remain infamous—fascism, Stalism, Maoism—were deeply optimistic ones: they were movements of historical renewal the likes of which can be sought only in certain religious uprisings whose participants were confident of gaining divine favor. The pessimists whom Fukuyama conjures up have very little to do with the thought of either the nineteenth or the twentieth century; they are, rather, rivals for "pure prestige" and have no reality outside this imaginary rivalry. What Fukuyama seeks to wrestle from his rival is authority. Whether the pessimist succeeds in representing reality or only indicates his great "depth," he remains an authoritative voice, and all the more so if the dictum "things are getting worse" contributes to the worsening of things.

The optimist whom Fukuyama then represents not only runs the risk of revealing himself to be lacking in seriousness; the very nature of his optimism makes it impossible for him to claim certain kinds of authority: he can claim neither the priestly authority of "depth" nor the political authority by virtue of which pronouncements are transformed into historical reality. Under the rubric of "optimism" Fukuyama plays out the loss of these modes of authority. The authority he can claim is, by contrast, purely scholarly: it does not consist in making things happen by announcing that they will, nor in making oneself distinct by announcing that one is distinct, but in making claims that may turn out to be generally recognized as accurate. This is less a mode of authority than an indication of its loss. The announcement of "the end of this history" that arises on the basis of this loss—as opposed to the apocalyptic announcements of the priest or the catastrophic calls of certain optimistic ideologies—is ironic from the start: once announced, we are supposed to do nothing but wait and see if the end of history, like changes in the weather, will come about.

III

The tacit recognition that an announcement as momentous as the one proposed by Fukuyama's title is of no historical significance and can claim only historiographical authority is by no means insignificant. It indicates something about the time in which this announcement is made. When Kant set out to write his "Idea for a Universal History," he first tried to understand what he was doing when he wrote and what kinds of effects his writing might have. His essay of a few pages spends nearly as much time on these problems as on the actual shape of a future universal history, and the very brevity of the essay is understandable in terms of its overall strategy. Kant understood the "Idea for a Universal History" to be an impetus for "Nature" to produce a philosophical historian who would, in turn, promote the final purpose of nature and thereby make good on Kant's otherwise illegitimate talk of "Nature" as agent. And Kant is scarcely alone: no philosopher—whether classical, premodern, or modern—has made pronouncements on the character of historical change, much less on the end of history, without thorough considerations of the promises they enact and the effects they promote; every philosopher, in other words, has worried over the depth and extent of his authority. These considerations have often been conducted under the general title "philosophy and tyranny" and have gravitated toward the question of the need for, and the possibility of, a philosopher-king. Fukuyama's failure to treat with any seriousness the historical power of his own announcement testifies less to a specific thesis he proposes—the thesis, namely, that tyranny will die out as the end of history comes to its completion—than to the one mode of authority he seeks to claim: scholarly authority, a mode of authority that consists primarily in a claim to have been the first one to have made a solid case for something.

Fukuyama never claims to be the first one to have announced "the end of history," nor even the first one to have done so in a generally secular context. The authority of his announcement does not consist in the newness but rather in the solidity of his case, and solidity can in this case be achieved only by disregarding as much as possible the metaphysical intentions of his predecessors, including the intention on the part of certain predecessors to overturn metaphysics and begin philosophy anew. Thus Fukuyama presents Hegel's philosophy of history as the complete fulfillment of Kant's "Idea for a Universal History," although the metaphysical principles on which the latter stands are everywhere at odds with those from which Hegel developed his system. Thus Fukuyama divests himself of Hegel's metaphysical program and keeps away from his *Science of Logic*. Thus Fukuyama conceives of Nietzsche as a Platonist who simply wants to give *thymos* its due, not a genealogist who subjects Platonic psychology to ever more incisive critiques and ever more devastating attacks. Thus Fukuyama shies away from the enormous complications and contradictions of Kojève's ontology, complications and contradictions that have quite rightly been seen as formative for thinkers as different from one another as Sartre, Lacan, and Foucault. And when Fukuyama does tread on this territory he takes false steps. In a footnote, for example, he cites Leo Strauss's critique of Kojève for failing to comprehend how deeply Hegelian thought commits its proponents to a dialectics of nature, but this critique has no effect on Fukuyama's own performance.[2] Kojève, as Strauss perceives, wishes to cut and paste the most systematic thinker the West ever produced; in this regard, or in this disregard for the fearsome consistency of Hegel's thought, Kojève could take lessons from Fukuyama.

Yet Fukuyama does not disregard the problem of metaphysics altogether. Whereas in certain contexts he recommends that we look to the "empirical flow of events" in order to put to rest "our pessimism," in contexts less conducive to optimistic scenarios he warns us not to look "simply at empirical evidence" but instead to pose the problem of "man as man" (138). The pursuit of this problem is supposed to lead to the disclosure of a "transhistorical standard," which in turn will free us from our historical perspective; or, more exactly, it will "free us from the tyranny of the present" (138). Freedom from the present in favor of an eternal presence, freedom from men as they are in favor of "the first man": these are descriptions of the classical metaphysical projects that Nietzsche's "psychological" studies were meant to unmask. If Fukuyama pursued these puzzles with any degree of vigor or, more modestly, if he could make his project square with the very different ones of Hegel, Nietzsche, and Kojève, he would perhaps be in a position to explain what it meant for him to announce the end of history now—under the tyranny of the present. Instead, he relates his project once again to his earliest predecessor: "The mere fact that human nature is not created 'once and for all' but creates itself 'in the course of *historical* time' does not spare us the need to talk about human nature. . . . For example, if as Kant suggests man's reason cannot be fully developed except as the result of a long and cumulative social process, this does not therefore make reason any less 'natural' an aspect of man" (138). If Kant ever suggested any such thing, he would have annulled his own moral theory, since it is based on the possibility that pure reason can be practical at any time and under any condition. Fukuyama's representation of his predecessor reaches an even higher order of confusion in the footnote to this remark: "Kant describes Nature as a volitional agent standing outside of human beings; we may however understand this as a metaphor for an aspect of human nature existing potentially in all people, but realized only in the course of their social and historical interaction" (364n9). Nature is a metaphor for an aspect of one species' nature, which means that Nature must be thought on analogy to one of its parts viewed from an unspecified perspective. No wonder Kant's program has to be amalgamated with those of Hegel and Kojève: on its own it is hardly comprehensible, much less compelling.

Fukuyama never presents his forays into the problem of "man as man" as independent contributions to the stabilization or the overturning of any plausible metaphysics. These forays are merely supplemental: they deliver additional—and this time nonempirical—arguments in support of a thesis drawn from the putative observation of "the empirical flow of events" (70). A dose of metaphysics helps solidify the case. Without having to investigate the ontological premises of any thinker from the ground up, Fukuyama can nevertheless gain the kind of freedom metaphysics has traditionally offered: freedom from the "tyranny of the present," which has traditionally been understood as freedom from activity in life. The more solid the case, the less one has to ask what it means to make world-historical pronouncements now, and the less one has to do this, the easier it is to convert Kant's complex rhetorical strategy into a simple matter of metaphor. All the paraphernalia of *The End of History and the Last Man*—its lengthy talk of the Mechanism, its conflation of Hobbes and Hegel, its treatment of Nietzsche without the doctrine of the eternal return of the same, and so forth—are meant, by contrast, to solidify a case for doing nothing, or nothing of historical importance—a case, in short, for the end of history. Metaphysical motifs appear in *The End of History and the Last Man* for one reason: to supplement Fukuyama's account of desire. This account needs to be supplemented because on its own it cannot make sense of those desires that do not seek satisfaction in empirical objects but seek out other things. Since all metaphysical thinkers, regardless of their intention toward metaphysics, are on the track of these nonempirical objects of desire, all are treated as one.

IV

The End of History and the Last Man is evidence of a desire: the desire on the part of its author to distinguish himself from the crowd of contemporary pessimists. But it does not unambiguously express a desire, not even the desire for the end of history to come to completion. Not only is the expression of desire exposed to equivocation, but the very word *desire*, as Fukuyama uses it, is equivocal: it designates the drive of "economic man" toward those empirical things that make him happy, on the one hand, and it designates something quite different when it is brought into relation with the question of recognition, on the other. The oddity of Fukuyama's procedure, and the degree to which it differs from Hegel and Kojève, cannot be underestimated. Instead of distinguishing between desire and, say, "need," which would leave open the question whether cases of need were not also cases of desire, Fukuyama speaks everywhere of desire and yet wishes to distinguish desire from itself—to distinguish, that is, desire from the desire for recognition.

When ambiguity threatens, new words—or newly valued ones—come to the rescue. Thus Fukuyama, without so much as a comment about what he is doing, returns to the Greek vocabulary of desire in order to make up for a deficiency in modern ones. The ancient world may be incapable of satisfying desire, but it is at least capable of satisfying the desire for a satisfactory vocabulary of desire. Regression to this vocabulary then rescues desire from its contemporary confusion. The exoticism of the Greek term *thymos* does not make "the desire for recognition" recognizable—how could a foreign word do so?—but, instead, distances desire from the language in which it is expressed. Expression of desire, as a result, can no longer be so straightforward. And the reason why Fukuyama would engage in this linguistic regression is readily apparent: his case rests on the separation of desire from the desire for recognition. The economic-technological "Mechanism" owes its continuous development to the former, whereas the discontinuities to which liberal democracy has been subject are ascribed to the latter.

But Fukuyama cannot conceal the degree to which desire and *thymos* are implicated in one another. If the desire for recognition did not share something in common with desire, it would be a mistake to call it "desire" in the first place, and if this mistake in modern languages could be made up only with an appeal to dead ones, then the very ability of our language, perhaps even any living language, to express desire unambiguously is greatly compromised. But even the miraculous language of the Greeks gives out, for, as Fukuyama admits in a footnote, it is no less confusing than living languages in these matters: "Strictly speaking, the desire for recognition can be considered a form of desire like hunger or thirst, only one whose object is not material but ideal. The close relationship between *thymos* and desire is evident in the Greek word for desire, *epithymia*" (369n2, ch. 16).

Strictly speaking, then, desire is always desire. Its expression exposes it to an ineluctable confusion: its object could be either "material" or "ideal"—or both. What appears to be a material object of desire may very well be a ruse: it may be desired only for the sake of recognition; it may identify who one is; it may, that is, grant the desiring subject a title or a name. And Fukuyama recognizes this complexity of desire, like so many other ones, in an oblique way: in his account of *Leviathan*, he mentions Hobbes's reflections on the "trifles" that so often have a prominent role in contests of pride. Such trifles are the trophies of recognition; they are the signs by which one is recognized as a member of a certain class, the titles one earns, the names one makes for oneself. The relation of desire and the desire for recognition is so close that every object of desire, to speak in Platonic terms, participates in both materiality and ideality. Indeed, the relationship may be even closer: what Fukuyama calls *desire* and translates back into Greek as *epithymia* may be nothing more than an epiphenomenon of the other desire, the desire to be desired by the other, a desire that may then take the form of mistaking certain solid things for objects of desire. Even if this reduction of *epithymia* to an epiphenomenon is deemed unacceptable— Fukuyama attributes such a move to Nietzsche[3]—desire is still exposed to an ineluctable confusion. Every desirable object can function as a trifle, and no struggle for recognition can do without its trophies, the signs of being recognized as someone. And this goes even for the most dire cases. The fact that a material object is desired in order to keep one alive does not make desire unequivocal; on the contrary, remaining alive, keeping one's body in motion, may very well be a matter of pride—and nothing else.

If the word *desire* is exposed to this kind of equivocation, it is because desire itself is equivocal, but the nature of this confusion has yet to be decided. The classification of desirable objects into "material" and "ideal" is, to say the least, quite primitive and owes its origin less to Plato than to Hobbes. For Plato still lived in a climate of rhetoric; he understood that the desire for recognition had its locus in speech, not in private "mental contents." For this reason sophists and rhetors were his most challenging rivals. The desire for recognition is not satisfied by something "ideal" but, rather, seeks satisfaction in certain modes of speaking: in encomia, in testimonials, in titles, in names. The locus of this desire is language. The expression of a desire is therefore not only exposed to equivocation; such expression can be what is desired *in every desire*. And on this every claim to authority—or every claim to accountable authority—counts: those who harken to authority do not desire something in particular but desire that the authority express its desire. Fukuyama reduces rhetoric—as the expression of desire and as desire in expression—to the status of "ideality" and, by doing so, solidifies his case: announcements of historical proportion are not themselves the loci of desire, the places in which desire acts and is activated, but are at the very most evidence of a desire.

V

All this talk of lack and language would seem to be far removed from the grand historical schema of Fukuyama's book were it not for the fact that his argument for the end of history hinges on a certain linguistic lack: the absence of any universalizable alternative to the language of liberal democracy for the legitimization of political institutions and therefore the lack of a language other than that of liberal democracy in which authority can be exercised as a matter of course. This lack is supposed to say something about the state of desire—namely, that it is satisfied, that historically relevant desires are lacking. And this is true, it is said, because no desire escapes the horizons of liberal democracy. In short, desire now knows no unsatisfiable lack except the lack of a certain discourse, a lack of a universizable alternative to the discourse of liberal democracy. No doubt this lack is the place to locate not a historical but an historiographical desire, a desire to better Fukuyama by inventing—or citing, or revising, or renewing—another discourse which could henceforth be used to legitimate future political institutions. But this gesture, which is inevitable from the perspective of the theory of desire adumbrated in *The End of History and the Last Man*, hardly does justice to the linguistic fact Fukuyama comes across.

The fact is this: there is a linguistic lack. And this lack lets us know, according to Fukuyama's analysis, that liberal democracy is the politico-economic structure best suited to make good on every historically relevant lack. The lack of a certain discourse is, therefore, the last lack. It is one lack liberal democracy cannot satisfy. But—and here is the source of Fukuyama's peculiarly inflected optimism—this lack is *purely linguistic*. It has no relation to anyone's experience, or if it does manage to secure some sort of relation to life, it is only the highly unhistorical life of the historiographer faced with the problem of coming to terms with the announcement of the end of history. The confidence with which Fukuyama makes an announcement about world-history resides in his certainty that this linguistic lack will never translate into a real lack, a historical lack, a lack that will have the power to transform historical reality. The lack of desire thus takes up residence in language alone, and—so Fukuyama contends—there it will remain. It is from this contention that the case for "the end of history" ultimately draws its authority.

The fact that Fukuyama's announcement of the end of history enacts nothing, makes no demands, and discovers no new desires converges with the ineluctable fact from which the case for this announcement seeks confirmation: the fact that there is a lack of alternatives to speaking the language of liberal democracy. For this fact gives support to Fukuyama's case only if the absence of a certain language is as inert as the presence of this very announcement. Fukuyama's contention rests on the supposition that the expression of desire is so univocal, and univocal in such a way, that the lack of a certain language is evidence of an absence of desire. For, so the argument runs, if desires were not satisfied, if the desire for tangible things and the desire for recognition were not taken care of, wouldn't another language have arisen by now to express whatever desires remained unsatisfied? If, however, language does not simply express desire, if expression itself is a locus of desire—and everything Fukuyama says about Hegel points in this direction—then the lack of a language to compete with the language of liberal democracy cannot be used as evidence about the reality of the institutions it sanctions. At most, the lack of an alternative language is a sign that has to be read.

VI

The End of History and the Last Man could also be called "The Tower of Babel Rebuilt." For an indispensable point of support for its case rests on the emergence of a universal language of political life. The universal language that, according to certain medieval traditions, the tyrant Nimrod enlisted in the service of his own glorification has once again arisen under the rubric of liberal democracy. Such is the irony of history: what once served the tyrant's desires now proclaims his illegitimacy. And it is not difficult to see why those who are made uneasy by irony find all talk of a "new world order" spooky or even blasphemous. But one thing is certain: if Fukuyama's account of the universality of a particular political discourse has merit, a universal language allows for the rebuilding of the Tower of Babel—whatever that may mean. The last words in *The End of History* are a warning, or a promise, of just such a possibility: those who "set their eyes on a new and more distant journey" (339) are not removed from those who wish to "make a name" for themselves in the shape of a building that reaches toward the ever receding heavens.

The single victorious language of legitimation is the ground on which any new Babel will be built; it alone will be able to justify old institutions and make newly established ones legitimate. And yet this ground, this universal language of political life, is unstable from the start. Its name is not even clear. Usually Fukuyama calls the one discourse capable of lending legitimacy to any political institution "the language of liberal democracy," but at other times it is simply "the language of democracy," as though the word "liberal"—with its implicit appeal to greater and greater freedom—designated a moment of destabilization. Nowhere are the tremblings to which this linguistic ground is subject more strongly felt than at the point where it first enters into Fukuyama's argument:

> What is emerging victorious, in other words, is not so much liberal practice, as the liberal *idea*. That is to say, for a large part of the world, there is now no ideology with pretensions to universality that is in a position to challenge liberal democracy, and no universal principle of legitimacy other than the sovereignty of the people. Monarchism in its various forms had been largely defeated by the beginning of the century. Fascism and communism, liberal democracy's main competitors up till now, have both discredited themselves. If the Soviet Union (or its successor states) fails to democratize, if Peru or the Philippines relapse into some form of authoritarianism, democracy will most likely have yielded to a colonel or a bu-

reaucrat who claims to speak in the name of Russian, Peruvian, or Philippine people alone. Even non-democrats will have to speak the language of democracy in order to justify their deviation from the single universal standard. (45)

Not only *will* nondemocrats have to speak "the language of democracy," they *already* have done so: liberal democracy's main competitors, communism and fascism, also sought legitimacy in the principle of popular sovereignty, the difference among the "competitors" lying less in their appeal to "we the people" than in the methods they employed to name, constitute, and give voice to their respective peoples. If Fukuyama fails to subscribe fully to Kojève's sublime indifference—what does it matter which competitor wins the vast wars of the twentieth century as long as the principle expressed at the battle of Jena triumphs?—then he is caught in a perplexing conclusion: a single universal language of legitimation triumphed, and yet history still happened. And history still happened because the "language of democracy" does not specify the name of the people who are sovereign; it could only name the principle of sovereignty, and the chosen name of this principle is, universally, "the people." The universality of this name doubtless makes possible a universalizable discourse of legitimation, but the very generality of the name—the fact that it names only a principle—denies its nominal status. Something is lacking in the triumphant "language of democracy": the names of the people who are everywhere acknowledged as sovereign.

"The language of democracy" can lend legitimacy to any political institution because any political institution can be claimed in the name of a people. But the name of the people lies outside this language's jurisdiction. Every one of these names—and one need only look at the role call of the United Nations to recall their proliferation—is potentially a matter of dispute; not one of them can claim anything more than a provisional legitimacy. And the name of the element that makes "popular" names into an always unstable matter is, of course, "liberalism." Certain languages of democracy make it impossible to dispute the name of the people in whom political institutions are granted legitimacy—this is what fascism tries to accomplish—but if the language of liberal democracy is indeed of a distinct order, it is because it leaves open this question: there is always something illegitimate—or, less drastically put, something only provisionally legitimate—about this name, something that cannot be justified according to the institutions founded in its honor. If each name of a people is only provisionally legitimate, if each one is less a proper name than a promise, the language of liberal democracy not only has a future; it is always only futurial. The name of the people is the locus of a constantly shifting melee of desires.

" 'Come, let us build a city, and a tower, with its top in heaven, and let us make us a name; lest we be scattered abroad upon the face of the earth.' "[4] These builders are not only unnamed, they lack a name for themselves, and this lack gives rise to a desire: the desire to make a name, the desire to be recognized under this name, the desire not simply to be desired by the other but the desire to be desired by the absolutely Other, who, also unnamed, understands this desire as an intolerable provocation: " 'Behold, they are one people, and they have all one language; and this is what they begin to do; and now nothing will be withholden from them, which they purpose to do.' " This all takes place even though—or, more accurately, precisely because—the language in which the builders of the city seek to make a name for themselves is universal. The desire to make a name for oneself does not stop when there is only one "political" language, only one language through which the founding, building, and maintaining of cities are accomplished; indeed, it does not stop when there is only one people. Then it begins in earnest. For the made-up name, if it were ever to be secured, would let the people recognize itself as one. A secure name would guard against a certain "scattering," but a desire for a name in the face of this scattering only confirms the confusion of all desire: it seeks something "material" as well as "ideal," and yet neither of these terms does justice to the confusing desirability of self-made names. "Making a name" makes up for the lack in the universal language of political life because every new—or newly valued—name for the people makes language once again into the locus of desire. No divine agent is needed to foment confusion; on the contrary, the more universal the language of political life, the more desirable a made-up name, the greater the confusion.

VII

Under the threat of the disintegration of another "universal" language of political life—the language of Catholicism—the concept of the *katechon* was developed. The *katechon* is supposed to "hold back" the acceleration of this disintegration; it is a bulwark against confusion, and its ultimate end is to keep the world from falling into the hands of the master of confusion, the Anti-Christ.

Fukuyama, too, speaks of a *katechon*: "Standing as a bulwark against the revival of history and the return of the first man is the imposing Mechanism of modern natural science that we described in Part Two of this book, the Mechanism driven by unlimited desire and guided by reason" (336). Only the confidence in this Mechanism gives life to Fukuyama's optimism. Without this confidence he would be in the same position as those pessimists of the past who, having abandoned the idea of sacred history, returned to the conception of world-history as a natural cycle of rises and falls. But the *katechon* in which he places his confidence could not be further removed from the one that was supposed to preserve the institutions sanctioned by the one "catholic" language. For, unlike the Church, the Mechanism cannot confer recognition on anyone. According to Fukuyama's account, this is precisely what defines "the Mechanism": it can satisfy every desire but the desire for recognition, and this is because it neither expresses desire nor, as a result, exercises authority. The bulwark against the fall into chaos no longer presents itself as a decisive voice but as a mute Mechanism. This muteness then has its own function: it makes this new *katechon*, unlike its predecessor, univocal. Or so it is supposed to be: the towering technological Mechanism simply creates and satisfies ever more desires for tangible things and, at least according to the logic of Fukuyama's argument, although not his more nuanced presentation of the "rational desire," these things are never "trifles," never the modes of expression in which people make a name for themselves.

The muteness of the Mechanism may make it univocal, but it also has its disadvantages: the Mechanism cannot speak for itself, and so it takes time for its meaning to come to light. In the meantime—which is the time before the end of history has come to completion and the time in which the sheer reality of the Mechanism outweighs its meaning— historiographical discourse remains dissociated from historical reality: "it would seem that the chief threat to democracy would be our own confusion about what is really at stake. For while modern societies have evolved toward democracy, modern thought has arrived at an impasse, unable to come to a consensus on what constitutes man and his specific dignity" (337). Confusion, as one might expect all along, is the impasse to the satisfaction of desire and therefore to the completion of history, and it is the kind of confusion that not only lets one speak without knowing what one says but indeed encourages this kind of talk: "Today, everybody talks about human dignity, but there is no consensus as to why people possess it'' (296). Everybody talks about dignity because there is only confusion, for nothing is more conducive to desire—and dignity is very much a matter of desire—than confusion. This confusion over dignity does not take place "despite the fact that history is driven in a coherent direction" (338), but because of this very coherency, or, better yet, because of that which gives history its irreversible directionality: the mute Mechanism, the Mechanism without meaning, the Mechanism in its sheer reality.

The desire for recognition is not satisfied with "ideal" things, and yet whatever does satisfy this desire—certain modes of speech by which people name, know, and mistake themselves—is not quite real either. Fukuyama emphasizes that liberal democracy satisfies the desire for recognition better than others only *in reality*: "If it would not qualify as the most just 'in speech,' it might serve as the most just regime 'in reality' " (337). In speech, then, there ought to be other, more just regimes—those "republics" from whose standpoint the inadequacies of real regimes come to light. But this opposition of "in speech" to "in reality" at the end of history not only runs counter to the Hegelian mode of thought on which Fukuyama supports his case; it also goes against the fact on which this case stands or falls: the lack of alternatives "in speech" to liberal democracy. Something must have happened to the language of political life such that it can no longer express the desire for a just polity. Or, conversely, something must have happened to this language such that there is everywhere talk of justice but this talk does not give rise to the language of a more just regime. Talk of justice—or dignity—remains less than a language: it is fragmented, disjoint, confused, and yet ever more vociferous.

Only one thing could have made the talk of desire—and justice, like dignity, is every bit a matter of desire—incapable of coming up with a language: a *shock*, or many shocks, each one unique, and each one an eruption of something real, something that gives rise to an ever-increasing number of names and vocabularies precisely because it escapes everyone. Fukuyama blames the confusion of moral vocabularies on one such shock: "cultural relativism (a European invention) has seemed plausible to our century because for the first time Europe found itself forced to confront non-European cultures in a serious way through the experience of colonialism and de-colonization" (338). The seriousness of this experience, or any experience, lies in an exposure to reality. Once exposed in this way old names, vocabularies, and languages are shattered to the point where new ones—or newly valued ones—have to be invented again and again.

The experience of colonialism and decolonization is one shock, but it is not the only one. Fukuyama mentions some of them in the course of his presentation. But he makes sure not to mention one: the mute Mechanism itself, the bulwark against the return to chaos. This is not the source of all shocks; there may be no such source. But the Mechanism goes its way *without recognition*, and this, as always, is a shock. Fukuyama entertains none of the fantasies so dear to much science fiction that a Mechanism, under the auspices of some super-computer, will come to recognize everyone; rather, his optimism consists in the hope that the Mechanism will be recognized as the supreme creation of univocal desire. But until this recognition takes place, until the Mechanism becomes meaningful—"untils" that are perhaps as fanciful as the dreams of science fiction—the Mechanism cannot help but deliver one shock after another. Deflecting these shocks is then the task of political language, and none so far has been more adept at doing so than the language of liberal democracy. For it has been able to foster the proliferation of "popular" names, the invention of new moral vocabularies, the production of new discourses of desire, and the incessant yet always fragmented talk of justice. The confusion of tongues gives the one remaining language of political life with any claim to universality its strength to deflect shock after shock, for in each case of confusion something of these shocks—their singularity, their uniqueness—is preserved.

VIII

These remarks were broken off on the day that the leader of the Liberal Democratic Party, Vladimir Zhirinovsky, gained a significant victory in the election of the new Russian assembly. He does not pretend to speak the language of liberal democracy but has done something a stroke better: he has simply taken its *name*. And this victory, which owes its origin in no small measure to a certain "shock therapy," may very well give rise to another shock, one that the language of liberal democracy will have to handle this time without being able to call itself, without a certain equivocation, "liberal democracy."

Notes

1. See Immanuel Kant, *Perpetual Peace and Other Essays*, trans. Ted Humphrey (Indianapolis: Hackett, 1983), 29. This is the best edition of Kant's writ-

ings on history in English, and it can be supplemented with *The Conflict of the Faculties,* trans. Mary Gregor and Robert E. Anchor (New York: Abaris, 1979).

2. Fukuyama, 364: "Leo Strauss notes that even within [!] Kojève's Hegelian system, a philosophy of nature is still 'indispensable.'" On the contrary, Strauss rightly emphasizes that one cannot simply pick and choose from Hegel's system, and that if one is committed to his philosophy of history, one is therefore committed to his philosophy of nature and indeed to his theology. The distress caused by these commitments played no small role in the dissolution of the Hegelian system into academic and Marxist versions of materialism in the course of the nineteenth century.

3. See Fukuyama, 334: "Rather than being one of three parts, as it had been for Plato, *thymos* became the whole of man for Nietzsche." A reading more in accord with both the spirit and the letter of Nietzsche's writing would balk at the expression "the whole of man." What Fukuyama does not want to discuss is "the will to power," which is not limited to man, which impels man "beyond" himself, and which thereby escapes categories of recognition and identification.

4. Genesis 11: 4.

13

Reflections on *The End*
of History, Five Years Later

Francis Fukuyama

When I showed a draft of my original article "The End of History" to a political theorist friend in early 1989 and asked for his opinion, he said: "You will be misunderstood." This judgment proved quite prophetic: after its publication in *The National Interest* that summer, it elicited a flurry of misinterpretations, many related to its supposed relevance to American foreign policy (it had none). Part of the reason that I enlarged the article into *The End of History and the Last Man* was to correct these misinterpretations by presenting the argument at much greater length. Surely, I thought, a 400-page book would go a long way to setting the record straight. I should have known better, of course; what you are is what you are *recognized* as being, to use one of the book's central concepts. We exist not "in ourselves," but only in an intersubjective social context; and in that context, what I said was that events would somehow stop happening, or there would be perpetual peace.

Nonetheless, I have been asked to look again at my arguments in 1994, in light of the significant events that have taken place in the real world since 1989, and in light of the criticisms that have been made of my article and book. While I have little confidence that a third attempt to clarify will actually serve that purpose, I will nonetheless try.

My book consists of two distinct arguments: the first an empirical evaluation of various events, both contemporary and historical, and the second a "normative" or theoretical one that seeks to evaluate contemporary liberal democracy.[1] The empirical part has been attacked the most relentlessly. Virtually every week I read a story in the papers that contains some variant on the words, "As we can see, history has not ended but is only now beginning. . . ." (This phrase has now been

239

used by Margaret Thatcher, Mikhail Gorbachev, George Bush, Hosni Mubarak, Anthony Lake, and a host of lesser lights; I propose a moratorium as it now represents the total bankruptcy of the speechwriter's art.) The normative or theoretical part has been attacked also, usually by a different and more serious group of readers, who argue that I got Hegel wrong, or Kojève, or Nietzsche, or one of the other philosophers mentioned in the book. And finally, as Greg Smith points out, there is a major question as to the way that the two parts of the book relate to one another. The normative part of the book has been criticized for being based on "mere" empiricism and vulnerable to changes in a turbulent world scene. Alternatively, I have been charged with moving to inadmissible normative arguments when the empirical analysis failed.

I will take on each of these groups of criticisms, beginning with the relationship of the empirical to the normative argument, then moving to the empirical argument itself, and finally to the most difficult issue, the normative or theoretical question.

I. The Relationship Between the Empirical and Normative Arguments

Perhaps the most common misunderstanding of my argument (of which I am sure none of the readers of the current essay are guilty) is that the phrase, "the end of history," is a simple empirical statement describing the current condition of the world. These critics believe I was asserting that there would be no more war, struggle, or conflict, and their criticism takes the form: "As we can see, history has not ended because X happened," where X is something they regard as bad: the Gulf War, the Yugoslav conflict, famine in Somalia, a coup in Moscow, the LA riots, poverty, drug use, you name it. A colleague of mine who is working for the Agency for International Development in Bangladesh sent me what is probably the ultimate of this form of critique: a local Dhaka columnist denounced the idea of the end of history because a Bangladeshi had been bumped off of a British Airways flight (this evidently showed that racism still existed in the world).

A somewhat more sophisticated version of this criticism asserts that the reality of the post-cold war world is not democracy, but virulent nationalism. By this account, everyone was euphoric in 1989 after the fall of the Berlin Wall, thinking that the world was turning democratic and capitalist, but in fact it was returning to a premodern world of tribalism and ethnic passion run amok. The situation in Bosnia proved that modernity was a thin veneer; even in Western Europe, the upsurge in anti-foreigner violence showed that liberal democracy rested on very weak foundations. The institutions of world order like the United Nations, the European Community, or NATO, proved to be woefully inadequate in maintaining a common level of civilized behavior, and the future was likely to look much uglier than the past.

These sorts of issues are not irrelevant to the argument (and will be dealt with at greater length in the following section), but they fundamentally miss the point of the phrase "the end of history." The latter is not a statement about the *is,* but about the *ought:* for a variety of *theoretical* reasons, liberal democracy and free markets constitute the best regime, or more precisely the best of the available alternative ways of organizing human societies (or again, if one prefers Churchill's formulation, the least bad way of doing so). Liberal democracy most fully (though not completely) satisfies the most basic human longings, and therefore can be expected to be more universal and more durable than other regimes or other principles of political organization. It does not *completely* satisfy them, however, which means that the resolution of the historical problem cannot be brought to a close.

This is a normative, not an empirical statement, but it is a normative statement based in crucial ways on empirical evidence. It is of course possible to construct a best regime "in speech," as Socrates did in the *Republic*, that has no chance of ever being realized on earth. Most college students (at least, before they became so earnestly careerist) have sat around their dorm rooms late at night imagining a perfectly just society that would be just as perfectly impossible to bring into being, for reasons they will come to understand in another ten or fifteen years. No one likes the moral implications of capitalism, or imagines that the way it distributes gains is perfectly just. Socialist schemes of distribution are arguably fairer;[2] their chief problem is that they don't work. The latter is not something one can determine theoretically or on a priori grounds. When writing *Capitalism, Socialism, and Democracy* in 1943, Joseph Schumpeter argued that there was no reason why socialist economic organization should not be as efficient as capitalism. He dismissed the warnings of Hayek and von Mises that centralized planning boards would face problems of "unmanageable complication," gravely underestimated the importance of selfish incentives in motivating people to produce and innovate, and falsely predicted that centralized planning would reduce economic uncertainty.[3] None of this could have been known without the experience of real-world socialist societies trying to organize their economies according to socialist principles and failing.

If the Soviet Union had entered on an era of explosive double-digit growth in the 1970s and 1980s while Europe and the United States stagnated, our view of the respective normative merits of capitalism and socialism would be very different. The normative argument, therefore, is crucially and obviously dependent on empirical evidence.

The normative assertion that liberal democracy is the best available regime depends, then, not simply on a theoretical view of the adequacy of its moral and political arrangements, but also on empirical verification of its workability. If liberal democracies all failed shortly after being established (as European conservatives like Joseph de Maistre believed the American experiment would fail), or if liberal democracy proved successful only on Kiribati or Vanuatu, but nowhere else, we would not take it seriously as a moral alternative. On the other hand, its moral adequacy is not simply dependent on its workability, durability, or power: there have been many and various bad regimes (or at least, regimes constructed on principles diametrically opposed to those of liberal democracy) that have been very successful as historical enterprises. Might does not make right, though might may be a *condition* for right.

The assertion, then, that liberal democracy constitutes the "end of history" does not depend on the short-term advances or setbacks to democracy worldwide in 1994 (or 1989, or 1939, or 1806, for that matter). It is a normative statement about the principles of freedom and equality that underlay the French and American revolutions, to the effect that they stand at the end of a long process of ideological evolution, and that there is not a higher set of alternative principles that will in time replace them. This normative statement, to repeat, cannot be divorced from empirical fact. Empirical fact alone cannot prove or disprove its validity, except perhaps at the very unlikely extremes (i.e., the complete disappearance of liberal democracy, or the total universalization of it, or the appearance of an angel announcing the millennium). Empirical fact does not and cannot arm us with a deterministic methodology for predicting the future. What empirical fact can do, on the other hand, is to give us greater or lesser degree of *hope* that the normative statement is true. In this respect, empirical fact plays the same role that Kant's proposed "universal history" does in his essay of the same name. As Susan Shell points out, the purpose of this reading of history for Kant is to give us hope, and therefore perhaps to assist in the accomplishment of moral and political progress in the world. I have been accused, particularly in France, of being the "last Marxist;" of having a linear, deterministic, or mechanical understanding of history; or generally of espousing some "strong" version of historicism. If one goes back to *The End of History and the Last Man*, however, it should be clear that I was proposing a very weak version. I asked whether "it makes sense for us once again to speak of a coherent and directional History of mankind that will eventually lead the greater part of humanity to liberal democracy." To "speak of History" is only to say that the question is once again meaningful, and not that it is possible to answer the question with a strong version of historical progress.

Thus the truth of the assertion of the "end of history" did not in any way depend on the events of 1989. It could have been asserted with equal validity ten years earlier, at the height of the Brezhnev era; it was asserted in the late 1930s on the eve of World War II (by Kojève); and in the aftermath of the Battle of Jena in 1807 (by Hegel himself). The statement was not absurd in any of these cases, despite the turbulent and bloody "history" (in the conventional sense of the word) that took place before and after each was enunciated, for in every case they signified that the principles of the French Revolution were normatively the best available principles of political organization. Indeed, the flow of empirical events has given us greater *hope* that it is true with each repetition: in 1807, there were only three working democracies; in 1939, there were thirteen; while in 1989 there were more than sixty. Thus, if the question is asked "Have the events of the past few years (the Gulf War, Bosnia, Somalia, etc.) made you rethink the hypothesis?" the answer is obviously *no*. There may be somewhat less hope, but the normative argument concerning liberal democracy is not affected by the short-term flow of empirical events; it rests on other, broader grounds. Nor is there empirical evidence that an alternative set of normative principles is taking hold: fascism may be winning politically in Serbia, but no one (even, I would guess, in Belgrade) sees Serbia as an attractive generalizable model for the future.

There is, of course, a higher level question to be answered concerning the relationship of the empirical to the normative question, namely, how does one arrive at normative statements at all? The whole thrust of modern thought teaches us that there can be no such thing as a rational derivation of values from facts, or values grounded on a concept like nature. How one resolves this conundrum is of course the essence of the Strauss-Kojève debate, which will be taken up in Section III below.

II. The Empirical Argument

The empirical case that there is such a thing as "History" in the Marxist-Hegelian sense is perhaps the easiest to demonstrate of the various points made in *The End of History and the Last Man*. It is of course not fashionable to speak of History in this sense, particularly among professional historians who are trained to be narrowly empirical. But I would argue that virtually everyone believes in the existence of a directional history (though not necessarily in an "end" of history) on some level, and that the burden of proof is in fact on those who argue that history in this sense does not exist.

First, to define our terms, by "History" or "universal history" we mean a coherent and directional transformation of human societies that affects the whole, or nearly the whole, of mankind.

The starting point for a discussion of whether History in this sense exists is emphatically not in the events of the past few years, but in the concept of economic modernization. Prior to the scientific revolution of the sixteenth and seventeenth centuries in Europe, there could be a high degree of continuity in history: Chinese civilization, whether one looks at political organization, family life, or economic production, did not look terribly different in the Han dynasty than it did in the Sung or even Qing periods. But with the development of the scientific method, a process of economic development began that has encompassed virtually the whole of humanity.

The logic of this development process is determined by the progressive nature of scientific knowledge and its embodiment in technology through research and development. Science unfolds, once the scientific method is discovered, out of what is at least a twofold process: on the one hand, there is something like the desire for "utility maximization" described by neoclassical economists, and on the other a desire for recognition that leads human beings to seek mastery over nature. But while this process serves human ends and occurs through human agency, the internal logic of the process is determined ultimately by the laws of nature, which impose upon it a certain regularity. The second law of thermodynamics is not culturally determined; it is no different in Japan or Rwanda than it is in the United States. Technology provides a uniform horizon of production possibilities at any given level of scientific knowledge, and forces all societies employing technology to organize themselves in certain ways. It is now clear, forty years after the elaboration of "modernization theory," that there are a variety of paths to modernity, and that all societies will not necessarily resemble England or the United States in their development histories (indeed, in certain respects England and the United States differed considerably from one another). Late developers do things differently from early ones; there are cultural aspects to economic organization; the State can play varying roles in promoting or retarding the process. But the broad outlines of the process—urbanization, rational authority, bureaucratization, an ever-ramified and complex division of labor—are constant between cultures.

What is remarkable about the process of economic modernization is its universality as a goal. For a while there was one nation, Burma, that explicitly stated that it did not want to modernize, but now, even "Myanmar" has gotten on the treadmill. The only parts of humanity not aspiring to economic modernization are a few isolated tribes in the jungles of Brazil or Papua New Guinea, and they don't aspire to it because they don't know about it. Societies that at one point did not want to modernize or rejected further social change (for example, Japanese renunciation of certain types of new weapons in the Tokugawa period) were eventually forced to adopt technology with all it implied because of the decisive military advantage that technology conferred. There are, of course, small communities in the developed West like the Amish who keep alive an earlier level of technology (not, I would note, neolithic but nineteenth century), and ideologically committed environmentalists, who want to reverse the process of industrialization. But the aspiration to economic modernization is one of the most universal characteristics of human societies one can imagine.

Though the tendency toward capitalism has historically been much less universal than the desire for economic modernization per se, I argued in *The End of History and the Last Man* that technology necessarily points toward market-oriented forms of economic decision-making. What is even less universal than capitalism is the preference for liberal democracy. Nonetheless, as a purely empirical matter, there is an extraordinarily strong correlation between high levels of industrial development and stable democracy.[4] With modernization, there has been a corresponding growth in the legitimacy of the idea of human equality, the phenomenon noted by Tocqueville at the beginning of *Democracy in America*. There has been considerable argument as to why this correlation exists: at one extreme, the case has been made that democracy is culturally determined; it flows in some sense from Christian cultural systems and it is merely an accident that the world's earliest developed countries were also Christian nations; it is Christianity, and not development per se, that leads to democracy.[5] On the other hand, it can be argued that there is a certain hierarchy of human goals, with the satisfaction of economic needs preceding in some sense the need for recognition. With advancing socioeconomic status comes an increasing demand for recognition in the form of political participation. As an empirical matter, the most interesting test cases are now in Asia: Japan, Korea, Taiwan, and other Asian countries are not culturally Christian, and yet there has been a distinct correlation between level of economic development and stable democracy there as well. This suggests that while there may be cultural elements to the correlation, the correlation itself is not ultimately culturally determined but applies universally.

As noted earlier, the argument for the existence of a universal history would have to be made in a relatively weak form. That is to say, there is nothing necessarily linear, rigid, or deterministic about saying that the progressive unfolding of modern natural science determines in broad outline the economic modernization process, which in turn creates a predisposition toward liberal democracy. Marxists tended to state their theories of history in a very strong form: feudalism *inevitably* gives way to capitalism, which *inevitably* collapses from its own internal contradictions and gives way to socialism, etc. The misuse of such deterministic theories to legitimize political terror by Lenin and Stalin has given them a justifiably bad name. On the other hand, many people who reject Marxism would accept a weak form of this theory, for example that put forth by Max Weber, which accepted the fact that history has a directionality but which allowed for vast discontinuities like the Reformation not explainable by any unitary theory.

A universal history understood as modernization can and has been attacked from a postmodernist perspective. Why ''privilege'' the story of economic development, or identify it with History itself? Is this not a Euro-, phallo-, or whatnot-centric story? Why not tell another story, say, the story of indigenous peoples crushed by modernization, or the story of women, or the story of family life, each of which would follow a very different trajectory? What about the story of all those years prior to the invention of the scientific method; were these not worthy of being called history? Who is the teller of the Universal History, and what are his interests in telling the story in this manner?

Modernization theory collapsed in the 1970s under the weight of such attacks, but it should not have. The transition from a premodern society to an industrial society is one that affects virtually every other ''story'' in a fundamental way, and it affects virtually all societies in some manner, whether or not they have modernized successfully. The postmodernist professor who asserts that there is no coherent direction to history would most likely never contemplate leaving his comfortable surroundings in Paris, New Haven, or Irvine and moving to Somalia; he would not raise his children under the hygienic conditions prevailing in Burundi, nor teach postmodernist philosophy in Teheran.

While there is a reasonable empirical basis for constructing a directional universal history, the empirical grounds for arguing that the historical process has an end or goal are much weaker. To begin with, the phenomenon of modern natural science is open-ended; it does not, as far as we know, have an end point where we will know everything there is to know about the physical universe. And if our lives and our forms of social organization are governed by the inner logic of the development of science, we cannot know with finality what social arrangements will be dictated by a given level of scientific knowledge in the future.

Moreover, while it might be possible to assert that something broad like economic modernization is a virtually universal goal, any particular set of political arrangements like liberal democracy is rather unlikely to emerge out of the merely empirical data as the immanent goal of the historical process. The present confusion over the nature of the post-communist world order is testimony to the lack of consensus on how to interpret the data. Some will deny that there has been any particular trend toward democracy. Others, like G. M. Tamás, will assert that what Western liberals have identified as democracy in contemporary Eastern Europe is actually a depoliticized version of democracy, one that is bound to emerge in the West as well. Others will assert that individualistic democracy has been stripped of any real meaning in Japan and other places in Asia where the form of democracy has been observed. And finally, there will always be reasonable doubts about the cohesiveness and irreversibility of democracy in places where it by common consensus already exists, such as Western Europe or even the United States.

Thus, empirical fact can lead us to assert that there is such a thing as History. Empirical fact can probably also falsify the notion of liberal democracy as an "end of history" under several conditions: if liberal democracies around the world collapsed as communist systems did in the late 1980s; if a society based on genuinely different principles arose somewhere in the world and looked like it was a going concern over a long period of time (my candidate is an Asian "soft authoritarian" state); or if some earlier nonliberal principle returned and gained widespread legitimacy (for example, if American women lost the right to vote or slavery became legal once again). Empirical fact by itself, however, does not provide us a basis for talking about an end of history. As stated above, all it can do is give us a certain basis for hope.

III. The Normative Argument

The first question that arises is how, at the end of the twentieth century, anyone can put forward a serious "normative" argument concerning the goodness (or badness) of liberal democracy. God having been killed off in the nineteenth century, the entire thrust of twentieth-century philosophy from Heidegger to the postmodernists has been to kill God's secular replacement, enlightenment rationalism, as well. Modern thought has sought to undermine the very notions of metaphysics, nature, natural right, and the like, on which any philosophical concept of "the good" could be built. This, I take it, is the reason for Peter Fenves' unhappiness with my "forays into the problem of 'man as man' " or the "doses of metaphysics" that appear in the book. I use them, in his view, as illegitimate buttresses to an empirical argument, as if I hadn't heard the news that metaphysics is no longer permissible—somewhat like a modern social scientist using biblical authority to cover a gap in his survey data.

It is not my purpose here, nor was it my purpose in *The End of History and the Last Man,* to defend traditional metaphysics against its modern critics. This is certainly well beyond my abilities. I find, however, that many of the epigones of Nietzsche and Heidegger themselves assume the impossibility or falsity of traditional metaphysics and spend their careers playfully deconstructing the Western philosophical tradition, without thinking through the disastrous consequences of their actions. Richard Rorty is a telling case in point. Anyone listening to Rorty understands that he is very committed to a certain set of rather conventional liberal values: he does not like what Ronald Reagan did to the poor, he does not favor totalitarian regimes, he is against "ethnic cleansing" and other atrocities in Yugoslavia. Yet he is equally if not more committed to demonstrating that there is no philosophical basis for these commitments: they are just a matter of sentiment, of the surrounding moral climate, of education, of pragmatic adjustment to experience. Fortunately, his surrounding moral climate is the relatively benign one of Charlottesville. The country in which he lives is a liberal democracy; the politics, for all its problems, are moderate, and a Jamesian pragmatism may indeed be sound moral and political advice. But what if one were growing up not in Charlottesville, but in Navortny's post-1968 Prague? While Rorty claims Václav Havel as a "postmodern" politician, Rorty's own advice would have led the young Havel not to jail and dissidence, but to a career as a reform Communist. For an individual living in the even less benign environments of Hitler's Germany, or the Serbia of 1993, the "sentimental education" provided by the local environment might have led to even less palatable moral choices. They would be unpalatable from Rorty's own point of view, yet Rorty's attack on the possibility of philosophy and moral knowledge leaves him no ground on which he can criticize a phenomenon like "ethnic cleansing."[6]

Many postmodernists seem to think that their critique of traditional philosophy leads to a kind of depoliticized, deideologized *faut de mieux* liberalism. A postmodernist liberalism would rest not, like the American Declaration of Independence, on the "self-evident" truths of human equality or natural rights, but rather on the mutual exhaustion of all other fundamentalisms, ideologies, or philosophies, and would do no more than give free play to the individual's self-creation (or in the case of Havel, his moral being). This, and not a universalist enlightenment doctrine, seems to be what G. M. Tamás argues was the meaning of democracy for his generation of Eastern European dissidents. Their common cause with traditional American liberals, or neoconservatives, on a human rights agenda during the days of communist tyranny was, he argues, more an accident than a real convergence of thought.[7] This also seems to be the meaning of Peter Fenves's "Tower of Babel": contemporary liberal democracy is actually a cacophony of different languages, but since the "language of liberal democracy" is the only one left standing in the ring, it has convinced itself that it is a universal language.

This line of argument seems to me to be very problematic insofar as its proponents do not have the courage or the resolution of either Nietzsche or Heidegger in seeing it to its logical conclusions. For any doctrine that undermines the "ideologized" version of liberalism likewise undermines the egalitarian principles on which that liberalism rests. A postmodernist liberalism may remain safe from external threat in a world populated exclusively by other such liberal states—in other words, if postmodernists knew they were living at the end of history. But by their own premises they do not and cannot know this. They have no reason in principle not to expect the rise of new "fundamentalisms" (whether traditional or modern, at home or abroad), and have only the very weak armor of their own intellectual premises to protect them once they do arise. The denial that there can be a knowable concept of "man as man," or a consensus on the question of human nature or the basis of human dignity, means that any discussion of liberal rights will simply amount to "rights talk," with no principled way of adjudicating the conflicts and contradictions that will inevitably arise.[8] While such a society will continue to thrive for a time on the basis of pre-postmodernist habits, I do not understand how it could defend itself from external enemies in the short run or sustain either polity or community over the long run.

The "crisis of modernity," then, is a very real one. Both Strauss and Kojève were aware of the *aporia* of modern thought, and both believed that a way out was the most urgent of problems. This is why I believe the Strauss-Kojève debate was one of the most important of twentieth-century discussions, because these two thinkers tried to address this problem from diametrically opposite positions, those of history and of nature.

Without reviewing that very complicated discussion in detail, it seems to me that Strauss shows quite convincingly that history does not in the end provide a way out. As pointed out above (section II), the empirical fact of history provides us with nothing more than a *hope* that it is directional and purposeful. While Hegel asserts that history is radically different from nature, the product of free human self-creation, we cannot know whether this history is unique without a larger teleological theory of nature: perhaps there is another universe or another time in which our history has unfolded in an identical manner, not the product of free human creation but of a natural process of which we are simply not cognizant.

Moreover, we have a major problem with the knowability of "the end of history." As Tom Darby points out, the end of history for Hegel lies not in the appearance of Napoleon as such, but in the appearance of the dyad Napoleon-Hegel. That is, Hegel is the philosopher who truly understands Napoleon's significance; he is not speculating about "imaginary kingdoms" but understands the underlying rationality of the world's seemingly meaningless flow of events. He understands that Napoleon is not just another ambitious adventurer, but is ushering in the universal and homogeneous state that will realize the possibility of universal recognition. In doing so, Napolean makes it possible for man to achieve a self-knowledge, an awareness that he is a being that seeks recognition and is satisfied by universal recognition. And Napoleon becomes something more than an adventurer by the fact of his having been "interpreted" by Hegel.

But how do we know that Hegel was right about Napoleon? The end of history is not immanent in the empirical facts of history, as noted above. Hegel would argue (with considerable empirical justification, even with the hindsight of nearly two hundred years) that the French Revolution and Napoleon ushered in the principle of universal recognition. But how, then, does one know that man is a being that seeks recognition, and is satisfied by universal recognition? It is possible to regard universal recognition as a kind of Kantian rule of transcendental reason (or, in the language of a contemporary Kantian like Rawls, something like the rule that arises out of the ''original position'') that would be valid regardless of our knowledge of empirical facts about the world, and would apply to rational beings whether they were human or not. For Hegel to represent much of an advance over Kant in this regard, we would have to understand and accept much of the argument of the *Science of Logic* and the critique it contains of Kantian metaphysics, a task that seems at once formidable and dubious. It is dubious not simply because I have never succeeded in working my way through this book, but because it seems to me very unlikely that man's final knowledge of himself should rest on a book so obscure, and about which there is so little consensus even among Hegel specialists.

It seems to me that one of the sources of Kojève's great appeal is that he offers a highly anthropologized reading of Hegel, in which our understanding of the role of recognition in history does not depend on our knowledge and acceptance of the *Science of Logic,* but rather on the degree to which Kojève's anthropology corresponds to our own observation or intuition of ''man as man.'' That is, its appeal lies in the plausibility of his explanation of man as a being that works and struggles over pure prestige, and in the degree to which this explanation is revealing of a deeper level of motivation when we view the empirical facts of history. The adequacy of this highly anthropologized Hegel stands or falls on the basis of what amounts to an account of human nature, that is, the trans-historical concept of man as a being that seeks and is satisfied by recognition. This, in the end, is why I was driven back to Plato and his tripartite account of the soul, because Plato's account of *thymos* seemed to me to provide an alternative language in which we could discuss recognition as an *anthropological* phenomenon.

Victor Gourevitch and other critics are undoubtedly right that one cannot reconcile unreconcilables: Plato and Hegel, nature and history. Orthodox Hegelians will argue, doubtless correctly, that this highly anthropologized version of Hegel is not, in fact, Hegel. They may further argue that it is not Kojève, either, and therefore could not be the synthetic philosopher Hegel-Kojève. The charge that I am not seeking to understand Hegel as Hegel understood himself, that I am using bits and pieces of this most systematic of philosophers, is doubtless true, and is one that I accepted in the book itself. But one can still make an argument about a universal history without use of the concept of history in the Hegelian sense (i.e., of man's free self-creation in opposition to nature). I would argue that this procedure is implicit to some degree in Kojève's work itself, when it calls on us to understand man as a being for whom recognition is primary. Whatever Hegel's self-understanding, it is both an interesting and an important question to uncover the degree to which the historical process can be properly understood as the result of an "anthropologized" struggle for recognition.

A much more central criticism of this argument is the one made in the essays by Tim Burns, Victor Gourevitch, and in a somewhat different framework, Peter Lawler. The question can be put simply: how is it possible to have *recognition* without a prior *cognition?*[9] That is to say, what is the value of the universal recognition underlying liberal democracy, a recognition that is not based on a knowledge of what it means to be a good or excellent human being? Recognition as it appears in Hegel or Kojève is a purely formal matter. That is, one is recognized equally and universally for being a human being, a free being undetermined by nature and therefore capable of moral choice. There can be no other formal solution to the problem of recognition, because no other form of recognition can be universalized and therefore made rational. One might wish to say that being a brilliant physicist or concert pianist or even a devoted father is a worthy way of life deserving of recognition, but recognition of such qualities cannot be universalized because not all human beings are brilliant physicists or pianists or fathers. To recognize those qualities means to denigrate those who do not possess them. All forms of *megalothymia* are hostile, ultimately, to the *isothymia* on which liberal democracy is based. One is reduced, then, to recognizing a kind of moral lowest common denominator, a free being that can negate nature. By this Hegelian scheme, one can distinguish between a human being and a rock, a hungry bear, and a clever monkey, but one cannot distinguish between the first man who kills his fellow human being in a battle for pure prestige and a Mother Teresa who sacrifices her worldly happiness to follow the dictates of God.

Tim Burns and Victor Gourevitch make similar points about my comparison of Hobbes and Hegel. In *The End of History and the Last Man,* I argued that Hegel provides a broader and deeper understanding of human motivation, not because Hobbes does not understand the desire for recognition, but because he seeks to subordinate it to rational desire. Hegel, I argued, understood that even in modern polities men do not live for the rational pursuit of bread alone, but seek recognition, and that the Hegelian universal and homogeneous state honored this honor-seeking side of modernity by making universal recognition the basis of all rights. Both Burns and Gourevitch argue, properly, that in this respect both Hobbes and Hegel share the narrowing of perspective characteristic of modern thought. Hobbes and Hegel deny the possibility of an original cognition; that is, they both deny the existence of cognizable human goodnesses or excellences, goodnesses or excellences that exist "by nature," that are inherently worthy of recognition. While Hegel's point of view may be broader than that of Hobbes in the sense that he understands the irreducibility of isothymia, and honors it politically, he shares with Hobbes the principle that rights must be formal and not substantive. The state, in other words, can only recognize the right to *free* speech, not good or excellent speech.

While I accept this criticism (and indeed, I anticipated much of it in *The End of History and the Last Man*), I still believe that the distinction between Hobbes and Hegel is crucial in one key respect. Tocqueville in *Democracy in America* talks about the American "passion for equality:" how equality is the founding principle of democracy, how the passion has spread ineluctably over the centuries, and how it has come to affect all aspects of the social life of a democracy over time. Yet he never really explains what is meant by the "passion for equality." Surely it does not mean a passion for physical equality: Americans do not aspire to be equally strong or tall or handsome. It does not refer exclusively to equal political or legal rights, since these were *in principle* established with the founding of the country (with the well-known and ever-narrowing circle of exceptions: the propertyless, racial minorities, women, tomorrow perhaps homosexuals). Nor does it refer to an equality of economic station: Lockean principles of property have been widely accepted, and therefore Americans have accepted a fair degree of economic inequality throughout their history.

The "passion for equality" refers, above all, to a passion for equal recognition, that is, an equality of respect and dignity. I believe that the major currents of contemporary American politics—feminism, gay rights, the rights of the handicapped or of Native Americans—are merely the logical present-day manifestations of the same isothymia that Tocqueville described in the 1830s. Contrary to what most economists and rational-choice theorists argue, this desire for equal recognition cannot be reduced to economic motives; instead, much of what passes as economic motivation has to be understood in terms of the struggle for equal recognition. In this respect alone, Hegel is a better guide for understanding our politics than is Hobbes.

None of this, however, speaks to the legitimate question of what the original cognition is that underlies recognition. Is not "man as man" something more than a being capable of negating nature? And if this is indeed the central question, should not the faculty of cognition have been emphasized to a much greater extent relative to the desire for recognition?

The centrality of the issue of cognition underlies, I assume, Peter Lawler's repeated question of whether it is possible to have a sense of human dignity without God, or without making the distinction between man and God. His own answer to his rhetorical question is, I assume, *no*: only God can provide us with the original cognition to know what is truly worthy in His sight, and therefore only God can open the way for us to express ourselves, as moral beings, in something other than the blind fury of Hegel's "first man" and his struggle for pure prestige.

My answer to Lawler's question is: if the question of man's dependence on God is meant in a practical sense, that is, if he is asking whether a liberal society is sustainable without religion and other premodern sources of constraint and community, the answer is probably *no*. If his question is meant in a theoretical sense (i.e., are there other sources of cognition besides God?), the answer is, *I don't know*. It may be that God is the only possible source for such knowledge; if so, and if God has indeed died, then we are in a lot of trouble and need desperately to find another source on which to base our belief that human beings have dignity. Enlightenment rationalism is not the solution but part of the problem. Hobbes and Hegel are constitutive thinkers in that tradition, but the self-undermining character of their thought is what has landed us in this predicament in the first place. Tim Burns, following Strauss, suggests another approach, which some have labeled "zetetic": to find our way, not by holding fast to unexamined demands on the world or unexamined presuppositions about justice (which gave rise to abstractions like the first man or man-in-the-state-of-nature), nor with an effort, desperate or otherwise, to ground unexamined beliefs; but to find our way, rather, by engaging in or observing dialectical arguments with political or moral human beings on the question of justice and its relation to the good, in order to come into a genuinely rational life. It is certainly the case that while postmodernists believe that there is no rational systematic philosophical view of the whole that would allow us to come to a consensus on what constitutes specific human excellences, virtually everyone (postmodernists included) has opinions as to what those excellences are. We live in a world dedicated to isothymia, and yet see evidence of megalothymia all around us: while all of us believe we are entitled to equal respect, no one in his heart of hearts believes equal respect is all there is to life, or thinks that life would be worth living if there was no room for unequal respect based on some degree of excellence or achievement. And since, in Peter Fenves's words, the content of that respect is constituted by *logos,* there remains the possibility that *logos* can be subject to rational discussion and ultimately to some measure of consensus.

Let me turn for a moment to a different question. I am accused by both Theodore von Laue and Peter Fenves of—as odd as it may seem—being insufficiently reductionist in my analysis of the underlying forces of history on the one hand and the nature of desire on the other. These critiques are quite different. Von Laue asserts that "[t]he most crucial flaw is Fukuyama's blindness to the centrality of power," which he notes is "a common failure among Americans." He then goes on to draw up his own thumbnail "universal history," in which all the varied phenomena of history, from power politics to economics to religious enthusiasm to family relations, can be seen as manifestations of an underlying struggle for power. Fenves, on the other hand, takes me to task for distinguishing between simple desire, which I portray as something like the "utility maximization" of traditional "economic man," and the desire for recognition, which is attached not to material but to ideal objects. Fenves's point, as I understand it, is that all desire is constituted by language, and all desire therefore partakes of a "nonmaterial" quality, even those desires that are conventionally thought of as material or economic in nature.

Any attempt to construct a universal history necessarily involves a high degree of abstraction and simplification from the enormous mass of empirical historical fact, and therefore will always be open to the charge of reductionism. Much of my book was implicitly an attack on the economic reductionism of Marxism and an attempt to recover the greater richness of human motivation embodied in the concept of the struggle for recognition. It seems to me that in constructing any kind of universal history, one should as a matter of course prefer less reductionist to more reductionist theories, consistent of course with the need to construct a general theory in the first place. In this respect, trying to reduce the larger patterns of history to a simple struggle for power seems to me a step backward rather than a step forward, one that I criticized at some length in my discussion of power politics. Those who seek to reduce everything to power forget to ask the question, power for what? Is it desired for its own sake, or is it a fungible commodity to be converted into other goods? I doubt seriously that it is the former: can one understand Luther's motives in launching the Protestant Reformation, or those of the American founding fathers, without reference to the ends that they sought to achieve, and for which power was only a means? If, alternatively, power is simply a fungible commodity sought as a means to other ends, then one hasn't advanced a theory of history by saying that everyone seeks power. In the absence of a discussion of ends, it becomes tautological, just like the argument of those economists who define "utility" so broadly that it includes any end actually pursued by human beings.

Fenves's critique is considerably more subtle. I had tried to disaggregate economic motivation into what was truly economic in a conventional sense (that is, the satisfaction of basic needs like food and drink), and an ideal dimension in which people sought recognition of their dignity through the acquisition of material goods. I thought this added a layer of nuance to our understanding of desire. Fenves seems to be arguing that I didn't go far enough: economic motivation in the former sense doesn't exist at all—as he says, "remaining alive, keeping one's body in motion, may very well be a matter of pride—and nothing else." I doubt it—at least, the *and nothing else*, which makes things a bit too subtle. While there is potentially a thymotic dimension to virtually everything, sometimes one eats because one is hungry. I don't know how else one would explain the phenomenon of cannibalism.

I would like to conclude with the question raised by Fenves, as to why I raised the question of the end of history at this particular juncture in history.[10] He (and a legion of others, such as von Laue) asserts that I am an "optimist," and tries to uncover the position from which an optimist might understand his own activity. If history is indeed over, there is no historical necessity for optimism: the proclamation of an optimistic point of view becomes a matter of vanity, of one's reputation as a historiographer. I do not, it seems, have the serious purpose or self-understanding of Kant, who by raising the question of progress in history hoped to contribute to the end of progress.

The problem with this analysis is that it begins with the assumption that I am fundamentally optimistic. In fact, Susan Shell is much more correct in characterizing *The End of History and the Last Man* as a "most pessimistic of optimistic books." As noted earlier, one can be optimistic in the sense of being able to discern a "universal history" in the mass of empirical data, and one can be optimistic concerning the long-term prospects for liberal democracy. But to be optimistic in any philosophical sense about our situation requires that one know that liberal democracy is a good thing. This, as I stated at several points in the book, is not something we can take for granted. One can conclude, provisionally, that liberal democracy satisfies the different parts of the soul more completely than its competitors, but one has to know whether the soul exists, and if so, of what it consists. The question that is prior to the empirical one is an epistemological one. There has to be a ground for the "original cognition," and one can at least begin the search by revisiting the debate between Strauss and Kojève.

The present *aporia* brings me to the larger reasons for writing the book. We are at a unique juncture in history when, most people would admit, liberalism does not have many serious competitors. There is only "one language," that of liberal democracy. But our preference for liberal democracy was conditioned for many years by the enemies of liberal democracy. We knew that liberal democracy was better than communism or fascism, but we deferred addressing the question of whether liberal democracy was choiceworthy in itself, or whether we could conceive of preferable arrangements, if not among actual regimes, then among some that could only now be imagined. The time for that discussion has come, and it seems to me that our initial attempts to address the question show the nakedness of our position.

It is clear to me that the postmodernist answer, that no ground exists, either for an original cognition or for liberal democracy itself, is politically, morally, and humanly intolerable. And in this respect, it is impossible to be anything but pessimistic.

Notes

1. The first argument corresponds to Part II of *The End of History and the Last Man*, while the second is contained in Parts III–V. I do not like the word "normative" because it implies that there is a multiplicity of "norms" or "values" among different societies, or within the same society, about which there can be no rational consensus and no rational discourse, as opposed to "empirical" facts, about which consensus can, through application of the proper method, be reached. However, my meaning will probably be clearer, particularly to social scientists, if I use the term "normative" rather than, for example, "theoretical."

2. That they are arguably fairer does not mean they are actually fairer; equal distribution of economic gains would be fair only if people were equally deserving of them.

3. For a more extended analysis of *Capitalism, Socialism, and Democracy,* see Francis Fukuyama, "Capitalism and Democracy: The Missing Link," *Journal of Democracy* 3 (July 1992): 100–110.

4. For a review of the extensive social science literature that confirms this point, see Larry Diamond, "Economic Development and Democracy Reconsidered," *American Behavioral Scientist* 15 (March–June 1992): 450–99.

5. See, for example, Samuel Huntington, *The Third Wave* (Lexington: University of Kentucky Press, 1992).

6. In the light of the alleged inability to make rational moral distinctions, it is perhaps not surprising that Rorty compares the Serbs to Thomas Jefferson. See his "Human Rights, Rationality, and Sentimentality," in Stephen Shute

and Susan Hurley, eds., *On Human Rights: The Oxford Amnesty Lectures 1993* (New York: Basic Books, 1993), pp. 111–34.

7. See G. M. Tamás, "The Legacy of Dissent," *The Times Literary Supplement*, May 14, 1993. [Ed. note: When writing this essay, Mr. Fukuyama did not have access to the essay by G. M. Tamás that appears in this volume.]

8. This problem I alluded to in *The End of History and the Last Man,* p. 296.

9. I owe this formulation to Charles Griswold.

10. In his formulation, I "proclaimed the end of history"; in fact, I never proclaimed anything but merely raised the *question* of the end of history.

Index

Napoleon, 200–204, 211, 250
nationalism, 5, 11, 48–49, 53n5, 105, 114, 212–13, 240
nature, 3–5, 11–12, 14, 18, 20n25, 20n26, 26, 28, 39–40, 42, 52, 65, 67–69, 71–72, 79n8, 82, 83–85, 88, 111, 116, 120–21, 123–26, 138–41, 148–49, 152, 156–57, 187, 189, 202, 210, 212, 224, 225–26, 244, 250–51
negation, 19n22, 65, 70, 73, 75, 86–87, 97, 117–18, 138–39, 199, 200, 202, 253
neoconservatism, 4, 96, 104–5, 249
Nietzsche, Friedrich, 7–9, 11, 16n4, 18n19, 24, 30, 39, 42–43, 45, 49, 50, 64, 66, 75, 85, 88, 103, 112, 116, 119–20, 124, 133, 139, 140, 157–60, 166n15, 211, 225–26, 228, 237n3, 248–49

Oakeshott, Michael, 93–94, 107n11, 108n25
optimism, 28, 31, 37, 39, 40, 43, 58, 198, 211, 221–25, 230, 234, 256–57

Pangle, Thomas L., 43, 79n18, 109n27, 127n4, 129n22
pessimism, 30, 37, 42, 45, 221–23, 250–57
philosophy, 18n19, 21n31, 58, 67, 71, 84, 92, 96, 122–23, 138, 140, 148–49, 160, 183, 187, 190, 197–98, 206–7, 213, 224
Plato, 11–12, 17n13, 19n22, 44, 47, 53n1, 59, 83, 103, 111–12, 121–26, 133, 136, 159–63, 170n72, 199, 207, 213, 215n21, 225, 229, 251
political philosophy, 8–9, 15, 18n19, 20n26, 21n31, 98–99, 136–37, 150, 157
postmodernism, 4, 8, 9, 10, 14, 15, 16n4, 17n10, 17n12, 42, 63, 77,

78n2, 92, 109n28, 163, 212–13, 246, 248–49, 254–57
power, 26–28, 34, 102, 146, 200, 209, 213, 255
progress, 30–31, 40, 52, 58, 134, 184, 189, 200, 202, 209, 242–43, 256
progressives, 15–16, 58–59, 92, 158

rationalism, 71, 78, 85, 121, 144, 148, 152, 157, 161–63, 254; modern, 58, 63–65, 67, 71, 76, 139–44, 149–52, 156–57, 163, 172, 175, 183, 243, 248, 252–54
Rawls, John, 5, 20n24, 250–51
recognition, dialectic of, 11, 25, 35, 42, 44–45, 49, 67–70, 74–75, 86–87, 97–98, 102–3, 105, 116–19, 135–36, 141–45, 151, 154–55, 182, 203, 233, 235, 244, 251–53
relativism, 36, 55, 120–21, 125, 138–40, 157–60, 164, 213, 235, 248–49
religion, 5, 27, 35–36, 42, 45, 48–49, 52, 58, 64, 74–76, 89, 91, 100, 114, 132–33, 148–51, 153, 162, 175–78, 181, 183, 187, 254
right, the, 4, 9, 15n, 49, 132, 140, 157, 158
Romanticism, 91–92
Rorty, Richard, 17n11, 50, 84, 248–49
Rousseau, Jean-Jacques, 5, 12, 19n24, 47, 50, 54n6, 68–76, 92, 123, 136, 152–56, 163
Russia. *See* Soviet Union

Sartre, Jean-Paul, 73, 225
satisfaction, 12, 20–21n27, 39, 42, 44–47, 56–58, 63, 66–74, 77–78, 88–89, 97–98, 115, 118, 134, 136–37, 141–43, 156–57, 159–60, 168n48, 186–89, 198–99, 201, 209–10, 212–13, 222, 227,

About the Contributors

Timothy Burns is assistant professor of political science at Southwest Texas State University, San Marcos. This is his first book. He has written articles and papers on Homer, Thucydides, Xenophon, and Augustine, and is currently at work on a study of the problem of piety and justice in Thucydides.

Tom Darby is professor of political science at Carleton University in Ottawa, Ontario. He is the author of *The Feast: Meditations on Politics and Time* (1982, 2nd ed., 1990), editor of *Sojourns in the New World: Reflections on Technology* (1986), and editor, with Bela Eged and Ben Jones, of *Nietzsche and the Rhetoric of Nihilism* (1988). He is currently at work on a novel, *Life at the End of History*.

Peter Fenves is associate professor of German and comparative literature at Northwestern University. He is the author of *A Peculiar Fate: Metaphysics and World-History in Kant* (1991) and *"Chatter": Language and History in Kierkegaard* (1993), and he is editor of *Raising the Tone of Philosophy: Late Essays by Kant, Transformative Critique by Derrida* (1993). He is now at work on *Language on a Holiday: Wittgenstein, Benjamin, Heidegger*.

Timothy Fuller is professor of political science and dean of Colorado College, Colorado Springs. He is editing the papers of Michael Oakeshott and overseeing the publication of the selected works of Oakeshott. In the series, *Michael Oakeshott on Religion, Politics and the Moral Life* was published in October 1993.

Francis Fukuyama, former deputy director of the Policy Planning Staff, U.S. Department of State, is currently a resident consultant at the RAND Corporation in Washington, D.C. The English edition of his *The End of History and the Last Man* (1992) won the *Los Angeles Times* Book Critics Award (Current Interest category), and the Italian edition won the *Premio Capri* International Award. He is also the author of numerous articles on Soviet and Russian foreign policy, international relations, and political economy. He is now completing a book on the cultural roots of economic behavior, to be published in 1995.

Victor Gourevitch is the William Griffin professor of philosophy at Wesleyan University, Middletown, Conn. He is the editor and translator of *The First and Second Discourses Together with the Replies to Critics and Essay on the Origin of Languages* (1986), and editor, with Michael S. Roth, of Leo Strauss's *On Tyranny: Including the Strauss-Kojève Correspondence,* revised and expanded (1991). He is also the author of "Rousseau's 'Pure' State of Nature," *Interpretation, A Journal of Political Philosophy*, 16 (Fall 1988).

Joseph M. Knippenberg is associate professor of politics and chairman of the Division of History, Politics, and International Studies at Oglethorpe University in Atlanta, where he has taught since 1985. He is the author of a number of articles on Kant, most recently in *Kant and Political Philosophy: The Contemporary Legacy*, Ronald Beiner and W. J. Booth, eds. (1993). He has held fellowships from the John M. Olin and Earhart foundations, and is currently a Salvatori Fellow in Academic Leadership with the Heritage Foundation. He is co-editor of a forthcoming collection of essays on literature and politics.

Peter Augustine Lawler is professor of political science at Berry College, Mount Berry, Georgia. He is the author of *The Restless Mind: Alexis de Tocqueville and the Origin and Perpetuation of Human Liberty,* and editor, with Robert Schaefer, of *The American Experiment* and *American Political Rhetoric*.

Susan Shell is associate professor of political science at Boston College. She is the author of *The Rights of Reason: A Study of Kant's Philosophy and Politics* (1980) as well as articles on German Idealism, Rousseau, the American Constitution, and the current state of the humanities. She is currently at work on a book-length study of Kant's theory of community.

Gregory Bruce Smith is associate professor of political science at Trinity College, Hartford, Connecticut. He has also taught at the University of Chicago, University of Pennsylvania, Carleton College, and American University. He is the author of *Between Eternities: Deflec-*

tions Toward a Postmodern Future (1994), as well as articles on technology and environmentalism, Heidegger, Derrida, Nietzsche, and Plato. He is currently at work on a book of essays entitled *Environmentalism and Political Philosophy.*

G. M. Tamás, one of the leaders of the last European dissidence, is now an opposition member of the Hungarian parliament, director of the Institute of Philosophy of the Hungarian Academy of Sciences, and a reader in philosophy at the University of Budapest Law School. Many of his works have been published in the West, including *L'oeil et la main* (1985) and *Les Idoles de la tribe* (1990). An extended American version of the latter, *Tribal Concepts*, is scheduled to appear in 1994.

Theodore H. Von Laue is the Jacob and Frances Hiatt professor of history emeritus at Clark University, Worcester, Massachusetts. Born in Germany in 1916, he has lived and taught in the United States since 1937. He is the author of many scholarly articles and the following books: *Leopold Rank, the Formative Years* (1950), *Sergei Witte and the Industrialization of Russia* (1963), *Why Lenin? Why Stalin?* (1964) expanded into *Why Lenin? Why Stalin? Why Gorbachev?* (1992), *The Global City* (1969), and *The World Revolution of Westernization* (1987).

David Walsh is professor and chair of the Department of Politics, Catholic University of America, Washington, D.C. He is the author of *The Mysticism of Innerworldly Fulfillment: A Study of Jacob Boehme* (1983) and *After Ideology: Recovering the Spiritual Foundations of Freedom* (1990). He is the author of articles on Hegel, Nietzsche, Dostoyevsky, Eric Voegelin, and others. He is currently completing a book on the historical and contemporary debates surrounding liberal democracy.